THE GENERAL
& THE TEXAS

Pictorial History of the Andrews Raid, April 12, 1862

by Stan Cohen & James G. Bogle

THIS LITHOGRAPH WAS ISSUED IN 1903 BY THE NASHVILLE, CHATTANOOGA & ST. LOUIS RAILWAY SOON AFTER THE ENGINE WAS PLACED ON DISPLAY IN THE UNION DEPOT IN CHATTANOOGA, TENN. THE PRINT IS 12" x 19" AND WAS AVAILABLE UNTIL 1969 WHEN THE SUPPLY WAS EXHAUSTED.

PICTORIAL HISTORIES PUBLISHING CO., INC.
MISSOULA, MONTANA

LIBRARY OF CONGRESS
CATALOG CARD NUMBER No. 99-70473

ISBN 1-57510-060-6

First Printing May 1999

Typography by Janyce Taylor & Leslie Maricelli

Cover Graphics by Mike Egeler, Egeler Designs

FRONT COVER PHOTOS FROM THE WILBUR G. KURTZ COLLECTION
BACK COVER PHOTO SHOWS THE *GENERAL* ARRIVING AT KENNESAW, GEORGIA,
APRIL, 14, 1962. PHOTO L&NRR

SITES ASSOCIATED WITH THE ANDREWS RAID

• THE KENNESAW CIVIL WAR MUSEUM IS LOCATED IN A FORMER COTTON GIN WHICH WAS RENOVATED AS THE HOME FOR THE *GENERAL*, RAID ARTIFACTS AND CIVIL WAR MEMORABILIA. IT IS LOCATED AT 2829 CHEROKEE STREET, KENNESAW, GEORGIA 30144.

• THE ATLANTA CYCLORAMA BUILDING IS LOCATED IN GRANT PARK AT 800 CHEROKEE AVE. SE, ATLANTA, GEORGIA 30315. IT HOUSES THE FAMOUS 1885-86 PAINTING OF THE 1864 BATTLE OF ATLANTA AND THE LOCOMOTIVE *TEXAS*.

• THE CHATTANOOGA NATIONAL CEMETERY IS LOCATED BETWEEN CENTRAL, HOLTZCLAW AND BAILEY AVENUES IN CHATTANOOGA, TENNESSEE. A MONUMENT TO THE RAIDERS AND THE BURIAL SITES OF EIGHT OF THEM ARE LOCATED WITHIN THE CEMETERY.

PICTORIAL HISTORIES PUBLISHING CO., INC.
713 So. 3rd St. W.
Missoula, Montana 59801
(406) 549-8488   phpc@montana.com

 # Introduction

There were many, many daring exploits conducted during the American Civil War, both on the land and on the sea. They involved incursions far behind enemy lines on both sides, from small raiding parties to full regimental strength.

The Andrews Raid, more commonly known as "The Great Locomotive Chase," involved a small raiding party of 22 troopers from several Ohio regiments and two civilians including James J. Andrews, the leader. It was a very risky venture, for the purpose of disrupting rail traffic between two important Southern supply cities—Chattanooga, Tenn., and Atlanta, Ga. Isolating these points would give the Federal army a chance to strike deep into the heart of the Confederacy.

Many myths have grown up through the years, through the printed word and movies about the raid. The story is be treated pictorially and will contains the largest collection of appropriate photos ever produced in one book. Dozens of books and two major motion pictures have been produced over the years about this one-day affair on April 12, 1862.

This book is a tribute both to those daring raiders and their Confederate pursuers and to the healing process that occurred between adversaries years after the war was over.

Most of the writing and research for this book comes from James G. Bogle of Atlanta, who has written much and who has amassed the largest collection of photographs, books and art work of anyone. His help has transformed my idea into this book. I am sure I speak for all the other authors whom Jim has helped. He opened his huge archives to me and trusted me with most of the photographs and newspapers reproduced in this volume.

The chapter on the movies was researched and written by John Cassidy of Simi Valley, Calif. It was published by my publishing company in 1986 under the title *Civil War Cinema, A Pictorial History of Hollywood and the War Between the States.*

Also my sincere thanks go to John Hunter and Harper Harris of the Kennesaw Civil War Museum; Keith Lauer of the City of Atlanta Parks, Recreation & Cultural Affairs, Cyclorama; Robert Fulghum, National Medal of Honor Museum, Chattanooga, Tenn., for their help and encouragement and to Richard Andre of Charleston, W. Va. Mike Egeler produced the cover artwork and Janyce Taylor and Leslie Maricelli of my staff were responsible for the pre-production work.

For a detailed written account of the raid, please check the enclosed bibliography.

Stan Cohen
Publisher

**Dedicated to the memory of Wilbur G. Kurtz who kept the
story of the "Great Locomotive Chase" alive.**

Photo Credits

All photos in this book are from the collection of James G. Bogle unless otherwise noted. The photos and other information in Bogle's collection were mainly gathered from the following sources:

Wilbur G. Kurtz
Louisville & Nashville Railroad
Edison H. Thomas
Charles B. Castner Jr.
Norman Beasley
Nashville, Chattanooga & St. Louis Railway
Atlanta History Center
National Archives

Georgia State Archives
Doug Byrum
Miss Holly Hewitt
Ms. Elizabeth Tone
Ohio Historical Society
Jolin Krause
Guy Hays

The Military Situation in the Southeast, Spring 1862

The object of the Andrews Raid, The Western & Atlantic Railroad was a vital link in the southeast area of the Confederacy. It connected Atlanta, Ga., and Chattanooga, Tenn., but also provided access by diverging routes to other major Southern cities such as New Orleans, Mobile, Montgomery, Charleston, Wilmington, Savannah, Augusta and points farther west and north. With these rail lines, men and supplies moved rapidly in this region.

The defense line of Confederate forces in the spring of 1862 extended from Richmond, Va., to Corinth, Miss. A rail line ran from Richmond to Memphis via Chattanooga, Knoxville and East Tennessee connecting the eastern and western sections of the Confederacy.

A focal point of Federal strategy in the spring was to take Chattanooga and sever rail transportation, thus the impetus for the Andrews Raid.

Andrews, a civilian, was engaged in espionage behind Confederate lines under the sponsorship of Federal officers. He would smuggle needed supplies south and at the same time bring back military information. In March 1862 Andrews got his employer, Gen. Don Carlos Buell to sponsor a raid to cut the Memphis & Charleston Railroad and the Western & Atlantic Railroad. The Raid did not succeed.

In the meantime, Gen. Ormsby MacKnight Mitchel had taken over command in the region from General Buell, who was sent to southwest Tennessee. Mitchel wanted to move southeast with his army and seize Huntsville, Ala., and then turn east in hopes of capturing Chattanooga. Andrews proposed that this time he make a raid to try and destroy the Western & Atlantic Railroad link to Chattanooga, thus isolating the city from Atlanta. In hopes of achieving success Andrews would take along his own railroad engineers.

At the time that Andrews and Mitchel were discussing plans for the raid on the railroad, a major battle was taking place farther west in Tennessee at a place called Shiloh or Pittsburg Landing. It resulted in a marginal Federal victory which would severely impact Confederate strategy in this part of the country.

FEDERAL ADVANCES - SPRING 1862

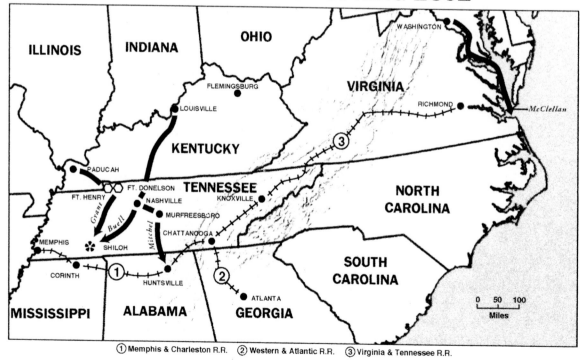

① Memphis & Charleston R.R.   ② Western & Atlantic R.R.   ③ Virginia & Tennessee R.R.

Maj. Gen. Ormsby M. Mitchel

Maj. Gen. Ormsby McKnight Mitchel was the commander of the Ohio Division of the 2nd, 21st and 33rd Ohio Infantry Regiments. Mitchel was in charge of the defense of Nashville, Tenn., with headquarters in the vicinity of Shelbyville. His plan was to advance on Chattanooga with the probability of liberating East Tennessee. He authorized James Andrews' plan to wreck havoc on the Western & Atlantic Railroad.

General Mitchel was born in Union County, Ky., in 1810 and graduated from the U.S. Military Academy in 1829. He served as assistant professor of mathematics, philosophy and astronomy at Cincinnati College. For a time he practiced law and at the time of the Civil War was director of the Dudley Observatory at Albany, N.Y. Upon entering the army he received a commission as brigadier-general of volunteers. From September to November of 1861 he was the head of the Department of the Ohio and had a division in the Army of the Ohio from December 1861 to July 1862. He led a brilliant expedition into Alabama which won him a promotion to major-general of volunteers. In September 1862 he was placed at the head of the Tenth Army Corps. He died at Hilton Head, S.C., of yellow fever on Oct. 27, 1862.

Maj. Gen. Don Carlos Buell

James Andrews, a civilian spy, worked for Maj. Gen. Don Carlos Buell during his 1862 campaign against Fort Donaldson in Tennessee. After Buell's army entered Nashville and while he was planning for further movement to the south, Andrews approached him with a scheme to cut the Memphis & Charleston Railroad by the destruction of the bridge over the Tennessee River at Bridgeport, Ala., and the bridges over Chickamauga Creek in north Georgia.

In March 1862 Andrews, with eight men, set out for Atlanta to do what damage he could, but when he failed to find the engineer who had agreed to help him, his group returned to Nashville without achieving any results.

Gen. Buell was a veteran of the Mexican War and in 1861 took charge of the Department and Army of the Ohio. He fought in Tennessee during the summer of 1862 and drove Bragg out of Kentucky, but he received so much criticism that he was replaced in October 1862 by Gen. Rosecrans and tried before a military commission. Buell resigned from the army in June 1864. He died in 1898.

Table of Contents

THE ANDREWS RAID MEDAL ISSUED BY THE GEORGIA CIVIL WAR CENTENNIAL COMMISSION IN 1962. DESIGNED BY JULIAN HARRIS OF ATLANTA, IT HAS A LIKENESS OF THE *GENERAL* ON ONE SIDE AND WILLIAM A. FULLER ON THE OTHER.

 # Participants in the Raid

There were 24 men involved in this event. Two of them were civilians: James J. Andrews, the leader, and William Campbell. The rest were soldiers, all volunteers, from General Ormsby McKnight Mitchel's Division of Ohio troops. Five men came from the 2d Ohio Infantry Regiment, nine from the 21st Ohio Infantry Regiment, and eight from the 33rd Ohio Infantry Regiment. It is not easy to determine from their files just what each man did as a member of his unit.

Of the 24 men, only 22 reached Georgia for the Raid. James Smith and Samuel Llewellyn dropped out at Jasper, Tenn., when they enlisted in a Confederate unit to avoid suspicion. This fact is often confusing because James Smith was awarded the Medal of Honor for his participation in the Raid. Of the remaining 22 men, two of them missed the train at Marietta on the morning of April 12, 1862. They were John Reed Porter and Martin Jones Hawkins. These two men did attempt to enlist in the Confederate Army later that day at Camp McDonald near Big Shanty (Kennesaw). They were soon identified as members of the Raiding Party and so treated thereafter. Thus, only 20 men actually participated in The Great Locomotive Chase—two civilians and 18 soldiers.

The average age of the Raiders was 24.5 years. Andrews and Robert Buffum were the oldest at about 33 years. James Smith was the youngest at 17 years, but he did not participate in the Chase. Of those who did, Jacob Parrott was the youngest with Samuel Robertson just a few months older.

For reasons not entirely clear from the record, all of the party were not court-martialled for their part in the Raid. James J. Andrews was quickly identified as the leader, and he was the first to be tried in Chattanooga. Twelve of the party were moved to Knoxville for trial, but only seven were actually tried. They were: William Campbell, Samuel Robertson, Marion A. Ross, John M. Scott, Charles P. Shadrach, Samuel Slavens and George D. Wilson. While the following men were taken to Knoxville, they were not tried: Wilson W. Brown, Robert Buffum, Elihu H. Mason, William J. Knight and William Pittenger. The reason these men were not tried was due, most likely, to enemy activity resulting in the adjournment of the court. The eight men who were tried were the eight men who were executed in Atlanta.

James Smith and Samuel Llewellyn are rarely associated with the Andrews Raiders even though they volunteered for the mission and later Smith was confined in the Swims Jail in Chattanooga during the same time as the rest of the Raiders and was also awarded the Medal of Honor for his part. Smith was released and returned to his Confederate unit, later escaping back to his Federal unit. Llewellyn made good his escape from the Confederate unit in which he enlisted and was quickly back with his Federal unit. Of the remaining 22 men, eight were tried and executed. Eight made good their escape from the Fulton County Jail in Atlanta on October 16, 1862. They were: Wilson W. Brown, Daniel A. Dorsey, Martin J. Hawkins, William J. Knight, John Reed Porter, John Alf Wilson, John Wollam and Mark Wood. The remaining six were exchanged on March 17, 1863, at City Point, Va.: William Bensinger, Robert Buffum, Elihu H. Mason, Jacob Parrott, William Pittenger and William H. Reddick. These six men were declared exchanged officially on June 26, 1863.

The first of the group to die after the War was Mark Wood on July 11, 1866. The last to die was John Reed Porter on October 15, 1923. Coincidentally, the last of the Confederate pursuers also died in 1923—Henry P. Haney who died in Atlanta on November 19, 1923. The eight who were executed are buried in the National Cemetery at Chattanooga, Tenn. The graves of eleven are scattered across the State of Ohio (Smith, Wollam, Llewellyn, Parrott, Porter, Bensinger, Knight, J.A. Wilson, Mason, W.W. Brown and Mark Wood.) The remaining five are buried across the country from New York to California: Pittenger in California, Reddick in Iowa, Dorsey in Kansas, Hawkins in Illinois and Buffum in New York. Buffum is buried in an unmarked grave, but his remains are known to be buried at the New York Correctional Facility at Auburn, New York, and a Medal of Honor marker has been placed in the vicinity. Others who have an official Medal of Honor marker at their graves are: Brown, Mason, Dorsey, Hawkins, Parrott, Pittenger, Robertson, Ross, Scott, Slavens, Smith and John A. Wilson.

Raiders' Profiles

James J. Andrews

- Six feet tall, approximately 185 pounds, clear complexion, gray eyes, abundant black hair, short curling beard, later to become luxuriantly full; about 33 on day of the raid.
- Born about 1829, Holiday's Cove, Va., (Now Wierton, W. Va.)
- Hanged June 7, 1862, near present-day intersection of 3rd and Juniper Streets NE, Atlanta, Ga.
- Buried temporarily at site of execution. Remains removed to National Cemetery, Chattanooga, Tenn., Oct. 16, 1887, near Ohio Memorial, Section H, Grave No. 12,982.
- Engaged to Elizabeth Layton of Flemingsburg, Ky., at the time of execution.
- Contraband merchant and trader between the lines. Leader of Andrews Raid, April 1862.
- Captured soon after Raid ended and identified as leader. Court-martialled at Chattanooga; sentenced to hang; escaped Swims Jail, Chattanooga June 2, 1862; recaptured June 3, 1862. Taken to Atlanta, June 7, 1862, and hanged about 5:00 p.m. that afternoon.
- Ineligible for Medal of Honor.

Jacob Parrott

- Five feet 8½ inches tall, dark complexion, black hair, black eyes; 18 years, 8 months, 25 days of age on day of the raid. Cabinet maker.
- Born July 17, 1843, Fairfield County, Ohio. Father died when he was six; mother died when he was 10.
- Dropped dead on South Main Street, Kenton, Ohio, Dec. 22, 1908.
- Buried Grove Cemetery, Kenton. Medal of Honor Marker at grave. (Requested by J.G. Bogle.)
- Married Sarah Lawrence, March 10, 1866, Kenton, Hardin County (d. Dec 6, 1911). Son John Marion married Edith Gertrude Brown, daughter of Raider Wilson W. Brown.
- Enlisted as Pvt. Co. K 33rd Ohio Inf. Regt., Nov. 18, 1861, Kenton, three years. Volunteered Andrews Raid April 7, 1862. Commissioned 2d Lt. Co. K 33rd Ohio Inf. Regt., May 3, 1863; 1st Lt. May, 25, 1864. Discharged Jan. 2, 1865, Savannah, Ga., expiration of term of service.
- Saw action at Battle of Ivy Hill, Ky., Nov. 8, 1861; in Andrews Raid; at battles of Stones River, December 1862; Tullahoma, Chickamauga, September 1863; Lookout Mountain; Missionary Ridge; in the Atlanta Campaign.
- Captured near Ringgold, Ga.; paroled via City Point, Va., March 17, 1863. Declared exchanged June 26, 1863.
- Awarded Medal of Honor March 25, 1863. Medal returned by family to U.S. Congress July 12, 1990; now on display in the U.S. Capitol Rotunda. Pension $30 per month effective February 1874, No. 125,044.

- Twenty-three years 3 months 11 days of age on day of the raid.
- Born Jan. 1, 1839, Stark County, Ohio, to Thomas B. Scott; mother unknown.
- Hanged June 18, 1862, at southeast corner of Fair Street (now Memorial Drive) and South Park Avenue, Atlanta, Ga.
- Buried temporarily at site of execution. Remains removed to National Cemetery, Chattanooga, Tenn., April 25, 1866, near Ohio Memorial, Section H, Grave No. 11,182. Medal of Honor marker at grave.
- Married Rachel M. Davis, Sept. 24, 1861. Findlay, Ohio. (Rachel Davis Scott remarried William C. Waggoner.)
- Enrolled as Pvt. Co. F 21st Ohio Inf. Regt. Sept. 6, 1861, for three years. Mustered as Sgt. Co. F 21st Ohio Infantry Regiment, Sept. 19, 1861. Volunteered Andrews Raid April 7, 1862.
- Saw action at Battle of Ivy Mountain, Ky., Nov. 8-9, 1861; in Andrews Raid.
- Captured near Lookout Mountain, April 19, 1862. Court-martialled Knoxville, Tenn., General Orders No. 54, 1862. HQ Department of East Tennessee, CSA.
- Awarded Medal of Honor Aug. 4, 1866. Receipt acknowledged by father Thomas B. Scott, by letter Sept. 18, 1866. Pension $8 effective June 18, 1862, to widow Rachel Scott.

John Morehead Scott

Robert Buffum

- Five feet 6$^{1}/_{2}$ inches tall, dark complexion, black hair, blue eyes, one upper front tooth missing; 33 years, 9 months, 5 days of age on day of the raid. Farmer. Drinking problem.
- Born July 7, 1828, Salem, Mass.
- Suicide July 20, 1871, Auburn, N.Y.
- Buried in unmarked grave, State Correctional Cemetery, Auburn, N.Y. Medal of Honor marker placed in vicinity, in Memory of Buffum, July 29, 1995.
- Wife Elizabeth.
- Served with John Brown in Kansas before the Civil War. Enlisted Co. H 21st Ohio Inf. Regt., Sept. 2, 1862, three years at Gilead, Ohio. Mustered Sept. 19, 1861, Findlay, Ohio. Volunteered Andrews Raid, April 7, 1862. Discharged May 24, 1863, to receive Commission as 2d Lt. Co. H 21st Ohio Inf. Regt. Declared exchanged June 21, 1863. AWOL June 22-Dec.12, 1863. Resigned for the good of service, April 28, 1864, Graysville, Ga.
- Saw action in Andrews Raid.
- Captured following Raid; sent to Knoxville, Tenn., May 1862 but not tried; exchanged via City Point, Va., March 17, 1863.
- Awarded Medal of Honor Mar. 25, 1863.

William Bensinger

- Five feet, 9 inches tall, light complexion, blue eyes, dark hair; 22 years, 2 months, 28 days on day of the raid. Railway employee at Lima and St. Marys, Ohio, five years after War.
- Born Jan. 14, 1840, Congress Township, Wayne County, Ohio, to Reuben and Hannah Feazel Bensinger.
- Died Dec. 19, 1918, McComb, Hancock County, Ohio.
- Buried Union Cemetery, McComb.
  No Medal of Honor marker at grave.
- Married Sarah A. Harris, Feb. 11, 1864, at Charlotte, Dickson County, Tenn. (b. May 26, 1846; d. Feb. 4, 1929.)
- Served with Co. G 21st Ohio Inf. Regt., Aug. 19, 1861, three years. Mustered Co. G 21st Ohio Inf. Regt., Sept., 19, 1861, Findlay, Ohio, three years. Discharged Aug. 20, 1863; Captain Co. C 13th U.S. Colored Inf. Regt. Discharged Jan. 10, 1866, Nashville, Tenn.
- Saw action in Battle of Ivy Hill, Floyd County, Ky., Nov. 8, 1861; in Andrews Raid; at Battle of Nashville, Dec. 1864.
- Captured April 13, 1862, near Ringgold, Ga.; escaped jail, Atlanta, Ga., Oct. 16, 1862. Recaptured Oct. 17, 1862; paroled via City Point, Va., March 17, 1863. Declared exchanged June 21, 1863.
- Awarded Medal of Honor March 25, 1863, Washington, D.C. Acknowledged receipt of engraved Medal on Nov. 10, 1863. Medal lost; duplicate issued July 30, 1894. Pension of $40 per month activated May 11, 1914.

Daniel Allen Dorsey

- Five feet 6 inches tall, light complexion, light eyes and hair; 23 years, 3 months, 11 days of age on day of the raid. Wrote diary and series on the raid for *The Ohio Soldier,* critical of William Pittenger. Roamed country, living out of suitcase.
- Born Dec. 31, 1838, Lancaster, Fairfield County, Ohio.
- Died May 10, 1918, Veterans Administration Hospital, Wadsworth, Kan.
- Married Annie C. Miller, March 9, 1865, Circleville, Ohio. Six children. Deserted family.
- Enlisted Aug. 27, 1861. Mustered Sept. 18, 1861, Co. H 33rd Ohio Inf. Regt., Portsmouth, Ohio. Promoted Cpl. Nov. 1, 1861. Volunteered Andrews Raid April 7, 1862. Promoted 2d Lt. April 27, 1863; 1st Lt. May 25, 1864; Hospitalized May 23, 1864, Lookout Mountain Tenn. Resigned with disability Aug. 24, 1864, Chattanooga, Tenn.
- Captured April 13, 1862, near Ringgold, Ga.; escaped Fulton county jail Atlanta, Ga., Oct 16, 1862. Rejoined Union lines Nov. 18, 1862, Somerset, Ky.
- Saw action in Andrews Raid; at Battle of Chickamauga, Ga., Sept. 1863.
- Awarded Medal of Honor Sept. 15, 1863. Pension $40 per month, No. 138123.

- Five feet 6¹/₂ inches tall, light complexion, light hair, blue eyes; 25 years, 2 months, and 18 days of age on day of the raid. Railroad engineer. Gave lectures on the Raid after the War.
- Born Jan. 24, 1837, Apple Creek, Wayne County, Ohio, to Matthew Knight; mother unknown.
- Died Sept. 26, 1916, Stryker, Ohio.
- Buried Stryker Cemetery, Sept. 30, 1916.
  No Medal of Honor Marker at grave.
- Married Emma F. Oldfield, Aug. 30, 1868, Defiance, Ohio. (b. Sept. 8, 1848; d. June 27, 1940).
- Enrolled Aug. 19, 1861, Co. E 21st Ohio Inf. Regt., three years, Findlay, Ohio. Mustered same unit Sept. 19, 1861. Transferred Co. G 115th Ohio Volunteer Inf. Regt., Mar 13, 1863. Volunteered Andrews Raid, April 7, 1862. Discharged Sept. 28, 1864, Nashville, Tenn, expiration term of service.
- Saw action in Andrews Raid; at Battle of Stones River, Dec. 31, 1862.
- Captured following the raid; taken to Knoxville, Tenn., for trial but not tried; escaped Fulton County jail Atlanta, Ga., Oct. 16, 1862. Rejoined Union lines Nov. 25, 1862, Somerset, Ky.
- Awarded Medal of Honor September 1863. Pension $30 per month at time of death.

William James Knight

- Five feet 6 inches tall, 175 pounds, dark complexion, light brown hair, blue eyes; 20 years, 5 months, 17 days of age on day of the raid. Coal miner, but wrote in September 1904 that he was "not very busy at it." Two-term member of House of Representatives, Ohio General Assembly, from Jackson County, Ohio, 1890-1893.
- Born Oct. 25, 1841, Pittsburgh, Pa., to natives of Monmouthshire, England.
- Died Aug. 14, 1915, Ohio Soldiers and Sailors Home, Sandusky, Ohio.
- Buried City Cemetery of Coalton, Ohio, near entrance. No Medal of Honor marker on grave.
- Enrolled as Pvt. Co. F 10th Ohio Inf. Regiment April 19, 1861, Pomeroy, Ohio, three months. Enlisted Co. L 33rd Ohio Inf. Regt, Sept. 10, 1861, three years. Mustered Oct. 11, 1861, Portsmouth, Ohio; promoted Cpl. Oct. 11, 1861; Sgt. May 20, 1862. Discharged Oct. 17, 1864, Villenou, Ga.
- Saw action at Battle of Perryville, Ky.; in Andrews Raid; enlisted in Confederate unit at Jasper, Tenn., then escaped to Union lines near Bridgeport, Ala., April 29, 1862; at Battle of Chickamauga, Ga., Sept. 20, 1863; wounded in chin; captured; paroled May 1, 1864.
- Pension $15 per month effective Oct. 27, 1911, per act of Feb. 6, 1907; $25 per month effective May 20, 1912, No. 1107-477.

Samuel Llewellyn

Elihu Harlam Mason

William Hunter Campbell

- Five feet 10$\frac{1}{4}$ inches tall, light complexion, blonde hair, blue eyes; 31 years, 19 days of age on day of the raid. Farmer.
- Born March 23, 1831, near Richmond, Wayne County, Ind.
- Died Sept. 24, 1896, at his home, corner of Perry and Maple Streets, Pemberville, Wood County, Ohio.
- Buried Pemberville Cemetery, Sept. 27, 1896, Block A, Lot No. 193. Medal of Honor marker at grave. Local marker nearby indicates he was awarded second Medal of Honor after Parrott.
- Married Nancy L. Kelley, Feb. 3, 1852, Wausau, Ind. (d. Nov. 27, 1905).
- Enrolled as Pvt. I Co. 21st Ohio Inf. Regt., April 26, 1861, Elmore, Ohio, three months. Mustered as Pvt. K Co. 21 Ohio Inf. Regt., Aug. 24, 1861, Wood County, Ohio, three years. Appointed Sgt. Sept. 19, 1861. Discharged for promotion 1st Lt. Co. L 21st Ohio Inf. Regt., April 10, 1863. Promoted Capt. Co. L 21st Ohio Inf. Regt., Dec. 30, 1864. Discharged for promotion 1st Lt. Co. B 21st Ohio Inf. Regt., June 10, 1863. Capt. Co. L 21st Ohio Inf. Regt., Columbus, Ohio, May 15, 1865.
- Saw action in Andrews Raid; at Battle of Chickamauga, Sept. 1863; at Battle of Dug Gap, Ga., Sept. 11, 1863.
- Captured at Bridgeport, Ala., April 19, 1862; escaped Fulton County Jail, Atlanta, Ga., Oct. 16, 1862. Recaptured Oct. 18, 1862; sent to Knoxville, Tenn., for trial but not tried; paroled via City Point, Va., March 17, 1863. Declared exchanged June 26, 1863. Captured again Chickamauga, Ga., Sept. 20, 1863; gunshot wound in hip; confined Richmond, Va., Nov. 20, 1863, Macon, Ga., May 7, 1864; paroled Dec. 13, 1864, Charleston, S.C.
- Awarded Medal of Honor March 25, 1863. Pension $24 per month approved July 7, 1884, No. 275,623.

- Weighed over 200 pounds; 22 years, 7 months, 3 days of age on day of the raid.
- Born Sept. 9, 1839, a few miles east of Salineville, Columbia County, Ohio, to Samuel and Sarah Hunter Campbell.
- Hanged June 18, 1862, at southeast corner of Fair Street (now Memorial Drive) and South Park Avenue, Atlanta, Ga.
- Buried temporarily at site of execution. Remains removed to National Cemetery, Chattanooga, Tenn., April 25, 1866, near Ohio Memorial, Section G, Grave No. 11,180.
- A civilian, visiting friends in 2d Ohio Inf. Regt. Grave marker indicates he was a member of 2d Ohio Inf. Regt. Court-martialled Knoxville, Tenn., General Orders No. 54, 1862, HQ Dept. East Tennessee, CSA.
- Ineligible for Medal of Honor.

- Five feet 11 inches tall, fair complexion, light hair, blue eyes; 22 years, 2 months, 11 days of age on day of the raid. Farmer, minister, author of several books about the Raid.
- Born Jan. 31, 1840, Jefferson County, Ohio, to Thomas and Mary Mills Pittenger.
- Died April 24, 1904, Fallbrook, San Diego County, Ca.
- Buried Odd Fellows Cemetery, Fallbrook, April 25, 1904. Medal of Honor marker placed on grave July 7, 1988.
- Married Wilhelmina (Winnie) Clyde Osborne of New Brighton, Pa., May 17, 1864. Six children.
- Enlisted Co. H 2d Ohio Inf. Regt. April 17, 1861, Camp Dennison, Ohio, three months. Enlisted as Cpl. Co. G 2d Ohio Inf. Regt. Sept. 5, 1861, Stubenville, Ohio. Mustered Sept. 11, 1861, Camp Dennison, three years. Promoted Sgt. March 13, 1862. Discharged with disability Aug. 14, 1863, Anderson Station, Tenn.
- Saw action in Andrews Raid.
- Captured April 15, 1862, near Lafeyette, Ga.; paroled via City Point, Va. Declared exchanged June 26, 1863.
- Awarded Medal of Honor March 25, 1863. Pension $24 per month, No. 166,444.

William C. Pittenger

- Five feet 8³/₄ inches tall, fair complexion, dark hair, hazel eyes; 23 years, 4 months, 28 days of age on day of the raid. Lived in Arkansas 1870-1883, McComb, Ohio, until 1888, then "roamed" as far west as Yakima, Wa., before returning to Ohio.
- Born Nov. 14, 1838, Delaware County, Ohio, to James and Opra Decker Porter.
- Last Raider to die, Oct. 15, 1923, 716 Meredith Street, Dayton, Ohio.
- Buried Union Cemetery, McComb, Ohio, Oct. 18, 1923. No Medal of Honor marker on grave.
- Enlisted Co. A 21st Ohio Inf. Regt., April 19, 1861, three months. Enlisted Co. G 21st Ohio Inf. Regt. Sept. 2, 1861, McComb, three years. Mustered Sept. 19, 1861, Findlay, Ohio, Co. G 21st Ohio Inf. Regt., three years. Promoted Sgt. Feb 1, 1863; 2d Lt. July 9, 1863; 1st Lt. Jan. 28, 1865, then commanding Co. I 21st Ohio Volunteer Inf. Regt. Discharged March 31, 1865, Goldsboro, N.C.
- Saw action at Battle of Ivy Hill, Floyd County, Ky., Nov. 8, 1861; in Andrews Raid; at Battle of Chickamauga, Ga., Sept. 20, 1863.
- Captured after Andrews Raid, April 14, 1862; escaped Fulton County Jail Atlanta, Ga., Oct 16, 1862. Rejoined Federal lines, Corinth, Miss., Nov 18, 1862. Captured Sept. 20, 1863; escaped near Augusta, Ga., June 27, 1864. Wounded on foraging expedition near Bentonville, N.C.; thrown from mule, suffering rupture and later hernia.
- Awarded Medal of Honor September 1863; acknowledged receipt of engraved Medal Aug. 1, 1864.

John Reed Porter

William Henry Harrison Reddick

- Five feet 8 inches tall, light hair, blue eyes; 21 years, 6 months, 24 days of age on day of the the raid. Farmer.
- Born Sept. 18, 1840, Bloomington, Monroe County, Ind.
- Died Nov. 8, 1903, Seventy-six Township, Muscatine County, near Letts, Iowa.
- Buried Lettsville Cemetery, Letts.
- Married Rachel Ann Stahl Reddick, March 6, 1864, Locust Grove, Adams County, Ohio.
- Enrolled Pvt. Co. B 33rd Ohio Inf. Regt., Aug. 18, 1861, Camp Morrison. Mustered August 27, 1861, three years. Promoted Cpl. Aug. 27, 1861. Volunteered Andrews Raid April 7, 1862. Discharged July 12, 1863, Cowan, Tenn., to accept commission as 2d Lt. July 13, 1863. Discharged July 25, 1865.
- Captured near Ringgold, April 12, 1862; paroled via City Point, Va., March 17, 1863.
- Saw action in Andrews Raid.
- Awarded Medal of Honor March 25, 1863. Pension $24 per month, No. 336,034.

Samuel Robertson

- Five feet 9 1/2 inches tall, sandy complexion, sandy hair, gray eyes; 18 years, 11 months, 11 days of age on the day of the the raid. Saw mill engineer.
- Born May 1, 1843, Taylorsville, Highland County, Ohio, to Samuel Robertson Sr. (b. March 15, 1798; d. Feb. 13, 1844) and Julia Ann Gater Robertson, (b. June 2, 1801), married March 11, 1824.
- Hanged June 18, 1862, at southeast corner of Fair Street (now Memorial Drive) and South Park Avenue, Atlanta, Ga.
- Buried temporarily at site of execution. Remains removed to the National Cemetery, Chattanooga, Tenn., April 25, 1866, near Ohio Memorial, Section H, Grave No. 11,177. Medal of Honor marker at Grave.
- Enrolled as Pvt. Co. G 33rd Ohio Inf. Regt., Sept. 1, 1861, Bourneville, Ohio, for three years. Mustered Sept. 12, 1861. Volunteered Andrews Raid April 6, 1862.
- Captured. Court-martialled Knoxville, Tenn., General Orders No. 54, 1862. HQ Department of East Tennessee, CSA.
- Saw action in Andrews Raid.
- Medal of Honor awarded September 1863. Pension $8 per month, No. 120,246.

Marion A. Ross

- Twenty-nine years, 6 months, 3 days of age on day of the raid.
- Born Oct. 9, 1832, near Honey Creek, Addison, Jackson Township, Champaign County, Ohio, to Levi (d. Dec. 25, 1863) and Mary Ruffner Ross.
- Hanged June 18, 1862, at southeast corner of Fair Street (now Memorial Drive) and South Park Avenue, Atlanta, Ga.
- Buried Temporarily at site of execution. Remains removed to National Cemetery, Chattanooga, Tenn., April 25, 1866, near Ohio Memorial, Section H, Grave No. 11,179. Medal of Honor marker at grave.
- Enlisted 2d Ohio Inf. Regt. April 15, 1861, three months. QM Sgt. Sept. 18, 1861; Regt. Sgt. Maj. Dec. 7, 1861. Enlisted Aug. 20, 1861, for three years. Mustered Aug. 27, 1861, Camp Dennison, Ohio.
- Captured. Court-martialled Knoxville, Tenn., General Orders No. 54, 1862. HQ Department of East Tennessee, CSA.
- Saw action at first Battle of Bull Run; in Andrews Raid.
- Awarded Medal of Honor September 1863.

- Five feet 7 inches tall, dark complexion, brown hair, blue eyes; 23 years of age on day of the raid. Came to United States about 1858. Machinist.
- Born Nottingham, England; christened Sept. 22, 1839, to William (d. July 29, 1892, aged 87 years) and Mary Wood, Germantown, Pa.
- First Raider to die after War, July 11, 1866, Toledo, Ohio.
- Buried Forest Cemetery, Toledo, Masonic Lot. No. 36, Section H, Grave No. 8, July 13, 1866. New marker on grave with engraved likeness of *General,* executed by Bo Coogler of Elberton, Ga.
- Enrolled as Pvt. C Co. 21st Ohio Inf. Regt., Aug. 29, 1861, Perrysburg, Ohio. Mustered Sept. 19, 1861, Findlay, Ohio, three years. Volunteered Andrews Raid April 7, 1862. Promoted Cpl. Feb. 1862. Discharged Feb. 9, 1864. Commissioned as 2d Lt. Co. F 21st Ohio Inf. Regt. March 1, 1864. Hospitalized Chattanooga, Tenn., May 9, 1864. Discharged Nov. 3, 1864, with disability due to wounds received at the Battle of Chickamauga, Ga., and again at Buzzard's Roost, Ga., Mar 9, 1864.
- Saw action at Battle of Ivy Hill, Nov 8, 1861; in Andrews Raid; at Battles of Stones River, December 1862; Chickamauga, September 1863, and Buzzard's Roost, May 1864.
- Captured near Bridgeport, Ala., escaped Fulton County Jail, Atlanta, Ga., Oct. 16, 1862; journeyed with John Alf Wilson. Picked up by Union gunboat, Gulf of Mexico Nov. 10, 1862. POW in Battle of Chickamauga, Sept. 20, 1863; paroled Chattanooga, Sept. 29, 1863.
- Awarded Medal of Honor September 1863. Pension $15 per month for disability, effective Nov 3, 1864.

Mark Wood

Samuel Slavens

- Five feet 8 inches tall, weight 180 pounds, stout build; 31 years of age on day of the raid.
- Born March 18, 1831.
- Hanged June 18, 1862, at southeast corner of Fair Street (now Memorial Drive) and South Park Avenue, Atlanta, Ga.
- Buried temporarily at site of execution. Remains removed to National Cemetery, Chattanooga, Tenn., April 25, 1866, near Ohio Memorial, Section H, Grave No. 11,176.
- Married Rachel Taylor (b. 1839; d. Feb. 6, 1907), Oct. 30, 1856, Pike County, Ohio.
- Enrolled Co. E 33rd Ohio Inf. Regt., Oct. 1, 1861. Mustered as Pvt. Oct. 11, 1861, Camp Morrow, Portsmouth, Ohio, three years. Volunteered Andrews Raid April 7, 1862.
- Saw action in Andrews Raid.
- Captured. Court-martialled Knoxville, Tenn., General Orders No. 54, 1862. HQ Department of East Tennessee, CSA.
- Awarded Medal of Honor; delivered to widow Rachel Slavens, July 28, 1883. Pension $24 per month to widow, No. 68,918.

Ovid Wellford Smith

- Five feet 9 inches tall, dark complexion, black hair, black eyes; 17 years, 5 months, 3 days of age on day of the raid. Machinist with Columbus & Indiana Central Railway at Columbus, Ohio, shops.
- Born Nov. 9, 1844, Fredericksburg, Va., to Rev. Samuel (d. Oct. 4, 1880) and Mary Smith.
- Died Jan 28, 1868, Columbus, of pneumonia.
- Buried Greenlawn Cemetery, Columbus, January 31, 1868, Section C, Lot. No. 84. Medal of Honor marker at grave. (Requested by James G. Bogle.)
- Enrolled as James Smith without parents' knowledge or permission Co. I 2d Ohio Inf. Regt., Aug. 15, 1861, Circleville, Ohio. Mustered Sept. 3, 1861, Camp Dennison, Ohio. Volunteered Andrews Raid April 7, 1862. Appointed Cpl. Sept. 25, 1862. Discharged Oct. 10, 1864, Camp Chase, Ohio, expiration of term of service.
- Saw action in Andrews Raid; at Battles of Chickamauga, Ga., Chattanooga, Ga., Missionary Ridge; in Atlanta, Ga., campaign.
- Enlisted Confederate unit Jasper, Tenn.; came under suspicion by Confederates; jailed in Swims Jail, Chattanooga; escaped.
- Awarded Medal of Honor July 6, 1864.

John Alfred Wilson

- Five feet 8 inches tall, sandy hair, blue eyes; 29 years, 8 months, 7 days of age on day of the raid. Author *The Adventures of Alf Wilson*.
- Born July 25, 1832, near Worthington, Franklin County, Ohio, to Ezekiel Wilson; mother unknown.
- Died March 28, 1904, Perrysburg, Ohio.
- Buried Union Hill Cemetery, between Perrysburg and Bowling Green, Ohio.
- Married Gretta Hale.
- Enrolled as Pvt. Co. C 21st Ohio Inf. Regt., Aug. 29, 1861, Findlay, Ohio, three years. Volunteered Andrews Raid. Discharged, Sept. 22, 1864, Atlanta, Ga., due to expiration of term of service.
- Saw action in Andrews Raid.
- Captured near Stevenson, Ala., April 24, 1862; escaped Fulton County Jail, Atlanta, Ga., Oct. 16, 1862; picked up by Union gunboat, Gulf of Mexico, Nov. 10, 1862. Hospitalized Murfeesboro, Tenn., May and June 1863.
- Awarded Medal of Honor September 1863. Medal on display at Freedom Foundation, Pa., as of 1992. Pension $24 per month, No. 258,375.

John Wollam

- Five feet 8 inches tall, slender, fair complexion, dark hair, blue eyes; 22 years of age on day of the raid. Slight beard and mustache. Farmer.
- Born 1840, Hamilton, Ohio, to Balser and Harriet Swanton Wollam (d. July 18, 1875), married Aug. 13, 1833.
- Died Sept. 25, 1890, Topeka, Kan.
- Buried Fairmont Cemetery, Jackson, Ohio, Sept. 29-30, 1890.
- Enrolled Co. C 33rd Ohio Inf. Regt. August 24, 1861. Mustered Aug. 27, 1861, Camp Morrow, Portsmouth, Ohio. Volunteered Andrews Raid. Discharged Oct. 10, 1864, Acworth, Ga., expiration of term of service.
- Saw action in Andrews Raid; at Battle of Chickamauga, Ga.; in the Atlanta, Ga., campaign.
- Captured April 1862; escaped Swims Jail, Chattanooga, Tenn.; recaptured 1862; escaped Fulton County Jail, Atlanta, Ga., Oct. 16, 1862. Reached Federal lines near Corinth, Miss., Nov. 18, 1862. Captured Sept. 19, 1863; escaped February 1864.
- Awarded Medal of Honor July 20, 1864. Pension $24 per month, effective July 16, 1888, No. 407,429.

Wilson Wright Brown

- Qualified locomotive engineer; 24 years, 3 months, 17 days of age on day of the raid.
- Born Dec. 25, 1837, Logan County, Ohio, to Harlan and Mary Ann (Polly) Colvin/Calvin.
- Died Dec. 25, 1916, 874 Forsyth St., East Toledo, Ohio.
- Buried New Belleville Ridge Cemetery, Dowling, Ohio. Medal of Honor marker at grave. Nearby Ohio Historical marker erected June 27, 1965, identifies him as Medal of Honor recipient.
- Married Clarissa Lowman, July 12, 1863, Marion Township, Hancock County, Ohio (d. Feb. 21, 1919, age 74). Seven children; daughter Gertrude married John W. Parrott, son of Andrews Raider Jacob Parrott and first to receive Medal of Honor.
- Enrolled Co. F 21st Ohio Inf. Regt., Sept. 5, 1861, Findlay, Ohio, three years. Mustered Sept. 19, 1861, as Pvt. Co. F 21st Ohio Inf. Regt., Findlay. Promoted Sgt. Nov. 1, 1862. Discharged May 15, 1864, with disability, Columbus, Ohio, Sgt.
- Saw action at Ivy Mountain, Ky., Nov. 8-9, 1861; in Andrews Raid; at Battle of Stones River, Dec. 31, 1862-Jan. 3, 1863; at Dug Gap, Ga., Sept. 11, 1863; at Chickamauga, Ga., Sept. 19, 1863. Wounded left knee, hand and captured; hospitalized at Stevenson, Ala; paroled, sent to Nashville, Tenn., hospital March 1, 1864. Furloughed from Nashville Hospital March 11, 1864.
- Captured near Bridgeport, Ala., April 19, 1862, after Andrews Raid; jailed Chattanooga, Madison, Atlanta, Ga.; escaped Atlanta Oct. 16, 1862. Reported behind Union lines, Somerset, Ky., Nov. 25, 1862. Not court-martialled.
- Awarded Medal of Honor Sept. 17, 1863. Pension $40 per month at time of death.

Philip Gephart Shadrach

- Enrolled in service under name of Charles P. Shadrack, also known as Perry; 21 years, 6 months, 27 days of age on day of raid.
- Born Sept. 15, 1840, Somerset County, Penn., to Robert and Elizabeth Shadrach.
- Hanged at corner of Fair Street (now Memorial Drive) and South Park Avenue, Atlanta, on June 18, 1862. Temporarily was buried near site of execution. Remains were removed to National Cemetery, Chattanooga, Tenn., April 25, 1866. Buried near Ohio Memorial, Section H, Grave No. 11,181.
- Never married.
- Enlisted as Pvt., Co. K, 2d Ohio Infantry Regiment.; served 3 years. Enlisted at Mitchell Salt Works. Volunteered for Andrews Raid, April 7, 1862, and was captured soon after.
- Court-martialled at Knoxville, Tenn., General Orders No. 54, 1862, Hq. Dept. of East Tenn., CSA.
- No Medal of Honor.

George Davenport Wilson

- Tall with spare frame, high cheekbones with overhanging brows, thin brownish hair, long thin whiskers and sharp gray eyes. Journeyman shoemaker.
- Born in 1830 in Belmont County, Ohio, to Elizabeth Clark and George Wilson. Father died April 14, 1861.
- Hanged June 18, 1862, at corner of Fair Street (now Memorial Drive) and South Park Avenue, Atlanta, Ga. Buried temporarily near site of execution, then remains removed to National Cemetery, Chattanooga, Tenn., April 25, 1866. Buried near Ohio Memorial, Section H, Grave 11,178.
- Married Martha Maple Wilson on Sept. 6, 1849, and divorced Feb. 8, 1861. One son, born Nov. 12, 1852, died in railroad wreck in August 1888. One daughter died in 1861.
- Enrolled Co. B, 2d Ohio Inf. Regt., Aug. 31, 1861, Franklin, Ohio, for three-year term. Volunteered Andrews Raid.
- Court-martialled at Knoxville, Tenn., May 31, 1862, General Orders No. 54, 1862, Hq. Dept. of East Tenn., CSA.
- No Medal of Honor.

Martin Jones Hawkins

- Six feet tall, dark complexion, black eyes and brown hair. Railroad engineer.
- Born 1830, Mercer County, Penn.
- Died Feb. 7, 1886, Quincy, Ill.
- Buried Feb. 9, 1886, at Quincy, Ill., Woodland Cemetery, Lot No. 182, Block 12. No Medal of Honor marker.
- Married Sarah F. Higgins on Sept. 10, 1866, Portsmouth, Sciota County, Ohio. She died Nov. 20, 1899.
- Enrolled Co. A, 33rd Ohio Inf. Reg., Aug. 5, 1861, Portsmouth, Ohio. Mustered Aug. 27, 1861, same unit, 3 years. Appointed Cpl. Aug. 17, 1861. Applied for commission in a colored regiment Dec. 5, 1863, examined and rejected Jan. 23, 1864. No reason specified. Reduced to Pvt. at his request April 24, 1864. Appointed Sgt. June 6, 1865, reenlisted as Veteran Volunteer, Jan., 1, 1864. Volunteered for Andrews Raid.
- Saw action in Andrews Raid. Captured April 13, 1862, near Dalton, Ga. Exchanged June 26, 1863. Discharged July 12, 1865, near Louisville, Ky.
- Awarded Medal of Honor, September 1863.

The Case of Private James Smith

The gravesite and real name of Private Smith was one of the last mysteries of the Andrews Raid.

James Smith's mother, Mrs. Mary Smith, applied for a pension on account of her son's military service on May 29, 1884, and gave her address as Parkersburg, W.Va., Wood County. She was then 77 years of age, and her husband, the Rev. Samuel Smith, had died at the age of 81 on October 4, 1880. Mrs. Smith stated in her application that she was the "Mother of (James Smith) Ovid Smith, who enlisted under the name of James Smith, at Circleville, Ohio, on the 15th of August 1861, in Company I, 2d Ohio Volunteer Infantry, who went in to the Army healthy and was afflicted with Rheumatism and Catarrh on his discharge. He enlisted without his parent's consent and was only 16 years of age but gave his age as 22.

"He was never well after his return but continued in bad health until his death on the 28th of January 1868, and was never married."

Mrs. Smith appointed S.F. Shaw, a lawyer of Parkersburg, as her attorney to prosecute her claim. Shaw wrote a covering letter addressed to the Honorable Commissioner of Pensions and stated: "Enclosed please find application for pension of Mrs. Mary Smith. This son for gallant service was given a Medal by Congress which I have here and will file with the papers when numbered. Ovid, who enlisted as James Smith, formerly lived here and was well-known in this city. No difficulty in proving the identify of the same."

Along with Mary Smith's pension application was additional information relative to James Smith's military service not heretofore obtained from theNational Archives. This data indicated that James Smith enrolled as a private in Lieut. Julius F. Williams, Company I, Second Ohio Volunteer Infantry Regiment on the 15th day of August 1861, at Circleville, Ohio, to serve three years, was mustered in on September 3, 1861, at Camp Dennison, Ohio, and was discharged from the service of the United States on the 10th day of October 1864, at Camp Chase, Columbus, Ohio. The record further indicates that James Smith was born in Fredericksburg, Va., was 22 years of age, 5 feet 9 inches tall, with dark complexion, black eyes, black hair, and by occupation, was a mechanic.

With this information, the writer got in touch with Harry D. Lynch, editor and publisher of the *West Virginia Hillbilly*, in December 1982, and asked him to publicize the matter and see if some reader in Parkersburg could help locate the resting place of James Smith. In early January 1983, word came from Charles E. Arnold of Vienna, and Wes Cochran of Parkersburg, that James Smith's parents were buried there in the I.O.O.F. Cemetery. More importantly, they enclosed a print from a microfilm copy of a portion of the *West Virginia Weekly Times*, Parkersburg, Thursday, February 6, 1868, with a death notice of Ovid W. Smith. The obituary states:

Died
In Columbus, Ohio on
January 28, 1868, Ovid W.
Smith, youngest son of the
Rev. Samuel and Mary Smith
of Parkersburg, W.Va.

This information was communicated to Doug Byrum in Columbus and he soon concluded that James Smith had to be buried in Green Lawn Cemetery, the oldest in Columbus. A visit to the cemetery revealed that he was buried there. The records of Green Lawn Cemetery reflect that Ovid W. Smith, was interred in the Samuel Smith lot, burial No. 3359, Lot No. 84, Section C, on January 31, 1968. The record also indicates that he was born on November 9, 1844, at Fredericksburg Va. That he died on January 28, 1868, at Columbus, Ohio, and that his parents names were: Samuel and Mary Smith. The cause of death was listed as pneumonia. The undertaker was Taylor, O'Hara and Company of Columbus. The inscription on his tombstone reveals his full name as Ovid Wellford Smith.

James Smith joined Corporal Samuel Lewellyn, of Company I, 33rd Ohio Volunteer Infantry Regiment, and together they started for Marietta. Near the town of Jasper, Tennessee, some 30 miles west of Chattanooga, they were sharply questioned as strangers. They decided to join a local Confederate Artillery unit, as they had been instructed to do by Andrews in such an event, with the intention of escaping later.

All went well until April 29, 1862, when their unit was engaged with elements of General Mitchel's Division, their parent unit, near Bridgeport, Alabama. During the course of the action, Llewellyn made a run for it and escaped over the Tennessee River bridge back to his own unit of the 33rd Ohio Volunteer Infantry Regiment. Smith was not able to get away. Llewellyn's action put Smith under greater suspicion and he was then placed under arrest and soon found himself in the Swims Jail in Chattanooga where Andrews' remaining 21 members of the party were. The jail was a two-story building and Smith was placed in the upper story whereas the rest were on the ground floor. In this way, it is doubted that Smith ever came in contact with other members of the party and they made no effort to recognize or communicate with him. Smith was there, apparently, because of questionable loyalty and not because he was known to be a member of the Andrews Raiding party.

At their initial meeting, Andrews had instructed the men if they were pressed too much about their presence or identity, to say they were from Fleming County, Kentucky, and going south to join a Confederate Army unit and, if necessary, to join and later escape back to their own lines. Andrews knew that no one from Fleming County, Kentucky, had enlisted in the Confederate Army and he felt this would be a safe course of action. It had the reverse effect in several instances, such as Porter and Hawkins, as it indicated to the Confederates that these strange men were all of the same party who had seized the train at Big Shanty. It is not known whether Smith and Llewellyn used the story. If they did, the information apparently was not conveyed to the Confederate authorities in Chattanooga and at the Swims Jail for Smith was not treated as a member of the Andrews Party.

It appears that Smith spent several months in the Swims Jail. On May 2, 1862, the other members of the party were moved from Chattanooga to Madison, Georgia, for a few days. Smith did not accompany the group. His service record indicates that he was on "detached service" during April and May, 1862, and that he was not present for duty until September 1862. Sometime during this period, he was released from the Swims Jail and returned to his Confederate unit. Then he was able to make good his escape and rejoin the 2d Ohio Volunteer Infantry Regiment. He was promoted from private to corporal on September 25, 1862, and this may have been related to his return from detached service. Sometime during May and June 1863, he was under arrest for "sleeping on post." This infraction probably caused his reduction in rank to private, and we find he was on furlough for some period in January and February 1864. Later, in 1864, he probably was fighting in the Atlanta Campaign under Gen. William T. Sherman, for the 2d Ohio Volunteer Infantry Regiment was part of Brig. Gen. William P. Carlin's First Brigade of Brig. Gen. John M. Palmer's 14th Corps of the Army of Tennessee. The regiment did not complete the campaign for it was ordered back to Chattanooga on July 27, 1864. Wilbur G. Kurtz was in Tiffin, Ohio, and in conversation with William J. Knight and Jacob Parrott, two members of the raiding party, was told that James Smith had been killed in the Atlanta Campaign.

The 2d Ohio Volunteer Infantry Regiment, after being withdrawn from Sherman's forces, made its way back to Ohio, where the unit was mustered out of the service on October 10, 1864, at Camp Chase. The members had served their three years. Private James Smith was among those discharged and his record indicated that he was then 19 years of age. This corresponds with his birth date of November 9, 1844, as indicated in the burial records of Green Lawn Cemetery, Columbus.

The first awards of the Medal of Honor, our Nation's highest award for valor, were made to those Andrews Raiders who were exchanged in March 1863. Subsequently, additional awards were made to others who had been executed and who had escaped. Eventually 19 of the 22 soldiers who had gone with Andrews were awarded the Medal of Honor.

On June 29, 1864, Brig. Gen. Edward Canby, Assistant General of the Army, wrote from Washington, to Maj. Gen. W.S. Rosecrans, Commanding Department of the Cumberland, Murfreesboro, Tennessee, as follows:

"The Secretary of War has received information of another survivor of the secret service expedition sent out by the late Gen. O.M. Mitchel, in April 1862—Private James Smith, Compy, I, 2nd Ohio Vols—who he intends to place on the same footing as the other men of his party, as regards compensation and medal.

"I am therefore instructed by the Secretary of War to enclose herewith a draft for one hundred dollars ($100), for which you will cause Private Smith to sign a receipt to be transmitted to the Chief Clerk of the War Department.

"His claim for commutation of rations while a prisoner will be made to Commissary General of Prisoners, and that for property lost or destroyed will be verified by affidavit and sent to the proper officer for final settlement."

James Smith's father wrote a letter applying for the medal and stating that his son had been one of the raiders and had been in a Confederate prison for some time. The record does indicate that on July 6, 1864, more than a year later, James Smith was awarded the Medal of Honor for being one of the Andrews Raiders.

It is not known for sure what James Smith did during those three years plus following his release from military service in 1864. The Columbus (Ohio) City Directory for 1867-68 reflects that Ovid W. Smith lived in Columbus and was working as a machinist for the Columbus and Indiana Central Railway Company whose office was located at 229 North High Street and whose shops were located one mile west of High Street on Railroad Avenue. Smith had given his occupation as "mechanic" when he enlisted in the service so it follows that he gained employment in that field following his discharge. The Columbus City Directory for 1866-67 indicates that Howard M. Smith lived on Maple Street west of North High Street. His occupation was listed as "railroad man." James Smith had an older brother whose name was Howard M. Smith and we can assume that James remained in Columbus after his military service and probably lived with this man, his brother, Howard, and they both worked for the Columbus and Indiana Central RR. This railroad subsequently became a part of the Pennsylvania Railroad System.

When James Smith died in 1868, his death was recorded in the Probate Court Records of Franklin County (Columbus) Ohio, and the data recorded is the same as previously discussed including his birth place as Fredericksburg, Virginia. The entry is probably based on the burial records for the information is the same. The lot in which Smith's remains were buried in Green Lawn Cemetery was owned by his father, The Rev. Samuel Smith, and so far as the records indicate, there is only one burial on the lot.

from *The West Virginia Hillbilly*, May 7, 1983

Profiles of Confederate Participants

Jackson Bond

- Section Foreman on the Western & Atlantic Railroad in 1862.
- Born August 24, 1829.
- Working at Moon's Station on the W&A RR the morning of April 12 when the Raiders came through. Provided Fuller and Murphy with the pole car and went with them to Ringgold. Worked for the W&A for 36 years.
- Listed with others for the Fuller Medal of 1950.

E. Jefferson Cain

- Physically frail and turbercular. Came to Atlanta, Ga., in 1857 from Pennsylvania.
- Born April 1827.
- Died of consumption Feb. 10, 1897.
- Buried Oakland Cemetery, Atlanta. Inscription on marker rather misleading: "Jeff Cain. The historic engineer of the W&A RR manned the famous *General* on the thrilling wartime run. It was he who drove the locomotive in the historic chase of the Andrews raders [sic.] May 12, 1862."
- Married Elizabeth Cain (b. 1835; died March 8, 1902. Buried beside her husband).
- Engineer on the Western & Atlantic Railroad, running the *General* on April 12, 1862. Remained with Fuller and Murphy in the chase as far as abandonment of *William R. Smith* north of Kingston, Ga.
- Listed with others for the Fuller Medal of 1950.

Fleming A. Cox

- Employed by the Memphis & Charleston Railroad.
- Born 1838.
- Died August 21, 1914 at the age of 76.
- Buried at Beauvoir, the Jefferson Davis Shrine, Biloxi, Miss., Nov. 16, 1912, based on service with 2d Georgia Infantry.
- Married Martha D. Cox (d. March 14, 1918; buried beside husband).
- A member of Fuller's Company of Independent State Railroad Guards. Served in Co. C 2d Georgia Infantry(?).
- On leave April 12, 1862, and aboard train pulled by *Catoosa* that day; joined the Chase at Calhoun, Ga.
- Listed with others for the Fuller Medal of 1950.

E. JEFFERSON CAIN

Henry P. Haney

- Fifteen years, 5 months of age at time of Raid. Fireman on the *Texas* with Peter J. Bracken. Left railroad and joined Atlanta Fire Department Jan. 6, 1885. Retired Dec. 2, 1919, as First Assistant Chief of Atlanta Fire Department.
- Born Nov. 25, 1846, to Thomas Haney (b. Belfast, Ireland, 1812; employed by Western & Atlantic Railroad first as engineer and later as shop machinist; d. July 20, 1901).
- Died Nov. 19, 1923.
- Buried Casey Cemetery, Atlanta.
- Listed with others for the Fuller Medal of 1950.

Peter James Bracken

- Per William A. Fuller on day of chase, April 12, 1862: "He wore a mustache and chin whiskers a little too large to be considered a goatee. They were very dark in his younger days. His hair was also very dark. He weighed about 140 pounds and was about 5 feet 9½ inches high. Yes, this was his appearance in 1862. In the time of our War, he, as the others of us did, wore a gray flannel shirt and dark gray clothers—vest open low down."
- Born Oct. 31, 1833, Philadelphia, Penn.
- Died May 26, 1909, Macon, Ga.
- Buried in unmarked grave. Holly Ridge, Rose Hill Cemetery, Macon. Marker (aranged by J.G. Bogle) made by C.S. "Bo" Coogler, Universal Memorial Company of Elberton, Ga. Transported and placed by Harry W. Barnwell, Clark Memorials of Macon. Memorial service and dedication on September 25, 1971, at grave.
- Married Louise Sewell Bracken, July 13, 1857 (b. February 1841, Macon; d. July 1909, Macon). Four sons, four daughters; grandaughters Mrs. John A. Pennington, Louisa Smith, Mrs. Mildred Miller.
- Engineer on the Western & Atlantic Railroad running the locomotive *Texas* on April 12, 1862, in the Great Locomotive Chase.
- Listed with others for the Fuller Medal of 1950.

William Allen Fuller

- Began working for the Western & Atlantic Railroad Sept. 8, 1855. Left January 1870 during Gov. Bullock's administration for two years to work for Macon & Western Railroad, returning to the W&A in 1876. Chief Marshall of Atlanta Sept. 2, 1865 to Oct. 15, 1865. In later years, became very possessive of the story of the Andrews Raid, taking others to task for not telling it his way.
- Born April 15, 1836, Henry County, Ga., to William Alexander Fuller; mother unknown.
- Died Dec. 28, 1905, Atlanta, Ga.
- Buried Oakland Cemetery, Atlanta. Inscription on imposing grave momument: "On April 12, 1862, Captain Fuller pursued and after a race of 80 miles from Big Shanty Northward on the Western & Atlantic Railroad, re-captured the historic war-engine *General* which had been seized by 22 Federal soldiers in disguise, thereby preventing the destruction of the bridges of the railroad and the consequent dismemberment of the Confederacy."
- Married Lulu Asher in 1850 (d. 1872); none of four children survived. Married Susan C. Alford in 1874 (d. Oct. 15, 1916); son William Alford Fuller and four daughters.
- Commissioned Capt. August 3, 1863, by Gov. Joseph E. Brown, 6 months Independent State Railroad Guards. Commissioned again February 23, 1864, same.
- Special Georgia Gold Medal Feb. 17, 1950, Georgia House Resolution No. 127-784e, Georgia Laws 1950, Atlanta, Foote & Davies, pp. 2914, 15-16; approved Feb. 17, 1950. Medal presented to son William Alford Fuller May 15, 1950.

WILLIAM ALLEN FULLER

Alonzo Dannger Martin

- Per Wilbur G. Kurtz description: "He is a chunky fellow heavy set. Sandy wiskers—great head of auburn hair, large blue eyes, dressed in civilian clothes." Employed by Western & Atlantic Railroad.
- Born 1838 to Harrison Thurmond Martin (b. Roswell, Ga., per 1850 census.) and Rixie Dannger (d. 1900, West Point, Ga.), married March 16, 1836.
- Buried Martin Plot, West Point, Georgia Cemetery
- Married Elizabeth Josephine Burney of Roswell Dec. 15, 1858, at Car Shed, Atlanta, Ga.
- Member of William A. Fuller's Company of Independent State Railroad Guards.
- Served as wood-passer on *Texas* during Great Locomotive Chase.
- Listed with others for the Fuller Medal of 1950.

Oliver Wiley Harbin

- Per Wilbur G. Kurtz at Oct. 28, 1907, interview, at Harbin's home in Tunnel Hill, Ga.: "Mr. Harbin is a magnificant speciman of manhood. He stands six feet two inches, and his actions speak of remarkable energy, vitality, and of one accustomed to doing things. Though the frost of 73 winters has settled upon hair and beard, he seems as active as when he ran locomotives with wide open throttles, and his blue eyes—though somewhat the worse for the sudden flashes of light from the fire-box and lantern—are not greatly dimmed, and their frankness, with his native geniality, at once commend him as one of God's honest men." Begin working with Rome Railroad 1848, becoming engineer in 1859.
- Born June 16, 1834, Dahlonega, Lumpkin County, Ga.
- Died Nov. 29, 1910.
- Buried Westview Cemetery, Atlanta, Ga.
- Married at age of 19.
- Engineer of *William R. Smith* on day of the raid with Conductor Cicero Smith, Fireman William G. Kirknodle and Brakeman/Baggageman Joe Lassiter, a free-black.
- Kurtz interview established the identity of the Rome Railroad locomotive used in the Chase as the *William R. Smith* and not the *Alfred Shorter.*
- Listed with others for the Fuller Medal of 1950.

OLIVER WILEY HARBIN

Stephen H. Stokley

- Settled in Oglethorpe County, Ga., having been driven from east Tennessee by bitter Union sentiment. Later located in Acworth, Ga., and was involved in the pursuit of Andrews Raiders. Moved to Lexington, Ga., 1863.
- Born Jan. 27, 1824, to Jehu Stokley, England; and mother Neil Stokley, South Carolina, one of three sons and six daughters. Lived on French Broad River, one mile from Del Rio, Tenn.
- Died Feb. 19, 1890, Crawford, Ga.
- Married first time to Ann Moore; two sons. Married second time to Miss McConnell. Married third time to Miss McConnell. Married fourth time to Mollie Latimer Upshaw.
- Listed with other for the Fuller Medal of 1950.

Anthony Murphy

- Came to Atlanta, Ga., in 1854. Foreman of Machinery and Motive Power for Western & Atlantic Railroad at time of the raid. Elected to Atlanta City Council 1866; served three terms. Inaugurated Atlanta Water Works 1866.
- Born Nov. 29, 1829, County Wicklow, Ireland, to Thomas and Elizabeth Keyes Murphy, one of eight children. Family emigrated to United States in 1838, settled in Schuylkill County, Penn.
- Died Dec. 28, 1909.
- Married Adelia R. McConnell, 1858 (b. Sept. 11, 1840, Hall County, Ga.; d. Dec. 13, 1916; buried Oakland Cemetery, Atlanta.)
- Listed with others for the Fuller Medal of 1950.

ANTHONY MURPHY

EDWARD R. HENDERSON

Edward R. Henderson

- Telegraph messenger, 1857, Dalton, Ga., then Atlanta 1859.
- Born Oct. 31, 1844, Bradley County, Tenn. to Joseph C. Henderson, a dealer in harness and saddlery, who moved to Dalton in 1854; mother unknown.
- Died Nov. 7, 1894, Smithville, Ga.
- Married Fanny Ross of Lake City, Fla; two sons Tally M. Henderson and Edward R. Henderson Jr.
- Had gone south to Calhoun the morning of the Raid checking on downed lines. Fuller picked him up at Calhoun, then dropped him at Dalton to send telegram to Gen. Ledbetter, Confederate commander at Chattanooga, Tenn.

N. White Smith

- Served as County Surveyor of Catoosa County, Ga., ten years.
- Gregg, in his pamphlet, states: "At Acworth, White Smith was sent to Allatoona by horse hoping that the engine (*General*) would be abandoned and he would be able to head them off. Seeing no one he joined the pursuit at Allatoona. Apparently Smith's participation ended at Kingston when the *Yonah* was given up for the *William R. Smith*.
- O'Neill in *Wild Train,* page 417, describing the ceremonies of 1891 at Chattanooga National Cemetery for the Ohio Memorial to the Raiders, states; "This time too, Anthony Murphy and White Smith stood with Conductor Fuller as representatives of the pursuing party of 1862."

Route Map of the Great Locomotive Chase
April 12, 1862

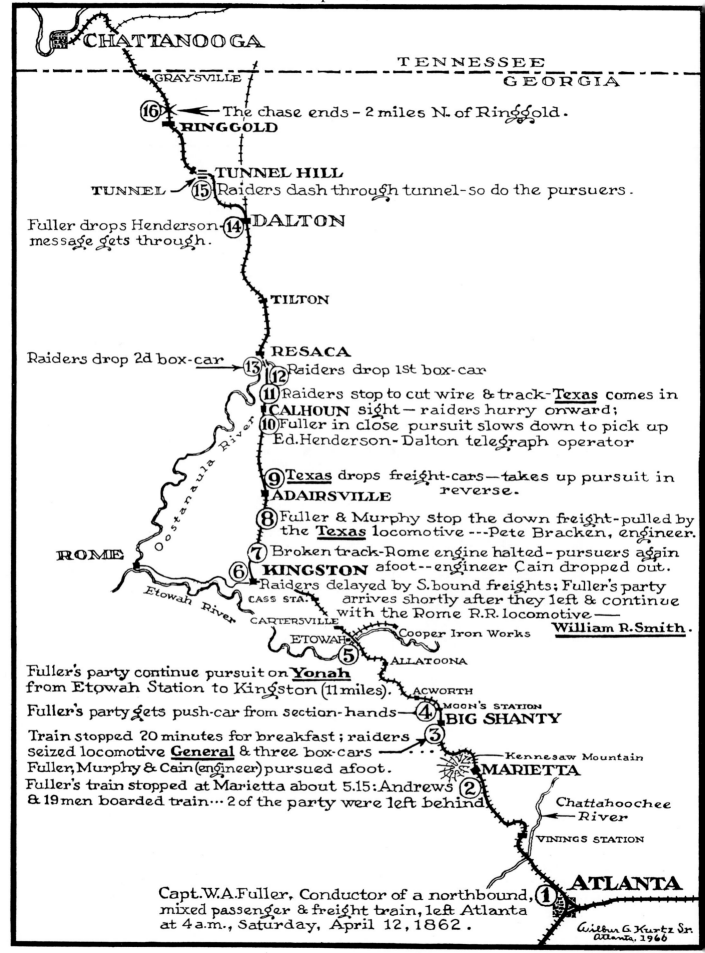

CHATTANOOGA

TENNESSEE

GEORGIA

GRAYSVILLE

⑯ The chase ends – 2 miles N. of Ringgold.

RINGGOLD

TUNNEL HILL

TUNNEL — ⑮ Raiders dash through tunnel – so do the pursuers.

Fuller drops Henderson— ⑭ **DALTON**
message gets through.

TILTON

Raiders drop 2d box-car ⟶ ⑬ **RESACA**

⑫ Raiders drop 1st box-car

⑪ Raiders stop to cut wire & track – **Texas** comes in

CALHOUN sight – raiders hurry onward;

⑩ Fuller in close pursuit slows down to pick up
Ed. Henderson-Dalton telegraph operator

⑨ **Texas** drops freight-cars – takes up pursuit in
reverse.

ADAIRSVILLE

⑧ Fuller & Murphy stop the down freight – pulled by
the **Texas** locomotive ---Pete Bracken, engineer.

⑦ Broken track-Rome engine halted – pursuers again

⑥ **KINGSTON** afoot – engineer Cain dropped out.

Raiders delayed by S. bound freights; Fuller's party
CASS STA. arrives shortly after they left & continue
with the Rome R.R. locomotive —

CARTERSVILLE

William R. Smith.

Cooper Iron Works

ROME

Oostanaula River

Etowah River

ETOWAH

⑤

ALLATOONA

Fuller's party continue pursuit on **Yonah**
from Etowah Station to Kingston (11 miles).

ACWORTH

MOON'S STATION

Fuller's party gets push-car from section-hands— ④ **BIG SHANTY**

③

Train stopped 20 minutes for breakfast; raiders
seized locomotive **General** & three box-cars
Fuller, Murphy & Cain (engineer) pursued afoot.

— Kennesaw Mountain

MARIETTA

Fuller's train stopped at Marietta about 5.15: Andrews ②
& 19 men boarded train ⋯ 2 of the party were left behind

Chattahoochee
River

VININGS STATION

ATLANTA

①

Capt. W. A. Fuller, Conductor of a northbound,
mixed passenger & freight train, left Atlanta
at 4 a.m., Saturday, April 12, 1862.

Wilbur G. Kurtz Sr.
Atlanta, 1966

The Great Locomotive Chase

On April 7, 1862, 22 volunteers were selected from the troops of Col. Joshua W. Sill's brigade. All were men from Ohio units – plus a civilian, William Campbell, who volunteered to go along. They were not given specific details of the mission but only warned of the hazardous nature of the enterprise. They went into Shelbyville to purchase civilian clothing and that night the group assembled on the Holland farm, one and one-half miles east of Shelbyville on the old Wartrace Road, and met Andrews for final instructions.

They were told to be at Marietta, Georgia, by midnight of April 10 so as to begin operations on April 11. Concurrently, General Mitchel's force would move on Huntsville. When Andrews and his party would show with a captured locomotive and word that the W&A RR was in ruins, Mitchel could then move on Chattanooga with greater ease.

As the raiders plotted that dark night in Tennessee, rain began to fall and would continue to fall for the next 10 days.

1860's PHOTOGRAPH OF CHATTANOOGA SHOWING THE CAR SHED THERE THAT WAS USED BY THE W&A RR.
NATIONAL ARCHIVES

WESTERN & ATLANTIC RR ROUNDHOUSE, ATLANTA, 1864, PRIOR TO DESTRUCTION BY GENERAL SHERMAN'S FORCES.

The 23 men who secretly met with Andrews that dark rainy night are (by regiment):

2nd Ohio Volunteer Infantry Regiment

Sgt. Maj. Marion A. Ross

Pvt. George D. Wilson, Co. B

Cpl. William Pittenger, Co. G

Pvt. James (Ovid Wellford) Smith, Co. I

Pvt. Philip G. Shadrach, Co. K (also known as Perry G. or Charles P., and last name sometimes spelled Shadrack)

William Campbell, of Salineville, Ohio (a civilian who took the place of a soldier)

21st Ohio Volunteer Infantry Regiment

Pvt. John A. Wilson, Co. C

Pvt. Mark Wood, Co. C

Pvt. William J. Knight, Co. E

Sgt. John M. Scott, Co. F

Pvt. Wilson W. Brown, Co. F

Pvt. William Bensinger, Co. G

Pvt. John Reed Porter, Co. G

Pvt. Robert Buffum, Co. H

Sgt. Elihu H. Mason, Co. K

33rd Ohio Volunteer Infantry Regiment

Cpl. Martin Jones Hawkins, Co. A

Cpl. William H. Reddick, Co. B

Pvt. John Wollam, Co. C

Pvt. Samuel Slavens, Co. E

Pvt. Samuel Robertson, Co. G

Cpl. Daniel Allen Dorsey, Co. H

Cpl. Samuel Llewellyn, Co. I

Pvt. Jacob Parrott, Co. K

Andrews closed his remarks to the raiders with concise instructions:

"Boys we're going into danger, but for results that can be tremendous. If we burn those bridges, General Mitchel can take and hold Chattanooga. But we'll have to be prompt. The last train for Marietta leaves Chattanooga at five in the afternoon. Be sure to catch it not later than Thursday, and I'll either be on it, or on an earlier one. Goodbye till then."

The group separated into smaller numbers and started overland to Chattanooga. They had three days to get there, a little more than 100 miles distant, in time to catch the train for Marietta.

By twos and threes they made their way generally following the present-day route of U.S. Highway 41 South and the Nashville & Chattanooga Railroad (now CSX Rail Transport), stopping at farms along the way for food and short naps, usually in a barn. As an explanation for their presence, they replied they were enroute from Fleming County, Kentucky, to Chattanooga with hopes of finding and joining a Kentucky-raised Confederate regiment. This story had been given them by Andrews, explaining that he knew there were no Confederate soldiers from Fleming County and thus they would not run the risk of being recognized by a Rebel soldier.

Progress of the men was slow. The drenching rains continued, and the Cumberland Mountains had to be crossed before they could reach Chattanooga. Several parties would come in contact with each other along the way and by Wednesday (April 9), Andrews had passed the word postponing the raid one day. He assumed General Mitchel would also be delayed at least one day due to the unexpected bad weather. Andrews' delay was to have a disastrous effect in the end.

At 5:00 p.m., Friday, April 11, most of the raiders departed Chattanooga on the southbound passenger train over the W&A RR, and reached Marietta around midnight. Only two of the party, Porter and Hawkins, had managed to get through in the original time allotted, arriving at Marietta on April 10. Two others, Smith and Llewellyn, did not reach Marietta at all, having been forced to enlist in a Confederate unit near Jasper, Tennessee, to avoid having to divulge their identity. That night Andrews and 21 of his men slept in Marietta. Most of them stayed at the hotel near the depot then known as the Fletcher House (and later as the Kennesaw House). The remainder of the party were in another hotel and Andrews made sure that both groups were instructed on the events to follow that morning.

At 4:00 a.m., Saturday, April 12, about the time Andrews and his men were getting up at their hotels in Marietta, the regular mixed passenger and freight train pulled by the locomotive *General* steamed out of the car shed in Atlanta. Jeff Cain was at the throttle that morning; Andrew J. Anderson was the fireman; and the conductor who was to figure so prominently in the adventure was William A. Fuller. Riding as a passenger was Anthony Murphy, foreman of motive power and machinery for the W&A RR, who was on his way to Allatoona to check on a water pump.

At Marietta, around 5:00 a.m., James J. Andrews and 19 of his raiders boarded the train with tickets to various points up the line. Only Porter

THE KENNESAW HOUSE WAS BUILT IN 1855 AS A SUMMER RESORT CALLED THE FLETCHER HOUSE. GENERAL SHERMAN HEADQUARTERED HERE ON JULY 3, 1864, AND IT WAS PARTIALLY BURNED IN NOVEMBER 1864. IT IS LOCATED ACROSS FROM THE MARIETTA WELCOME CENTER AND HOUSES THE MARIETTA MUSEUM OF HISTORY.

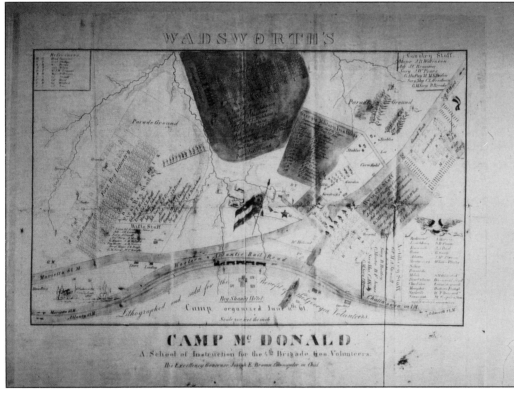

THE WADSMORTH'S DRAWING OF CAMP MCDONALD, BIG SHANTY, GA., 1861.

and Hawkins failed to get aboard, having overlooked paying a fee to a room waiter to awaken them that morning, thus missing the adventure completely.

Prior to boarding the *General* at Marietta, Andrews gave more instructions to the raiders:

"... get seats near each other in the same car and of course say nothing of our business on the way up. When the train makes the Big Shanty breakfast stop, keep your places till I tell you to go. If anything unexpected happens, look to me for the lead. Knight, Brown and John A. Wilson will go with me on the engine. The rest will go on the left of the train forward of where we'll uncouple it. Climb into the cars as quickly as you can when the order is given. If anyone interferes, shoot him, but don't fire unless you have to."

Three empty box cars were behind the locomotive that morning, bound for Chattanooga to bring back supplies and food from Tennessee. The cars were coupled next to the engine, thus fitting nicely into Andrews' plans for the concealment of his men. The box cars also afforded a basis for supporting his later contention that he was conducting an "emergency ammunition train" to General Beauregard and his troops at Corinth.

From Marietta to Big Shanty the railroad sweeps in a long bend, of some eight miles, around the foot of Kennesaw Mountain. The train chugged slowly, stopping at several intervening points, and reached Big Shanty about full daylight at 6:00 a.m.

As the train drew into the station, white tents, guards and recruits at Camp McDonald came into view. This military instruction camp had been established only recently and Andrews was unaware of it. It was located west of the railroad with the guard line coming to within 50 feet of the railroad track.

When the train stopped and the call came "Big Shanty! Twenty minutes for breakfast!" the conductor, engineer, fireman, and most of the passengers quickly covered the 40 feet over from the tracks to the porch of the Lacy Hotel (no longer standing).

Eating establishments along the railroad were as necessary as they were along stagecoach routes. The Lacy Hotel at Big Shanty was built by the W&A RR during the mid-1850s. It was leased to Lon Kendrick who operated it for awhile, and in 1859 subleased it to George M. Lacy who, with his family, operated it until forced to abandon the place in 1864, as Sherman's forces approached the Kennesaw Mountain front.

The hotel consisted of four rooms, two each above and below, a wide hall and stairs, a chimney at each end, and a porch of two levels. The kitchen was in a separate, one-story structure adjacent to the dining room. A picket fence enclosed the front yard except for a passageway from trackside to the entrance steps. On entering, the passengers encountered Mr. Lacy, who sat at the seat of custom with a bag of silver for change. Breakfast was 25¢ for grits, ham with red gravy, eggs, hot biscuits, flapjacks with butter, sorghum and coffee.

The *General*'s crew and *most* of the passengers seated themselves in Lacy's dining room, anticipating a pleasant, hearty breakfast.

Meanwhile, some of the passengers had remained outside. Andrews moved cautiously alongside the train toward the locomotive. With him were Knight, Brown and John A. Wilson, all experienced locomotive engineers. Knight hoisted himself onto the locomotive. He seized the throttle with nervous hands, keeping his eyes on Andrews. Other raiders sneaked behind the last box car and released the coupling. Andrews gave a signal and the other 16 raiders raced forward and threw themselves into the empty box car. Andrews swung aboard the *General* and nodded to Knight. And "The Great Locomotive Chase" was on.

Knight yanked the throttle and for an instant nothing happened. In his excitement he had thrown the power on too abruptly and made the driver wheels spin on the tracks. Sparks flew. Steam hissed beneath the engine. But shortly the wheels bit the rails and the train lurched away, gathering speed.

It all happened so suddenly that none of the

DRAWING OF THE LACY HOTEL BY WILBUR G. KURTZ.

nearby soldiers at Camp McDonald had time to appraise the situation, raise their muskets or give an alarm.

Meanwhile, Conductor Fuller, sitting at the breakfast table with Jeff Cain and Anthony Murphy, happened to glance out the window. He spied the strangers who had boarded at Marietta.

They had swung aboard his locomotive. Smoke was belching from the stack. His horror grew as the locomotive chugged from the depot. "Someone who has no right to has gone off with our train!" he shouted.

All three of the trainmen jumped to their feet and hurried from the hotel just as the train passed from sight.

The raiders had hardly escaped from Big Shanty before the *General* began to slow down. Knight was compelled to bring it to a dead stop. It was soon discovered that a damper had been left closed, causing a loss of boiler pressure. The *General* was virtually out of steam. Within minutes the fire was roaring again and steam pressure was on the rise. The *General* jerked and chugged toward running speed for what would be a thrilling chase of some 87 miles along the winding course of the W&A RR.

Before reaching Moon's Station, the raiders stopped to cut the telegraph wire and obstruct the track. There was no telegraph office at Big Shanty—one of the reasons Andrews chose that station to steal the train—but the raiders still felt safer having cut the line. However, they found that breaking the wire was not easy. John Scott, agile as a cat, had to climb the pole, break the insulators so the wire was loose, then swing down on it. Using a small hacksaw found on the engine, the wire was cut.

Andrews showed more excitement at this point than he had the previous several days. He felt they now had the advantage and that no one could harm them. "When we've passed one more train," he declared, "the coast will be clear for burning bridges and running on through to Chattanooga and around. For once boys, we've got the upper hand of the Rebels."

At Moon's Station, about two and a half miles into the Chase, the raiders found a track crew at work, and Brown obtained a crow bar from one of the track hands. This was their only tool with which to pry up spikes and obstruct track.

As they went on, Andrews instructed his engineer not to run too fast but to hold to the schedule. In this way the train would not attract undue attention. Also, when they met anticipated southbound

RAIDER JOHN M. SCOTT CUTTING TELEGRAPH ALONG THE RAILROAD LINE. COPIED FROM PITTENGER'B BOOK *CAPTURING A LOCOMOTIVE.*

WESTERN & ATLANTIC RR AND ALLATOONA PASS, GA., 1864.

trains they would be able to take the proper sidings to allow passage and avoid head-on collisions. The raiders had attached a red flag to the last car to indicate that another train was following the *General*. Andrews, of course, used this ruse hoping to confuse unsuspecting trainmen as to why the *General* was on the schedule of the morning mail and express train; the red flag might also help dispel

any suspicions about the unusual make-up of his train—a locomotive, tender, and just three box cars.

After passing through stations at Acworth and Allatoona, the raiders stopped again to cut the telegraph wire and to pry up a rail. While they felt sure no train was in pursuit, they wanted to be positive none could get by. Lifting the rail proved a difficult and time-consuming project without the necessary

VIEW OF KENNESAW MOUNTAIN FROM ALLATOONA HEIGHTS. HOUSE IN THE FOREGROUND STILL STANDS.

tools. After considerable effort they got the rail up and loaded it aboard one of the cars, thus leaving a considerable hindrance to a pursuing train.

In due time the *General* rounded McGuire's Curve and reached the Etowah River, passing easily over the great bridge. The raiders did not stop here, but the first serious cause for delay was apparent. On a side track, connecting a spur line that ran upriver to Maj. Mark Cooper's Iron Works, stood a locomotive. Smoke was rising from the stack, showing only too plainly that it was ready to go. It was the *Yonah*, used in switching box cars and gondolas from the iron works to the main line. Several men were gathered around the engine. At the first sight of the *Yonah*, Knight spoke directly to Andrews.

"We'd better destroy that," Knight said, "and this bridge with it."

Andrews shook his head. "It won't make any difference," he said. Moreover, he reasoned, destroying the *Yonah* would show clearly the mission of the crew when the intent was, to Andrews' knowledge, yet unsuspected.

The *Yonah* and the Etowah bridge left behind, the raiders passed on through Cartersville and continued without incident until they reached Cass Station. Here they took on wood and water for the thirsty *General*. William Russell, the wood tender at Cass, was curious about the short train and its purpose. With no hesitation, Andrews glibly stated that he was running an extra train through with powder and ammunition for General Beauregard at Corinth. General Grant was pressing him hard, according to Andrews, and ammunition was needed with the greatest haste. Russell knew of a battle going on (Shiloh) and Andrews' explanation appeared quite logical, so much so that Andrews was given a train schedule by Russell, who said he would also send his shirt to Beauregard if he needed it.

The raiders were now within seven miles of Kingston, resupplied with wood and water, and with a complete schedule of trains on the road. Kingston was a junction point with the Rome (Georgia) Railroad and there, at the Kingston siding, would be the morning train from Rome waiting for Conductor Fuller's *General* to pass. In addition, a local southbound freight was scheduled for passing. Thus Kingston was the first real complication the raiders would meet. Andrews had made himself familiar with the workings of the railroad at this point and they entered Kingston a few minutes ahead of schedule, confident of being able to steam through

with a minimum of delay. All the while, a slight but steady rain continued to fall across north Georgia, shrouding the hills and budding countryside in a gray mist.

Any possible success of the raid had been sacrificed the moment Andrews decided to postpone the event one day. General Mitchel had *not* postponed his plans as Andrews anticipated and with the capture of Huntsville on April 11, the Confederates were forced to ship goods out of Chattanooga, thus increasing the number of southbound trains. The extra traffic on the road caused complications for the raiders, slowing them down and facilitating pursuit.

The unexpected departure of the *General* and the three freight cars set all into commotion at Big Shanty. Fuller first supposed that the train had been taken by some deserting conscripts from Camp McDonald who would abandon it a short distance away. With this thought in mind, he set out on foot to recapture his train. Engineer Jeff Cain gave chase too. Anthony Murphy dispatched a rider to Marietta with instructions to telegraph the superintendent of the W&A RR that something was amiss at Big Shanty. Then Murphy ran after Cain and Fuller.

At Moon's Station, Fuller encountered Jackson Bond and his section crew. From them, Fuller learned that the captors of the *General* had stopped to ask for tools and were given a crow bar. This was an indication that perhaps they were not deserters from Camp McDonald but rather men with more devious motives. At any rate, Fuller borrowed the crew's platform car and with Cain and Murphy proceeded to kick and pole the vehicle down the big grade towards the Etowah River. Conductor Fuller knew the *Yonah* should be there, and he hoped to arrive before it left for its morning run to Cooper's Iron Works.

Beyond Acworth, Fuller, Cain and Murphy came across the place where the raiders had torn up the track. The puffing pursuers did not see the missing rail in time to stop and were thrown pellmell into a ditch as the platform car overturned. Within a few minutes they had the car back on the track, and only badly shaken, were on their way again to the Etowah. Arriving at the river before the *Yonah* had departed they seized the locomotive and quickly switched onto the main line and headed north toward Kingston, 14 miles distant, at full steam.

Fuller wrote later that they made these 14 miles in 15 minutes with the old *Yonah*, thus indicating a

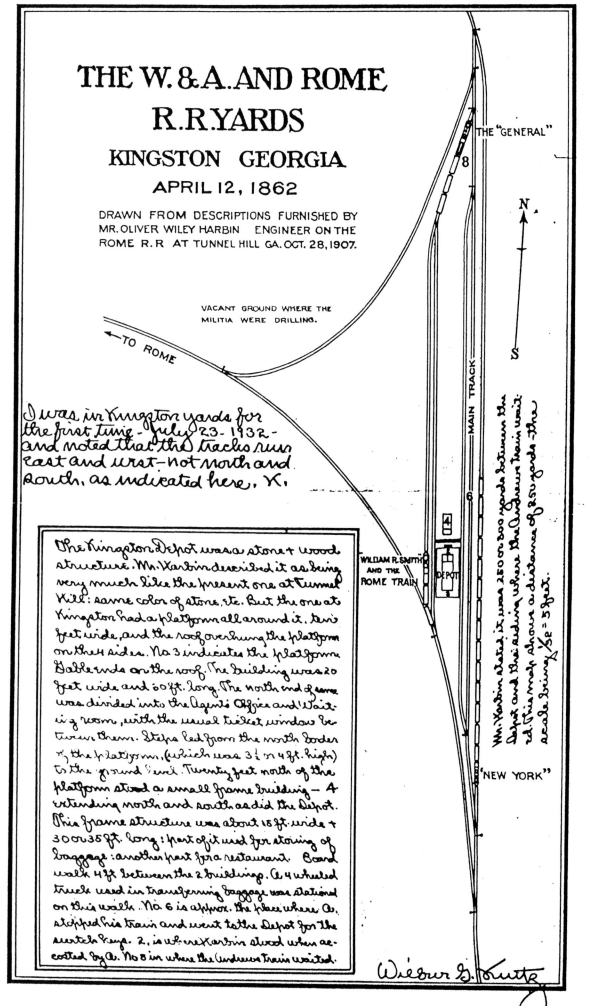

THE W. & A. AND ROME R.R. YARDS

KINGSTON GEORGIA

APRIL 12, 1862

DRAWN FROM DESCRIPTIONS FURNISHED BY
MR. OLIVER WILEY HARBIN   ENGINEER ON THE
ROME R.R AT TUNNEL HILL GA. OCT. 28, 1907.

THE "GENERAL"

8

N.

S

VACANT GROUND WHERE THE
MILITIA WERE DRILLING.

← TO ROME

MAIN TRACK

I was in Kingston yards for
the first time - July 23 - 1932 -
and noted that the tracks run
east and west - not north and
south, as indicated here. K.

6

Mr. Harbin stated it was 250 or 300 yards between the
depot and the siding where the Andrews train waited.
This map shows a distance of 250 yards - the
scale being 1/32 = 5 feet.

4

WILLIAM R. SMITH
AND THE
ROME TRAIN

DEPOT

The Kingston Depot was a stone + wood
structure. Mr. Harbin described it as being
very much like the present one at Tunnel
Hill: same color of stone, etc. But the one at
Kingston had a platform all around it, ten
feet wide, and the roof overhung the platform
on the 4 sides. No 3 indicates the platform.
Gable ends on the roof. The building was 20
feet wide and 50 ft. long. The north end of same
was divided into the Agent's Office and Waiting room, with the usual ticket window between them. Steps led from the north border
of the platform, (which was 3½ or 4 ft. high)
to the ground level. Twenty feet north of the
platform stood a small frame building — 4
extending north and south as did the Depot.
This frame structure was about 15 ft. wide +
30 or 35 ft. long: part of it used for storing of
baggage: another part for a restaurant. Board
walk 4 ft. between the 2 buildings. A 4 wheeled
truck used in transferring baggage was stationed
on this walk. No. 6 is approx. the place where A.
stopped his train and went to the Depot for the
switch keys. 2, is where Harbin stood when accosted by A. No 8 is where the Andrews train waited.

"NEW YORK"

Wilbur G. Kurtz

speed of over 55 m.p.h. If Andrews had taken Knight's advice to burn the Etowah bridge, the raiders would have prevented Fuller from continuing his pursuit on such even terms. Strange to relate, even with a locomotive standing under steam at the Etowah, the raiders did no damage to the tracks between the Etowah and Kingston. Removal of another rail might well have prevented Conductor Fuller from continuing his pursuit.

was late, and when it did arrive, the first sign the raiders noticed was the flags indicating another section was following. Still another section, making three trains in all, came in before the *General* was able to clear Kingston. While all this was going on, the raiders cooped up in the box car grew concerned over the delay.

Just four minutes after the raiders finally departed Kingston, Fuller, Murphy and Cain arrived

WESTERN & ATLANTIC BRIDGE OVER THE ETOWAH RIVER LOOKING EAST FROM FEDERAL LINES, 1864.

Andrews and his men spent a very frustrating hour and five minutes in Kingston before they were able to pull out. Kingston, being a junction point, had on hand a number of passengers and on-lookers that morning. The station attendants were inquisitive about strangers being there with Fuller's train and they demanded an explanation. The old switch tender, Uriah Stephens, did not believe Andrews and his story about rushing ammunition and powder through to General Beauregard at Corinth. Stephens was most reluctant to throw the switches for Andrews or to surrender switch keys to him. Further frustrating Andrews, a southbound freight

on the *Yonah*.

When Fuller and his party arrived at Kingston shortly after the *General's* departure they found nothing but confusion. Three southbound freights had pulled onto sidings to allow the *General* to speed on northward. Fuller realized quickly that it would be nearly impossible to move the freight trains around and allow the *Yonah* to pass. Consequently, he, Cain and Murphy again resorted to foot power and ran around the southbounds and beyond Kingston Station to where the Rome Railroad's locomotive, the *William R. Smith*, was standing under steam and ready to roll. Conductor Fuller and his party, having gained a few more volunteers at Kingston, seized the *William R. Smith* and headed northward with engineer Oliver Wiley Harbin aboard.

The rain began to fall in earnest as the raiders departed Kingston. While they were most anxious to get to Adairsville, where they expected to meet another southbound freight and pass it at the siding, they also realized the importance of obstructing the track again and cutting the telegraph wire. There was too much in the form of potential pursuit left at Kingston. The delay there had been costly and the raiders needed to get beyond the Oostanaula River at Resaca in order to burn the bridges and put the road out of commission.

A short distance north of Kingston they stopped to load some cross ties and other wood to use in bridge burning. Lifting a rail here seemed to take forever. Finally they had enough spikes loose to wrench the rail from the ties. Just as they were engaged in doing this, they heard faintly, but unmistakably, the whistle of a northbound locomotive to the south. It could only be in pursuit of them and no sound could have been more unwelcome.

The whistle boosted the raiders' adrenalin and with one convulsive effort they broke the rail. Quickly putting the broken pieces into one of the box cars, they pushed on to Adairsville with all possible speed.

As the raiders reached Adairsville, there waited the expected freight train. The *General* pulled in and stopped alongside the freight. At once a storm of questions was asked and Andrews tried to give reasonable answers. In fact, he asked a few himself as to what was going on at Chattanooga. He learned that General Mitchel was moving eastward from Huntsville (right on schedule, Andrews thought) and this was creating panic in Tennessee.

After the questioning, the southbound freight moved out of Adairsville toward Kingston. As it passed the *General*, Andrews, Knight, Brown, and Wilson could see the name of the locomotive on the boiler, *Texas*, an engine that before the day was ended would also take its place in history.

Now Andrews could sense the possible failure of his mission—that train whistle in his rear still echoing in his mind—and he ordered the engineer to let the *General* break loose, despite having been warned of other southbounds. Knight had been waiting for this word all morning. The *General* was in fine running condition. Knight had oiled her well during the long wait at Kingston and again had checked her over at Adairsville. A good head of steam had been built up. The three box cars were not a load for the *General* and the train made excellent time to Calhoun, where it nearly collided head-on with the southbound *Catoosa*.

The *Catoosa* crew, shaken by the close call, was unwilling to move out of the way until Andrews had given a proper explanation. His presence and movement without a flagman ahead was in violation of the rules of the railroad. Finally after much talk and persuasion, Andrews came out with a forceful "I've got to go on with no more delay!" Then he ordered the *Catoosa* to get out of his way.

Given in this form the order had to be obeyed or openly disputed. The crew of the *Catoosa* chose to comply and proceeded to let the *General* pass.

Away from Calhoun and on the main track to Chattanooga with no more trains to contend with, the raiders felt they were now free to accomplish their mission of burning bridges. The Oostanaula bridge at Resaca was just ahead and would be their first attempt.

Meanwhile, Conductor Fuller and his party aboard the *William R. Smith* proceeded north from Kingston. Fuller decided to ride as pilot and watch ahead for any obstructions on the track. Thus it was that he saw in time the missing rail. The *William R. Smith* came to a stop and completed its role in the stirring events of the day.

Again, it was necessary for Fuller and his associates to resort to movement by foot. After a run of some three miles they met the southbound *Texas*. Pete Bracken, the engineer, immediately recognized Fuller and reversed his engine to stop the train. Only Murphy was with Fuller at this point as Jeff Cain had given out and remained with the *William R. Smith*.

Fuller and Murphy quickly climbed aboard the *Texas* and told Bracken of the heist. Bracken threw the *Texas* in reverse and moved back to Adairsville where he got rid of the freight cars at a siding. The Great Locomotive Chase would continue in intensity now, with participants on both sides on somewhat more equal terms. The main differences were that the *Texas* was not burdened with box cars ... and was running backwards.

The *Texas* made the run in reverse to Calhoun in some 12 minutes. At Calhoun, the *Texas* crew picked up valuable reinforcements for their cause. Fleming Cox, an engineer on the Memphis and

Charleston RR, was on his way to Atlanta; caught up in the excitement of the day he climbed aboard the *Texas* and relieved 15-year-old Henry Haney as Bracken's fireman. Alonzo Martin also got on board and assisted in passing wood from the tender.

As the *Texas* left Calhoun, Conductor Fuller sighted a familiar face in young Edward Henderson, the assistant telegraph operator at Dalton, who had started south to find out what was wrong with the telegraph line. Fuller helped him aboard the *Texas*, still in reverse, and as soon as they got underway he scribbled a message for young Henderson to dispatch to Gen. Danville Leadbetter, commander at Chattanooga, as soon as they let Henderson off at Dalton. The message read:

My train was captured this a.m. at Big Shanty, evidently by Federal soldiers in disguise. They are making rapidly for Chattanooga, possibly with the idea of burning the railroad bridges in their rear. If I do not capture them in the meantime, see that they do not pass Chattanooga.

Having passed five trains, and remembering the sound of a locomotive whistle coming from his rear, Andrews concluded it was important again to obstruct the track. Thus, about three miles north of Calhoun the raiders stopped to remove yet another rail and cut the telegraph wire. While using a fence rail to pry the track loose, a loud and clear whistle came from the south. The raiders quickly stopped what they were doing and attempted to place the fence rail under the track, hoping to force the pursuers to halt. The *General* was soon racing again for Chattanooga.

Andrews, thinking of ways to spoil the pursuit and yet do it without force, decided to stop and reverse the *General* for a moment and kick a box car back at the engine chasing him. This might have worked had the *General* been on a grade. But on level track it was a simple matter for the pursuers to reverse their already backwards running engine and couple onto the rolling box car. After only a short delay, the *Texas* was again in hot pursuit.

The raiders were now nearing the Oostanaula bridge south of Resaca, their first objective. This bridge, along with many others on the W&A RR at the time, was a wooden covered bridge. (The present bridge stands on some of the supports that held the wartime structure.) All efforts were directed toward getting a fire started in the rear box car with a view to leaving it burning on the bridge and setting the bridge afire. All the wood they had

was soaked and even with coals from the firebox of the *General* it wasn't possible to get a roaring fire going.

As the raiders approached the bridge they slowed down and uncoupled the smoldering box car and left it on the bridge. As they sped on the raiders were disheartened to see their pursuers ease onto the span and push the smoking car on through; Fuller left both cars kicked back at him from the *General* on a siding at Resaca.

Beyond Resaca the raiders resorted to dropping cross ties on the track in hopes of slowing down the *Texas*. This proved futile, for the jettisoned ties bounced off the track.

A few miles above Resaca the *General* approached Green's Wood Station near Tilton, and was again in need of fuel. A quick stop was made at Green's for wood, and then for water at Tilton. But the pursuers were so close behind that the raiders could not satisfy completely the needs of the *General*. The stops did permit the building up of steam, which enabled the locomotive to take off in a hurry for Dalton.

The raiders passed Dalton at a high rate of speed. About two miles north of Dalton they stopped again to cut the telegraph wire. All but a few words of Fuller's message to General Leadbetter got through before the wire was cut by John Scott. This was enough to alert the authorities at Chattanooga. Before Andrews' men could pry another rail up, the pursuing *Texas* came into sight and once again the raiders had to flee in haste.

The remaining miles of the chase were a close race between the locomotives within sight and sound of each other now, making it impossible for the raiders to cause further obstructions. Even at Tunnel Hill, no effort was made to fight back at the pursuers, or damage or obstruct the tunnel.

Some accounts indicate that the raiders uncoupled their third and last box car on one of the Chickamauga bridges in an effort to burn it, but the preponderance of evidence indicates the third box car was still coupled to the *General* at the end of the chase.

After roaring through Tunnel Hill and then Ringgold, it soon became apparent that the chase was almost over. Fuel was about gone and water was running low on the *General*, whereas the *Texas* was well supplied.

The W&A RR comes into Ringgold from the south on a wide curve followed by a long stretch of straight track with an up-grade. The *General* was slowing down as it rounded this curve and headed out on the straight stretch. Andrews, realizing his mission had failed, gave his final command: "Jump off and scatter! Every man for himself!"

Thus ended The Great Locomotive Chase, at a point some two miles north of Ringgold.

The Andrews Raid had failed. The next attempt against the W&A RR would be made in April 1863, when Col. Abel Streight and his cavalrymen, mounted on mules, made a famous ride across northern Alabama and into Georgia, only to be captured by Confederate General Forrest's cavalry near Rome.

The final and successful attempt would occur in the spring of 1864 when Gen. William T. Sherman and his massive army fought southward almost four months along the W&A RR to capture the city of Atlanta.

TUNNEL HILL, GA., 1864. THE 1,477' TUNNEL WAS CONSTRUCTED THROUGH CHETOOGETA MOUNTAIN IN 1848 WITH IRISH AND SLAVE LABOR AND OPENED IN 1850. IT REMAINED IN USE UNTIL THE 1920'S BY WHICH TIME IT HAD BECOME OBSOLETE. THAT ERA'S LARGER STEAM ENGINES WOULD SCRAPE THE SIDES OF THE TUNNEL DURING THEIR PASSAGE, AND THE LAST TRAIN PASSED THROUGH IN 1928. A LARGER TUNNEL WAS SUBSEQUENTLY BUILT NEARBY. IT IS ONE OF THE OLDEST TUNNELS IN THE SOUTHEAST UNITED STATES.

BIG SHANTY, GA., DEPOT IN 1864 SKETCHED BY T.R. DAVIS FROM *HARPER'S WEEKLY*.

ACWORTH, GA., DEPOT IN 1864 SKETCHED BY T.R. DAVIS FROM *HARPER'S WEEKLY*.

Second Section | # The Morning Republican. | 16 PAGES TODAY

VOL. XX. NO. 121.   FINDLAY, OHIO, SATURDAY, APRIL 14, 1906.   PRICE THREE CENTS

DARING RAID OF ANDREWS AND HIS BRAVE MEN

Captured Rebel Train on Western & Atlantic Railroad in Connection With Mitchell Raiders -- Story as Told by Hancock County Man and Other Survivors.

BY RALPH R. MILLER.

Forty-four years ago Thursday Jas. J. Andrews, a citizen of Fleming county, Kentucky, with twenty-one volunteers from General Mitchell's division of the army of the Cumberland, captured Conductor W. A. Fuller's train on the Western Atlantic railroad at Big Shanty, a pretty little Georgia town, about twenty miles northwest of Atlanta. The capture of the enemy's train in the heart of the Confederacy makes an interesting story, especially for the younger generation. Special interest is attached to the story owing to the fact that William Bensinger, of McComb, this county, is one of the six survivors who was among the last to leave the engine when they were forced to desert it.

A representative of this paper while in conversation with Mr. Bensinger had the pleasure of hearing him relate the story of that daring exploit nearly a half century ago. Our informant was twenty-one years old then and a soldier in Co. G. Twenty-first Ohio, then quartered at Shelbyville, Tenn. The object of the raid was to burn the bridges between Atlanta and Chattanooga on April 11 and then Gen. Mitchell would move

a typical southern gentleman. He was reserved and fearless under all circumstances. Historians and men under his leadership as well, say that he expected to surmount all difficulties by strategy and always abhored a fight. On Monday night, April 6 orders were sent in regular military channels to the three Ohio regiments of Sill's brigade to have a man from each company for a special and hazardous duty. At the first meeting of the officers they arranged for experienced engineers. On the following day the required number of men were selected. The secret was, now known. They were to dress as private citizens and reach Marrietta, Ga. under disguise and be ready to capture the train on Friday morning, April 11. Andrews personally conferred with all his men, and advised them to go in small squads. They were to reach Chattanooga on Thursday and board various south-bound trains in the deepest secrecy as to who they were or what they were going to do. On Tuesday evening the men set out on their perilous journey towards Chattanooga. Andrews had arranged for a last conference with his men in a thicket near

hindering their progress and causing the great event to fall on Saturday, April 12. Early Wednesday morning the Cumberland mountains were reached. Some of the men were unused to mountains and lacked that peculiar instinct of knowing strange trails almost by night. Two of the parties met in the village of Jasper, one afternoon, but assumed the attitude of awkward country-fellows and passed unnoticed. One of these parties found lodging for that night at Widows Hall as old inn on a lonely cross-road. Others found lodging at the home of an old Tennessee planter. He was a typical southerner and was much enthused when the "Kentuckians" made known their intentions of joining the Confederate army. The little party of four were in advance and had crossed the Tennessee river safely. With few exceptions this was a hard proposition as the river was flooded and all ferrymen were afraid to venture across and besides this had strict orders to allow no one to cross. By the aid of neat sums of money the men persuaded the ferrymen to take them across. On Thursday night after all southbound trains had left the remainder of them reached Chattanooga. Some lodged at the Crutch said house while others lodged elsewhere. All appeared to be strangers and bid no consultation in public. During Friday they wandered about town, then a mere military village. Andrews met a part of the men here and bad-aided them in getting across the river merely by telling enough story. At the depot that night there was a large crowd, mostly of furloughed soldiers going back to Beauregard's

taking to the field, while the infantry kept the road. At this juncture the shrill whistle of a locomotive was heard. It was the early morning train bound for Chattanooga. The engine apparently saw the army and stops his train. A section was placed in the action and fired. The distance was great and the view was bad. The engine bounded away with a piercing scream and was soon lost to view around the bend. A train following was less fortunate. With a well-directed shot the engineer was killed and the locomotive disabled. The cavalry had now reached the town and galloping at break neck speed reached

men were nearing the end of their journey. Andrews had learned the railroad schedule and hoped to be successful even if they had been delayed one day. About midnight the conductor called out "Marietta." The goal was reached. A few short hours to wait. Every one was enthusiastic. The happy thoughts of giving the enemy a blow that would cut the Confederacy in twain made every nerve tingle with anxiety.

BURNED BRIDGES BEHIND HIM.

Gen. Mitchell was quite successful in the part he played in the raid. He broke camp on Tuesday and with his thousand infantry and cavalry moved southward into Alabama. The almost tropical rainfall made the forced march a very difficult one owing to the swollen streams and muddy roads. On Thursday the weather became settled-and sunshine and wind so drove the roads that the army was able to get within ten miles of Huntsville. At nightfall a strong picket line was thrown in all directions from camp.

Leader of the Intrepid Blue Coats, who was executed at Atlanta, June 7, 1862. The accompanying picture was made from the original given by Andrews to his sweetheart, Miss Elizabeth Layton, prior to his execution. After her death the picture was sent to Washington and is now in the archives there.

the telegraph office. The other divisions then rushed in from the side, followed by the infantry. The citizens were terror-stricken and rushed simultaneously through the streets looking for avenues of escape. All the railroad stock together with valuable messages were captured. There was no key to the cypher messages but Mitchell at once called for telegraphers from his command and soon read the messages. The most important dispatch was from Beauregard at Corinth to the Confederate secretary of war. It gave the great number of men he had and further stated that to resist

non passengers on the road they expected to return over the following day with the train in their possession. Mitchell suspected that something had happened to Andrews and his party and resolved to wait no longer. He bridges and wrought such damage would hinder the enemy. His to end the war with this great was now over. It cannot be his fault but due to the conditions existing. An explanation in the Atlanta journal of April 16 said: "It is not by any means certain that the substitution of Beauregard's whole army at Corinth would be so fatal a blow to us as would the burning of the bridges on the Western Atlantic road at this time as planned by Andrews and Mitchell." Thus it is seen that the expedition as planned was very important.

SHOWED HIS METTLE.

The greater part of the Andrews party found lodging at the same hotel in Marietta on Friday night. The gallant leader met with his men in their rooms during the after conference. He said: "We will buy our tickets for various places along the line to avoid suspicion. Have your revolvers loaded. Everybody must keep steady. Do not reconitre each other in any way on our short trip to Big Shanty. When the trainmen get off for breakfast we will uncouple the coaches from the box cars and be off. If any thing unexpected occurs look to our for advice. You and you (pointing to the engineer and fireman) get on the engine with me. The remainder get in the box car as best you can. If anybody interferes with you shoot them down, but do not

Famous engine, "General," stolen by the Yanks who constituted the Andrews raiders on their hair-raising run. Now in the Union Depot at Chattanooga, petted and admired by thousands each year.

dangerous than he had anticipated. Being one day late worried him very much but at no time did he think that all plans could not be executed. There were many more soldiers stationed at Big Shanty than at first reported. Moreover their picket line extended along the railroad which might be the means of side-tracking all plans. Several members of the company, while not lacking in courage, advocated the giving up of the proposed raid. Andrews exclaimed: "Boys, I have planned this raid and will be successful or leave my bones in Dixie." The trip was a failure and the latter was his fate together with seven companions.

STOP AT BIG SHANTY.

The next morning the men were up early excepting two who overslept and finally greatly missed the train. At the depot that morning were the usual number of passengers all bound for Chattanooga and intermediate points along the line. When Conductor Fuller came through the train taking up the tickets he glanced a moment at

(Continued on Page 10.)

WILLIAM BENSINGER
Of McComb, Hancock county, Ohio, one of the few remaining heroes of this famous and historical raid. Mr. Bensinger assisted in tearing up the track and burning the bridges as readily as the "General" passed over them.

Southern Confederacy

GEO. W. ADAIR..........J. HENLY SMITH,
EDITORS AND PROPRIETORS.
D. C. SMITH, M. D.,................ASSOCIATE EDITOR.

ATLANTA, GEORGIA:

TUESDAY, APRIL 15, 1862.

The Largest Daily Circulation in the State.

OUR TERMS:

The necessity for advancing the rates of subscription to the CONFEDERACY is imperative, and subscribers sending money on and after this day will receive the paper strictly in accordance with the following terms:

DAILY for one year.....................$7 00
"   for six months.................... 4 00
"   for three months.................. 2 00
"   for one month.....................   75

One dollar will pay for forty days.

WEEKLY—$2 per annum, invariably in advance

CLUB RATES FOR THE WEEKLY.

To a Club of Ten at one Post Office, where all the names and money and money are sent at once, we will send our Weekly at $1 50 per annum.

"IT IS NOW TOO LATE TO RETIRE FROM THE CONTEST. THERE IS NO RETREAT BUT IN CHAINS AND SLAVERY."—*Patrick Henry in the first Revolution.*

The Great Railroad Chase!

THE MOST EXTRAORDINARY AND ASTOUNDING ADVENTURE OF THE WAR!!

THE MOST DARING UNDERTAKING THAT YANKEES EVER PLANNED OR ATTEMPTED TO EXECUTE!

Stealing an Engine—Tearing up the Track—Pursued on foot, on Hand Cars, and Engines —Overtaken—A Scattering—The Capture—The wonderful energy of Messrs. Fuller, Murphy, and Cain—Some reflections, &c., &c.

FULL PARTICULARS!!

Since our last issue we have obtained full particulars of the most thrilling Railroad adventure that ever occurred on the American Continent, as well as the mightiest and most important in its results, if successful, that has been conceived by the Lincoln Government since the commencement of this war. Nothing on so grand a scale has been attempted, and nothing within the range of possibility could be conceived that would fall with such a tremendous crushing force upon us, as the accomplishment of the plans which were concocted and dependant on the execution of the one whose history we now proceed to narrate.

Its *reality—what was actually done*—excels all the extravagant *conceptions* of the Arrow-Smith hoax, which fiction created such a profound sensation in Europe.

To make the matter more complete and intelligible, we will take our readers over the same history of the case which we related in our last, the main features of which are correct, but are lacking in details, which have since come to hand.

We will begin at the breakfast table of the Big Shanty Hotel at Camp McDonald, on the W. & A. R. R., where several regiments of soldiers are now encamped. The morning mail and passenger train had left here at 4 A. M. on last Saturday morning as usual, and had stopped there for breakfast. The conductor, Wm. A. Fuller, the engineer, J. Cain—both of this city—and the passengers were at the table, when some eight men, having uncoupled the engine and three empty box cars next to it from the passenger and baggage cars, mounted the engine, pulled open the valve, put on all steam, and left conductor, engineer, passengers, spectators, and the soldiers in the camp hard by, all lost in amazement and dumfounded at the strange, startling and daring act.

This unheard-of act was doubtless undertaken at that place and time, upon the presumption that pursuit could not be made by an engine short of Kingston, some thirty miles above or from this place; and that by cutting down the telegraph wires as they proceeded, the adventurers could calculate on at least three or four hours the start of any pursuit it was reasonable to expect. This was a legitimate conclusion, and but for the will, energy and quick good judgment of Mr. Fuller and Mr. Cain, and Mr. Anthony Murphy, the intelligent and practical foreman of the wood department of the State Road shop, who accidentally went on the train from this place that morning, their calculations would have worked out as originally contemplated, and the results would have been obtained long ere this reaches the eyes of our readers—the most terrible to us of any that we can conceive as possible, and unequaled by anything attempted or conceived since this war commenced.

Now for the chase:

These three determined men, without a moment's delay, put out after the flying train—on foot, amidst shouts of laughter by the crowd, who, though lost in amazement at the unexpected and daring act, could not repress their risibility at seeing three men start after a train on foot, which they had just witnessed depart at lightning speed. They put on all their speed, and ran along the track for three miles, when they came across some track raisers who had a small truck car, which is shoved along by men so employed on railroads, on which to carry their tools. This truck and men were at once "impressed." They took it by turns of two at a time to run behind this truck and push it along all up grades and level portions of the road, and let it drive at will on all the down grades. A little way further up the fugitive adventurers had stopped, cut the telegraph wires and torn up the track. Here the pursuers were thrown off pell mell, truck and men, upon the side of the road. Fortunately "nobody was hurt on

our side." The truck was soon placed on the road again; enough hands were left to repair the track, and with all the power of determined will and muscle, they pushed on to Etowah Station, some twenty miles above.

Here, most fortunately, Major Cooper's old coal engine, the "Yonah"—one of the first engines on the State Road—was standing out, fired up. This venerable locomotive was immediately turned upon her old track, and like an old racer at the tap of the drum, pricked up her ears and made fine time to Kingston.

The fugitives, not expecting such early pursuit, quietly took in wood and water at Cass Station, and borrowed a schedule from the tank tender upon the plausible plea that they were running a pressed train, loaded with powder for Beauregard. The attentive and patriotic tank tender, Mr. Wm. Russell, said he gave them his schedule, and would have sent the shirt off his back to Beauregard, if it had been asked for. Here the adventurous fugitives inquired which end of the switch they should go in on at Kingston. When they arrived at Kingston, they stopped, went to the Agent there, told the powder story, readily got the switch key, went on the upper turn-out, and waited for the down way *freight train* to pass. To all inquiries they replied with the same powder story.— When the freight train had passed, they immediately proceeded on to the next station—Adairsville—where they were to meet the *regular down freight train.* At some point on the way they had taken on some fifty cross-ties, and before reaching Adairsville, they stopped on a curve, tore up the rails, and put seven cross-ties on the track—no doubt intending to wreck this down freight train, which would be along in a few minutes.— They had out upon the engine a red hand kerchief as a kind of flag or signal, which, in Railroading, means another train is behind—thereby indicating to all that the regular passenger train would be along presently. They stopped a moment at Adairsville, and said Fuller, with the regular passenger train was behind, and would wait at Kingston for the freight train, and told the conductor thereon to push ahead and meet him at that point. They passed on to Calhoun, where they met the down passenger train, due here at 4.20 P. M., and without making any stop, they proceeded—on, on, and on.

But we must return to Fuller and his party whom we have unconsciously left on the old "Yonah" making their way to Kingston.

Arriving there and learning the adventurers were but twenty minutes ahead, they left the "Yonah" to blow off, while they mounted the engine of the Rome Branch Road, which was ready fired up and waiting for the arrival of the passenger train nearly due, when it would have proceeded to Rome. A large party of gentlemen volunteered for the chase, some at Acworth, Allatoona, Kingston and other points, taking such arms as they could lay their hands on at the moment; and with this fresh engine they set out with all speed but with great "care and caution," as they had scarcely time to make Adairsville before the down freight train would leave that point. Sure enough, they discovered this side of Adairsville three rails torn up and other impediments in the way. They "took up" in time to prevent an accident, but could proceed with the train no further. This was most vexatious, and it may have been in some degree disheartening, but it did not cause the slightest relaxation of efforts, and as the result proved was but little in the way of the *dead game*, pluck and resolutions of Fuller and Murphy, who left the engine and again *put out on foot alone!* After running two miles they met the down freight train, one mile out from Adairsville. They immediately reversed the train and ran backwards to Adairsville—put the cars on the siding and pressed forward, making fine time to Calhoun, where they met the regular down passenger train. Here they halted a moment, took on board a telegraph operator, and a number of men who again volunteered, taking their guns along—and continued the chase—Mr. Fuller also took on here a company of track hands to repair the track as they went along. A short distance above Calhoun they *flushed their game* on a curve, where they doubtless supposed themselves out of danger, and were quietly oiling the engine, taking up the track, &c. Discovering that they were pursued, they mounted and sped away, throwing out upon the track as they went along the heavy cross-ties they had prepared themselves with. This was done by breaking out the end of the hindmost box car, and pitching them out. Thus, "nip and tuck," they passed with fearful speed Resaca, Tilton, and on through Dalton.

The rails which they had taken up last they took off with them—besides throwing out cross-ties upon the track occasionally—hoping thereby the more surely to impede the pursuit; but all this was like tow to the touch of fire, to the now thoroughly aroused, excited and eager pursuers. These men, though so much excited and influenced by so much determination, still retained their well known caution, were looking out for this danger and discovered it, and though it was seemingly an insuperable obstacle to their making any headway in pursuit, was quickly overcome by the genius of Fuller and Murphy. Coming to where the rails were torn up, they stopped, tore up rails behind them, and laid them down before, till they had passed over that obstacle. When the cross ties were reached, they hauled to and threw them off, and thus proceeded, and under these difficulties gained on the frightened fugitives. At Dalton they halted a moment. Fuller put off the telegraph operator, with instructions to telegraph to Chattanooga to have them stopped, in case he should fail to overhaul them.

Fuller pressed on in hot chase—sometimes in sight—as much to prevent their cutting the wires before the message could be sent, as to catch them. The daring adventurers stopped just opposite and very near to where Col. Glenn's regiment is encamped, and cut the wires, but the operator at Dalton *had put the message through about two minutes before* — They also again tore up the track, cut down a telegraph pole, and placed the two ends of it under the cross ties, and the middle over the rail on the track. The pursuers stopped again and got over this impediment, in the same manner they did before—taking up rails behind and laying them down before. Once over this, they shot on, and passed through the great tunnel, at Tunnel Hill, being there only five minutes behind. The fugitives still finding themselves closely pursued, uncoupled two of the box cars from the engine, to impede the progress of the pursuers. Fuller hastily coupled them to the front of his engine, and pushed them ahead of him, to the first turn-out or siding, where they were left —thus preventing the collision the adventurers intended

Thus, the engine thieves passed Ringgold, where they began to fag. They were out of wood, water, and oil. Their rapid running and inattention to the engine, had melted all the brass from the journals. They had no time to repair or refit, for an iron-horse of more bottom was close behind. Fuller and Murphy and their men soon came within 400 yards of them, when the fugitives jumped from the engine and left it—three on the north side and five on the South—all fleeing precipitately and scattering through the thicket. Fuller and his party also took to the woods after them.

Some gentlemen, also well armed, took the engine and some cars of the down passenger train at Calhoun, and followed up Fuller and Murphy and their party in the chase but a short distance behind, and reached the place of the stampede but a very few moments after the first pursuers did. A large number of men were soon mounted, armed, and scouring the entire country in search of them. Fortunately, there was a militia muster at Ringgold. A great many countrymen were in town.— Hearing of the chase, they put out on foot and on horseback in every direction, in search of the daring but now thoroughly frightened and fugitive men.

We learn that Fuller, soon after leaving his engine, in passing a cabin in the country, found a mule having on a bridle but no saddle, and tied to the fence. "Here's your mule" he shouted as he leaped upon his back and put out as fast as a good switch well applied could impart vigor to the muscles and accelerate the speed of the patient donkey. The cry of "Here's your mule" and "Where's my mule" have become national, and are general-

ly heard when, on the one hand no mule is about, and on the other when no one is hunting a mule. It seems not to be understood by any one, though it is a peculiar Confederate phrase and is as popular as it is from the Potomac to the Rio Grande. It is reserved for Fuller, in the midst of this exciting chase, to solve the mysterious meaning of this national by-word or phrase, and give it a practical application

All of the eight men were captured, and are now safely lodged in jail. The particulars of their capture we have not received. This we hope to obtain in time for a postscript to this, or for our second edition. They confessed that they belonged to Lincoln's army, and had been sent down from Shelbyville to burn the bridges between here and Chattanooga; and that the whole party consisted of nineteen men, eleven of whom were dropped at several points on the road as they came down, to assist in the burning of the bridges as they went back.

When the morning freight train which left this city reached Big Shanty, Lieut.-Cols. R. F. Maddox and C. P. Phillips took the engine and a few cars, with fifty picked men, well armed, and followed on as rapidly as possible. They passed over all difficulties, and got as far as Calhoun, where they learned the fugitives had taken the woods, and were pursued by plenty of men with the means to catch them if it were possible.

One gentleman who went upon the train from Calhoun, who has furnished us with many of these particulars, and who, by the way, is one of the most experienced Railroad men in Georgia, says, too much praise cannot be bestowed on Fuller and Murphy, who showed a cool judgment and forethought in this extraordinary affair, unsurpassed by anything he ever knew in a Railroad emergency. This gentleman, we learn from another, offered, on his own account, $100 reward on each man, for the apprehension of the villains.

We do not know what Gov. Brown will do in this case, or what is his custom in such matters, but if such a thing is admissible, we insist on Fuller and Murphy being promoted to the highest honors on the road—if not by actually giving them the highest position, at least, let them be promoted by *brevet*. Certainly, their indomitable energy, and quick correct judgment and decision in the many difficult contingencies connected with this unheard of emergency, has saved all the Railroad bridges above Ringgold from being burned: the most daring scheme that this revolution has developed has been thwarted, and the tremendous results which, if successful, can scarcely be imagined, much less described, have been averted. Had they succeeded in burning the bridges, the enemy at Huntsville would have occupied Chattaoga, before Sunday night. Yesterday they would have been in Knoxville, and thus had possession of all East Tennesse. Our forces Knoxville, Greenville, and Cumberland p, would, ere this, have been in the hands the enemy. Lynchburg, Va., would have en moved upon at once. This would have ven them possession of the Valley of Virgnia, and Stone Wall Jackson could have en attacked in the rear. They could have ossession of the Railroad leading to Charlotesville, and Orange Court House, as well the South Side Railroad leading to Petersurg and Richmond. They might have been le to unite with McClellan's forces, and tack Jo. Johnston's army, front and flank. is not by any means improbable that our rmy in Virginia, would have been defeated, aptured or driven out of the State this week. Then reinforcements from all the eastern nd south-east portion of the country would ave been cut off from Beauregard. The enmy have Huntsville now, and with all those esigns accomplished his army would have een effectually flanked The mind and eart shrink back appalled at the bare contemlation of the awful consequences which wo'd ave followed the success of this one act. When Fuller, Murphy and Cain started rom Big Shanty *on foot to catch that fugitive ngine*, they we e involuntarily laughed at by he crowd, serious as the matter was—and to most observers it was indeed most ludicrous; ut *that foot race saved us*, and prevented the onsummation of all those tremendous consequences.

One fact we must not omit to mention is he valuable assistance rendered by Peter racken, the engineer on the down freight rain which Fuller and Murphy turned back. He ran his engine fifty and a half miles—two f them backing the whole freight train up to a fairsville—made twelve stops, coupled to he two cars which the fugitives had dropped, u switched them off on sidings—all this, in *ne hour and five minutes*

We doubt if the victory of Manassas or Corinth were worth as much to us as the frusration of this grand *coup d'etat*. It is not by any means certain that the annihilation of Beauregard's whole army at Corinth would be so fatal a blow to us as would have been the burning of the bridges at that time and by those men.

When we learned by a private telegraph dispatch a few days ago, that the Yankees had taken Huntsville, we attached no great importance to it. We regarded it merely as a dashing foray of a small party to destroy property, tear up the road, &c, *a la Morgan*. When an additional telegram announced the federal force there to be from 17,000 to 20,000, we were inclined to doubt it—though coming from a perfectly honorable and upright gentleman, who would not be apt to seize upon a wild report to send here to his friends. The

coming to that point with a large force, where they would be flanked on either side by our army, we regarded as a most stupid and unmilitary act. We now understand it all. They were to move upon Chattanooga and Knoxville as soon as the bridges were burnt, and press on into Virginia as far as possible, and take all our forces in that State in the rear.— It was all the deepe t laid scheme and on the grandest scale that ever emanated from the brains of any number of Yankees combined. It was one that was also, entirely practicable on almost any day for the last year There were but two miscalculations in the whole programme. they did not expect men to start out at all to pursue them, and they did not expect these pursuers on foot to find Maj Cooper's old "Yonah" standing there all ready fired up. Their calculations on every other point were dead certainties, and would have succeeded perfectly.

This would have eclipsed anything Capt. Morgan ever attempted. To think of a parcel of Federal soldiers, officers and privates, coming down into the heart of the Confederate States—for they were here in Atlanta and at Marietta—(some of them got on the train at Marietta that morning and others were at Big Shanty;) of playing such a serious game on the State Road, which is under the control of our prompt, energetic and sagacious Governor, known as such all over America, to seize the passenger train on his Road, right at Camp McDonald, where he has a number of Georgia regiments encamped, and run off with it; to burn the bridges on this same road, and go safely through to the Federal lines—all this would have been a feather in the cap of the major men who executed it.

Let this be a warning to the railroad men and every body else in the Confederate States. Let an engine never be left alone a moment. Let additional guards be placed at our bridges. This is a matter we specially urged in the Confederacy long ago. We hope it will now be heeded. Further: let a sufficient guard be placed to watch the Government stores in this city; and let increased vigilance and watchfulness be put forth by the watchmen. We know one solitary man who is guarding a house of nights in this city, which contains a lot of bacon. Two or three men could throttle and gag him and set fire to the house at any time; and worse, he conceives that there is no necessity for a guard, as is sometimes away off duty, for a few moments—fully long enough for an incendiary to burn the house he watches. Let Mr. Shackelford, whom we know to be watchful and attentive to his duties. take the responsibility at once of placing a well armed guard of sufficient force around every house containing government stores. Let this be done without waiting for instructions from Richmond.

One other thought. The press is requested

by the Government to keep silent about the movements of the army, and a great many things of the greatest interest to our people. It has, in the main, patriotically complied.— We have complied in most cases, but our judgment was against it all the while. The plea is that the enemy will get the news, if it is published in our papers. Now, we again ask, what's the use? The enemy get what information they want. They are with us and pass among us almost daily. They find out from us what they want to know, by passing through our country unimpeded. It is con sense: it is folly, to deprive our own people of knowledge they are entitled to and ought to know, for fear the enemy will find it out We ought to have a regular system of pass ports over all our roads, and refuse to let any man pass who could not give a good account of himself—come well vouched for and make it fully appear that he is not an enemy, and that he is on legitimate business. This would keep information from the enemy far more effectually than any reticence of the press which ought lay before our people the full facts in everything of a public nature.

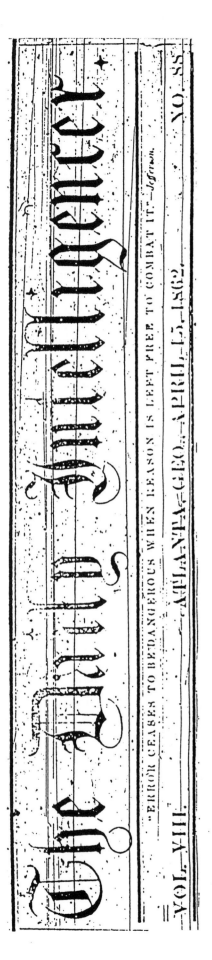

The Intelligencer.

ATLANTA, GEORGIA

Tuesday Morning, April 15, 1862.

LINCOLN'S SPIES, THIEVES, AND BRIDGE BURNERS.

On Saturday morning last, we were startled by intelligence telegraphed here from Marietta, that the Engine, with three cars attached to the mail train, from this place to Chattanooga, had been detached therefrom while the conductor, engineer, and train hands were breakfasting at Big Shanty, and had been steamed up the Road by unknown parties. Prompt measures were at once taken there to pursue the robbers. Mr. L. Kendrick, who, as soon as it was ascertained that the Engine was in possession of thieves, rode with speed to Marietta, and from there telegraphed the fact to this place. Major Rowland, the Superintendent, being absent up the Road, Mr. Walker, the Master of Transportation, immediately directed Mr. Kendrick to take an engine, and such armed force as he could get, and proceed at once to pursuit. This was done. But as our readers will be interested in a detailed account of this extraordinary and most audacious attempt of LINCOLN'S SPIES to rob, burn, and destroy the State Road, we give below the statement of Mr. Fuller, the conductor of the train from which the engine and three cars were detached by the Lincoln hirelings.

MR. W. A. FULLER'S STATEMENT.

On Saturday morning, I left at 4 o'clock, with the train, and reached "Camp McDonald" ("Big Shanty") at regular train time. While at breakfast, I heard the engine "exhaust" very rapidly and suddenly. I immediately rose up and stated to Mr. A. Murphy, who is Boss of the State Road Shop, but who happened to be a passenger that morning, and to Jeff Cain, my engineer, that something was wrong with the engine. We three then hastened out, and, much to our surprise, discovered that the engine with three cars was out of sight. It at once suggested to Messrs. Murphy and Cain, the propriety of following the engine to Chattanooga, if in no other way, on foot, and pursue till we overtook and captured the unknown thieves. But when I first got out, I enquired of a guard who was on the platform, "who had taken the engine off?" He replied that "he did not know him," but that "he was a tall, black-bearded man, wearing a military black overcoat, with a large cape." On foot, then, in double quick time, we three started in pursuit. I was the first to reach Moon's Station, some two and a half miles from "Big Shanty." There I found a hand car and returned a short distance to take in my companions, Messrs. Murphy and Cain, and we then, with a few men, whom we got at Moon's Station to push the car along, pursued on to within a

half mile of Acworth. At this point we found some thirty or fifty cross-ties laid on the track of the Road, to obstruct pursuit, and the telegraphic wires torn down some quarter of a mile. It took us some time to remove these obstructions. When we got to Acworth we took another hand car and some ten men, all armed, as well as ourselves, and pursued on till within a mile and a half of Etowah, where we were again impeded by the track's being torn up in a short curve, by which we were thrown into a ditch. Having extricated ourselves from this difficulty, we proceeded on to Etowah, where we took Major Cooper's engine, which was cheerfully delivered, and run by us from Etowah to Kingston. We also took on at Etowah a coal car for the purpose of carrying our men, who then had increased to about twenty, mostly citizens. When we arrived at Kingston, we found that the thieves had passed some twenty five minutes ahead of us. We were there told that they stated that they had been pressed by the Government to carry powder and ammunition to Beauregard—that Fuller, and the regular mail train, was behind, and would be on directly. This they did, to get the switch keys; and so plausible were their statements, that they completely deceived the agent at Kingston. At Kingston we changed engines—taking the Rome engine, which was already fired up, and which was kindly offered to us by Mr. Smith, the conductor. We pursued on thus till within four miles of Adairsville, where the track was again torn up, and cross-ties placed upon it. Mr. Murphy and myself then again took it a foot, at double quick, till we met the down Express train one and a half miles this side of Adairsville. This train we stopped and turned back to Adairsville where we switched off the cars and took the engine alone, Mr. Bracken, the engineer, running it. In this way, we still continued the pursuit, after having to stop to remove the obstructions of cross ties, &c., that the thieves had put at intervals on the shortest curves, in our way.

We reached Calhoun, where they had left about five minutes before our arrival there, and when about a mile and a half from that station we came in sight of them, where they had detached their hindmost car, and left it as an obstruction to our pursuit. This we coupled on to our engine and carried it on ahead in our pursuit, till we came to within a mile of Resaca, where they had detached another car. This we also coupled on ahead, and continued thus in pursuit till we reached Resaca, where we switched the two cars off, and without delay still continued the pursuit. In the mean time, it seems that they had loaded the third car which they had with cross-ties, and punching out the hindmost end of it, they dropped at intervals, as before, the cross-ties upon the track. These obstructions delayed us a little, but were soon removed. Beyond Dalton, about three miles opposite Col. Glenn's camp, the obstructions there

The Locomotive *General*

The *General* was built by the firm of Rogers, Ketchum & Grosvenor of Paterson, N.J., for the Western & Atlantic Railroad at a cost of $8,850.

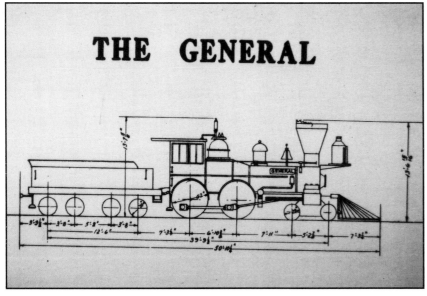

felt and Russia iron. The engine carried a working steam pressure of 140 pounds. The boiler contains 130 flues each eleven feet long and two inches in diameter. The leading truck, with four wheels, was built with a rigid center. The tender has two trucks of four wheels each, 30 inches in diameter and with inside bearings. The smoke stack of the old engine was of the balloon type known as a Radley and Hunter stack designed for burning wood as fuel. The engine had no live steam injectors but instead took water from the tender by a pair of ram type pumps which were activated by the crossheads. Therefore the boiler could not be supplied with water unless the engine was moving. There was no brake on the engine, and the hand brake on the tender was probably used when

Her construction number is 631, and she was completed in December 1855. She was built as an eight-wheel, wood-burning locomotive of the American type, with a 4-4-0 wheel arrangement, weighing about 50,300 pounds, with a gauge of five feet and cylinders 15 inches in diameter and a stroke of 22 inches. The four driving wheels, each 60 inches in diameter, were made of cast iron. The weight on drivers is 32,000 pounds, and the weight on the leading truck wheels is 18,000 pounds. The boiler was a type known as Wagon Top and was covered with

THE ROGERS LOCOMOTIVE AND MACHINE WORKS WERE LOCATED ON THE SOUTHEAST CORNER OF SPRUCE AND MARKET STREETS, PATERSON, NJ. THE FIRM WAS FORMERLY KNOWN AS THE ROGERS, KETCHUM & GROSVENOR, AND STARTED IN 1832. THEY ALSO OCCUPIED THE BUILDINGS ACROSS THE STREET, BY THE SIDE OF THE RACEWAY, WHERE THOMAS ROGERS BUILT THE JEFFERSON MILL IN 1831. THIS FIRM WAS ENGAGED IN THE MANUFACTURING OF COTTON, WOOL AND FLAX MACHINERY AND HAD LARGE IRON AND BRASS FOUNDRIES. THE BROWN STONE, TWO-STORY BUILDING AT THE LEFT WAS ERECTED IN 1835 WITH THE INTENTION OF GOING IN THE BUSINESS OF MAKING LOCOMOTIVES. WHEN THOMAS ROGERS DIED IN APRIL 1856, THE COMPANY REORGANIZED AND THE NAME WAS CHANGED TO ROGERS LOCOMOTIVE & MACHINE WORKS; THE OLD NAME OF THE FIRM IS STILL SHOWN WHEN THIS PPHOTO WAS TAKEN. THE LOCOMOTIVE IN THE CENTER WAS BUILT FOR THE NASHVILLE AND NORTH WESTERN, A FOUR WHEELER. IN FRONT OF THE STONE BUILDING CAN BE SEEN A NUMBER OF CANNONS, THE GOVERNMENT EXPERIMENTED HERE ON A NEW PROCESS FOR CASTING BRONZE CANNONS DURING THE CIVIL WAR. GREAT FALLS DEVELOPMENT CORP., PATERSON, NJ

Description of the Engine the *General*

DATE BUILT:	December, 1855	**BOILER PRESSURE:**	140 lbs.
NAME OF BUILDER:	Rogers Ketchum & Grosvenor	**GAUGE WHEN BUILT:**	5 ft.
	Locomotive Works,	**TRACTIVE EFFORT:**	9800 lbs.
	Paterson, N.J.	**SIZE OF CYLINDERS:**	15" x 22"
FOR WHOM BUILT:	Western & Atlantic Railroad	**PISTON RODS:**	2-1/4" diameter
TYPE:	8-wheel of 4- 4- 0	**TYPE OF VALVE GEAR:**	Stephenson, shifting link

WHEELS: Diameter:

Engine truck wheels 28" (cast iron)
Driver wheels 60" (cast iron centers)
Tender truck wheels 30" (cast iron)

VALVES:

	Type	'D' (slide)
	Travel	4-5/8 inches
	Lap	5/8 inches
	Lead	1/32 inches

LUBRICATION: Tallow   Pipes from tallow cups on boiler head in cab

SIZE OF JOURNALS:

Engine truck	4- 1/2 x 7 inches
Drivers	6 x 8 inches
Tender	3-1/2 x 6 inches

WHEEL BASE:

Engine trucks	5 ft. 3 inches
Driver or rigid	6 ft. 10 inches
Total engine	20 ft. 1 inch
Tender trucks	3 ft. 8 inches
Total tender	12 ft. 7 inches
Total engine and tender	39 ft. 4 inches
Length from end of push bar to face of tender coupler	49 ft. 4 inches

WEIGHT:

On engine trucks	18,000 lbs.
On drivers	32,300 lbs.
Total weight engine	50,300 lbs.
Weight of tender	11,700 lbs
Total engine and tender	62,000 lbs.

BOILER:

Type	Wagon top, crown bar stayed
Dia. first course	40 inches
Thickness of barrel	5/16 inches
Thickness of dome course	3/8 inches
Thickness of wrapper sheet	3/8 inches
Lagging and jacket	felt and Russia iron

HEATING SURFACE:

Flues	748.38 sq. ft.
Firebox	71.08 sq. ft.
Total heating surface	819.46 sq. ft.

GRATE AREA: 12.46 sq. ft.

FLUES:

Diameter	2 inches
Length	11 ft.
Number	130

FIREBOX:

Width	39 inches
Length	46 inches
Thickness of crown sheet	3/8 inches
Thickness of flue sheet	1/2 inches
Thickness of side sheets	5/16 inches
Thickness of door sheet	5/16 inches

SAFETY VALVES: Plain escaping type with spring scale in cab (two)

SIZE OF STEAM PIPES: 5 inches

BOILER FEED: 2 pumps operated by plungers attached to cross heads

TYPE OF SMOKE STACK: Balloon

FUEL USED: Wood

CAPACITY OF TENDER: Wood: 1.75 cords
Water 1750 Gallons

TYPE OF BRAKES: Hand brake on front tender truck

the engine was idle during terminal layovers. The way to stop the engine was for the engineer to pull back on the Johnson reverse bar and put the engine in reverse. Such a feature is unheard of today and has been for years....

When the *General* was ready for shipment from the Rogers, Ketchum & Grosvenor plant, she was placed on a heavy flat car and drawn by mules along Market Street in Paterson to the tracks of the Erie Railroad a mile away. The Rogers plant and its successors built over 6,000 steam locomotives, and the company always worked under the handicap of being far away from a main railroad track. The *General* was moved over the rails of the Erie Railroad to Philadelphia where she was loaded aboard a sailing ship for the thousand mile journey to Savannah. There she was placed on the rails of the Central Railroad of Georgia for the 191-mile run to Macon and then the 103-mile run to Atlanta over the rails of the Macon & Western Railroad.

The Annual Report of the W&A RR for 1856 reflects the fact that the *General* was placed in service on the Road in January 1856 for use in freight service. With five foot driving wheels, the *General* was equally capable of handling passenger trains.

Soon after the *General* arrived on the W&A RR, she was moved to the State Road Shops in Atlanta where the distinctive strap iron pilot was installed. All W&A RR locomotives were equipped with pilots of this type. This new pilot was made by Tom Haney, blacksmith in the Shops and father of young Henry Haney who later performed so well as fireman for Pete Bracken on the *Texas* during *The Great Locomotive Chase. . . .*

The *General* was handled well during the great chase and suffered only minor damage at the conclusion some two miles north of Ringgold. As soon as the chase ended, Anthony Murphy, foreman of Machinery and Motive Power at the State Road Shops and who was with Conductor William A. Fuller in the pursuing party, went aboard the *General* to check the water level in the boiler. He found it low. The *Texas* then pushed the *General* northward to Graysville where a more thorough examination was made and wood and water taken on. It was found that the brass journal bearing on the left side of the front axle on the leading truck had been damaged and would require replacement. The *Texas* then pulled the *General* to Ringgold where she remained until Tuesday, April 15, 1862, when Daniel Fleck, a machinist in the State Road Shops in Atlanta arrived with a new brass journal bearing. Fleck

replaced the bearing, and the *General* was ready to go back in service.

On May 2, 1862, the *General* again pulled a train with the Andrews Raiders aboard, hardly three weeks after the famous chase. All members of the Federal Raiding party were apprehended within a week of the Raid and were imprisoned in the Swims Jail in Chattanooga. The Confederate authorities, for reasons of security, decided to move the Raiders south to Georgia. They were placed aboard the southbound passenger train, pulled by the *General*, early on the morning of May 2, moved to Atlanta and thence over the Georgia Railroad to Madison where they were imprisoned in the old stone County Jail for a period of three days; then they were returned to Chattanooga.

The *General* continued in regular service, and the next record available indicates that she was almost under fire of the Federal batteries during the battle of Kennesaw Mountain on June 27, 1864. "When the battle began during the early morning General Johnston sent up a train load of ammunition, etc., to the Confederate lines at the eastern base of Kennesaw Mountain. The ammunition, etc., was unloaded and carried to the front as quickly as possible, but the engine and train were detained at that point, by order of General Johnston, to carry back the wounded at the close of the battle. During the entire morning the *General* and her train stood at the point where now is station Elizabeth, and some of the Federal bomb-shells, flying over the Confederate entrenchments, exploded almost in her neighborhood. In the afternoon wounded soldiers from Featherstone's Division, and others in that portion of the field, were placed aboard the train, and the *General* brought them down to Marietta, and thence on to Atlanta."

By the end of August, it was apparent to General Hood that Atlanta would have to be abandoned to the advancing Federal forces under General Sherman. Every effort had been made by Superintendent George D. Phillips and his staff of the W&A RR to move locomotives and rolling stock south over the Macon & Western RR and thus save this equipment from the Federals. The act of "refugeeing" equipment was also carried out by the other railroads that served Atlanta.

Around noon on Sept. 1, 1864, the *General* and the *Missouri* left Atlanta on the M&W RR, each pulling a train of military supplies picked up in the East Point Yards, namely ammunition, guns and Quartermaster supplies. Atlanta was beset from the

SEPT. 1, 1864 – GENERAL HOOD AND HIS CONFEDERATE FORCES, AS THEY LEFT ATLANTA, DESTROYED AMMUNITION AND SUPPLY TRAINS, INCLUDING FIVE LOCOMOTIVES, ONE OF WHICH WAS THE *GENERAL*. DRAWING FROM *HARPER'S WEEKLY*

AFTERMATH OF THE DESTRUCTION OF THE SCHOFIELD & MARKHAM ROLLING MILL. THE *GENERAL* WAS INVOLVED AND LOCATED JUST OUT OF THE PICTURE IN THE LOWER RIGHT HAND CORNER. NATIONAL ARCHIVES

direction of Jonesboro, but no one in Atlanta knew exactly where the Federal forces were. The trains came to a halt near Rough & Ready (present day Mountain View) when artillery of the 23rd Corps opened up, and both trains were backed to the car shed in Atlanta. They were then moved to the Georgia Railroad yards between Oakland Cemetery and the Schofield and Markham Rolling Mill. The supplies could not be removed, so the authorities decided to destroy them for the city was to be abandoned that night. Dave Young was the engineer assigned to the *General* at this time, and he was ordered to damage the engine sufficiently to render it useless to the Federals. This was hardly necessary in view of the damage incurred by the later burning of the car loads of ammunition and other supplies. The *Missouri* was run backward into a

line of cars, and the *General* was run backward into the *Missouri* and then the cars were set ablaze. The *Missouri* is reported to have been the last locomotive shipped south of the Mason & Dixon line before the Civil War. A third engine, the *Etowah,* was also involved in this movement as was the engine *N.C. Munroe* of the M&W RR and the *E.Y. Hill* of the Atlanta &West Point Railroad. A total of five engines and 81 cars of ammunition and other supplies went up in flames the evening of Sept. 1, 1864, as General Hood's Confederate forces left Atlanta.

This scene was vividly portrayed many years later by David O. Selznick in his production of *Gone With the Wind* with the burning of Atlanta. The five locomotives were badly damaged, and all the cars were destroyed.

In early September as General Sherman's forces

occupied Atlanta, Federal photographer George Barnard recorded several scenes with his camera. Among them was the locomotive that had been responsible for the hanging of eight men as spies, the *General*. . . .

The *General* was badly damaged during this conflagration, and she was carried as "captured property" by the U.S. Military Railroad Service as they took over operation of the W&A RR. She was also reported as "Captured in Atlanta" in the Annual Report of the W&A RR for the year ending September 30, 1864. On Oct. 21, 1865, after the War had ended and the W&A RR had been returned to its owner the State of Georgia for operation, John H. Flynn, master mechanic of the W&A RR, reported to Colonel Robert Baugh, Superintendent of the W&A RR, that the *General* was "Needing General Repairs."

There is some question as to whether the USMRRS repaired the *General* and put her back in service during the short period they operated the W&A RR in 1864 and 1865. It is believed that the USMRRS did nothing to repair the *General* and put her back in service. Master mechanic Flynn's report supports this contention. In 1866, Col. D.C. McCallum, General Manager of the USMRRS, rendered a report to the Secretary of War concerning the overall operation of the USMRRS during the War. He included in this report lists of the locomotives used by the USMRRS and certain data concerning each. He listed the *General* as "Captured and Returned." Such an entry suggests that the *General* was not repaired. The USMRRS had more than 200 good locomotives, most of them purchased new, to support General Sherman in his Atlanta Campaign, and they did not need to repair damaged engines such as the *General*. There were several instances when locomotives were wrecked and just left rather than expend the effort to repair them. Finally, the locomotive repair shops for the USMRRS in support of the Atlanta Campaign were located in Nashville, Tenn., and there is no evidence to indicate that the *General* was moved to Nashville for repair at this time.

The Annual Report of the W&A RR for the year ending Sept. 30, 1866, indicates that the *General* had been repaired, at a cost of $2,887.45 and was then in "Good Order" and was assigned to freight service. The *General* was reported to have run 2,560 miles that year which indicates that repairs were not completed until the latter part of the year. It is believed that these repairs were the first made to put the *General* back in service after the damage suffered on Sept. 1, 1864.

The Annual Report of the W&A RR for Sept. 30, 1867, indicated the *General* to be in "Good Order" having run 22,300 miles that year with repairs costing $759.38. This mileage is equivalent to over 80 round trips between Atlanta and Chattanooga. The engine had pulled 1,312 loaded cars and 1,400 empties for an average of 33 1/3 miles run per cord of wood consumed. The *General's* record was much the same for the year ending Sept. 30, 1868, when she ran 19,389 miles with repairs costing $497.75. She had pulled 1,343 loaded cars and 1,076 empties running 32 1/3 miles per cord of wood consumed. During the year ending Sept. 30, 1896, more repairs were reported at a cost of $2,260.70 and the *General* ran 13,222 miles with an average of 39 miles per cord of wood consumed, pulling 727 loaded cars and 313 empties.

It is not known for certain when the practice of numbering locomotives began. The USMRRS had their locomotives numbered, and it may be that the practice began among southern railroads at the close of the Civil War. Such was the case with the W&A RR. Their locomotives were assigned numbers in 1866 according to the date placed in service on the road, and the number was painted on the locomotive as was the name assigned to the locomotive. The *General* had the honor of being the 39th locomotive to be placed in service on the W&A RR, and that number was assigned to the engine. She also continued to carry the name, and until sometime after the restoration of 1892, the name *General* was painted in gold on the panel under the cab window. In 1880, the numbers were changed. Many of the early locomotives had been retired, sold or scrapped, and the change in numbering was apparently done to eliminate the gaps in numbers. Again, the numbers were assigned according to date placed in service of the oldest locomotive remaining on the roster. At this time, the *General* was the third oldest locomotive remaining in service, and she was assigned the Number 3, which she still carries.

The W&A RR began, from an operating standpoint, on May 9, 1850, when the track laying in the tunnel through the Chetoogeta Mountain was completed. From the beginning and through the Civil War, except for a period in 1864-65 when the Road was operated by the USMRRS, operation of the W&A RR was accomplished by the State of Georgia through a superintendent appointed by the governor and who reported to the governor. During the period of reconstruction following the Civil War, it became apparent that this was not the best way to run a railroad. Politics and graft were taking a heavy toll, and the railroad was not being operated in an efficient manner. Accordingly, on Dec. 27, 1870, the Road was leased to the Western & Atlantic Railroad Company for a period of 20 years. This company was formed for the purpose by Joseph E. Brown, wartime governor of Georgia, and twenty-two associates who agreed to operate the Road and to pay as rental the sum of $25,000 per month to the State of Georgia. The W&A RR Company took over the complete railroad to include locomotives and rolling stock. The *General* was included and was then valued at $2,000 and in running order.

Existing records of the W&A RR for the period operated by the State of Georgia, prior to 1870, are not complete. Annual Reports for the years 1863 and 1865 are not known to be available. Taking this fact into consideration and the fact that the *General* was not operable in 1864, the total mileage reported for this historic old engine during the period of State operation was 127,886 miles. The best year was 1867 when she ran 22,300 miles—all on a railroad only 138 miles in length.

In the early 1870s, the W&A RR Company began to rebuild the Road and to repair equipment. The War had taken a very heavy toll, and little had been done to rehabilitate the Road. During this time, the *General* was completely rebuilt in the W&A RR Shops in Atlanta. This rebuilding coincided with the change from wood to coal as fuel for the locomotives of the Road. The extra steam dome, ankle rails, strap iron pilot and balloon stack disappeared. . . . Since it had been converted to a coal burner, a diamond stack had replaced the balloon stack of wood-burning days. . . .

In 1886, the *Kennesaw Gazette* of March of that year reported on the *General* in this manner: "This famous locomotive is still on the Western and Atlantic Railroad, pulling a train. She is one of 'old issue,' but is retained in service, although her capacity is rather limited, when compared with the big 'ten-wheelers' and other modern locomotives which the ever-wide awake Western & Atlantic Railroad Company now possess." Joseph M. Brown, son of the wartime governor and president of the W&A RR Company Joseph E. Brown, served as Traffic Manager of the Road and also editor of the *Kennesaw Gazette.* The latter was a trade publication of tabloid size published for the benefit of employees and the public. This quotation indicates that he was always ready to advance the cause of the W&A RR Company which was then advertised and promoted as the "Kennesaw Route."

One of the most important achievements in the history of railroading in the United States was the change of gauge which occurred on June 1, 1886, on nearly 13,000 miles of railroads south of the Ohio and east of the Mississippi River. Most of the southern railroads were built to the five foot gauge, including the W&A RR, and the gauge was changed to four feet and nine inches, close to the standard gauge of four feet eight and a half inches of the railroads in the northern and western United States. This change made it practicable to interchange cars of all classes between the southern states and the rest of the United States. In the case of the W&A RR, the change was made during a 24 hour period. Track crews of sufficient numbers were placed along the 138 miles of track between Atlanta and Chattanooga and at the proper time moved one rail three inches toward the other to effect the new gauge. The work force engaged in this effort totaled 436 men. The work was started at 1:30 p.m. on May 31, 1886, and completed on June 1, 1886, at 10:00 a.m. Generally, the change of gauge on the locomotives was made by changing driving wheels which were made up ahead of time, though there were some other changes necessary in the running gear, etc. In the case of the *General* this was not done, probably due to her age and overall condition. The gauge of her drivers was changed by moving the tires in one and a half inches on each side. It appeared that the pony truck wheels were replaced as were those of the tender with new trucks of the new gauge.

The *Kennesaw Gazette* of Feb. 14, 1887, reported that the *General* was still in service on the road and had recently been photographed along with Conductor William A. Fuller and Captain Jacob Parrott. . . .

The April 15, 1887, issue of the *Kennesaw Gazette* was devoted to the story of the *General* and was headed "The Capture of a Locomotive Number." This account was written by Joseph M. Brown with the aid of Conductor William A. Fuller and was to be published in many forms during the seventy years that followed. An interesting feature of this issue is an illustration of the locomotive *General* on the front page. This illustration was made from a photograph taken of the engine sometime around 1886 or 1887. While the engine was then

DRAWING OF THE *GENERAL* FROM THE APRIL 15, 1887, *KENNESAW GAZETTE*, BASED ON A PHOTOGRAPH TAKEN IN 1886. (BELOW) WHILE THE *GENERAL* WAS A COAL BURNER AT THIS TIME, THE ARTIST REPLACED THE DIAMOND STACK WITH A WOOD BURNING STACK. NOTE ALSO THE PILOT (COW-CATCHER) ON THE REAR OF THE TENDER. THE *GENERAL* WAS IN SERVICE AT THIS TIME ON THE DALTON-CHATTA-NOOGA ACCOMMODATION TRAIN.

THE *GENERAL* IN ATLANTA IN 1887. CONDUCTOR WILLIAM A. FULLER IS STANDING TO THE LEFT AND JACOB PARROTT, ONE OF THE RAIDERS, IS IN THE CAB.

THE *GENERAL*, 1886 OR 1887.

still in operation and fitted with a diamond stack for burning coal, the artist gave the engine a balloon stack of the Radley & Hunter variety with which the *General* was equipped when burning wood as fuel. The likeness presented in 1887 resembles very closely the restored *General* of 1892. Another interesting feature in this drawing is the small cow catcher on the rear of the tender.

Joseph M. Brown, writing in the *Kennesaw Gazette* of April 15, 1887, gave evidence that the W&A's famous locomotive the *General* was still in good condition and capable of some speed. It seems that W&A passenger train No. 1, northbound, broke down near Chickamauga, and the passengers missed connections with the Cincinnati Southern Railway train at Boyce a few miles south of Chattanooga. The train was unable to go forward until the *General* pulling passenger train No. 19, overtook her. The *General* with nine coaches, two of which were heavy Pullman sleepers, proceeded from Chickamauga to Boyce making the run of six miles and a half in ten minutes. Brown concluded that this record was not being beaten by some of the big engines of modern build.

A few days later, the *General* was again in the news. The International Convention of Car Accountants was held in Atlanta April 19 through April 22, 1887. Approximately 100 of the delegates met in Chattanooga on the morning of Monday, April 18th and at noon boarded a special train for Atlanta via the W&A RR, pulled by the General...

In the *Kennesaw Gazette* of Sept. 1, 1887, Joseph M. Brown called attention to the fact that the "old *General* has of late been thoroughly overhauled and rejuvenated, and is now pulling one of the accommodation trains." During the overhaul, a small cowcatcher was put on the rear of the tender as was the custom for locomotives in accommodation train service when they would often be in a reverse position pulling the train...

Though small compared to other locomotives then in service, the *General* was referred to as a fast traveller. One remarkable run was cited while pulling train No. 19 from Atlanta to Kennesaw. The train left Atlanta nearly 45 minutes late with three coaches and a sleeping car. The *General* often ran at speeds of a mile a minute and pulled in to Kennesaw on time allowing the passengers to enjoy supper at the Railroad House operated by Judge G.T. Carrie at the regular time. Joseph M. Brown may have stretched this story a bit. The distance from Atlanta to Kennesaw is 28 miles by rail, and the schedule allowed one hour and 28 minutes including three stops for this run. In this instance the *General* practically cut the running time in half.

During March 1887 the W&A RR Company acquired three new modern locomotives from the Rhode Island Locomotive Works of Providence, R.I. These were ten wheelers and able to pull heavier loads than the eight wheelers like the *General* were able to do. For a time, this created a surplus of motive power on the W&A, and they assisted in the construction of the Atlanta & Florida Railroad from Atlanta to Fort Valley, by renting them the *General*. The *General* was employed in this service for a short time in late 1887 and early 1888...

In the Aug. 15, 1888, issue of the *Kennesaw Gazette*, Joseph M. Brown published a letter from his father, Joseph E. Brown, President of the W&A RR Company, addressed to the Secretary of the General Council of the Grand Army of the Republic. In this letter, Brown stated that: "I will consent to loan the engine, the *General*, to the Grand Army of the Republic during the period of the encampment without any charge whatever, except the charges, if any, that may be made by the companies north of Chattanooga for carrying the engine from Chattanooga to Columbus, Ohio, and back." He went on to state that the *General* was still in regular service and that "the engine has been rebuilt a time or two since the historical event to which you refer, (the Chase) but the machinery and framework are identically the same which formed part of the engine at the time of capture by Andrews' party." The *General* did go to Columbus, Oh., for this encampment and under her own steam. Joseph M. Brown issued a special number of the *Kennesaw Gazette* for this occasion. It was a reprint of the April 15, 1887, issue in which details of the Great Locomotive Chase were described. This extra issue was titled: "Extra Number, Complimentary to the Grand Army of the Republic, National Encampment, Columbus, Ohio, September 11, 1888." This encampment of the GAR was a special affair for the survivors of the Andrews Raiding party. They had a special reunion of their own, and Conductor William A. Fuller accepted an invitation to join them and was on hand for the occasion. The *General* was very popular among the veterans present. She was placed under a 24-hour guard to discourage souvenir hunters. Three photographs were taken of the engine and the survivors of the raiding party who were present including Conductor Fuller.

The latter made a very inspiring speech to the assembled veterans which was widely acclaimed.

After the reunion the *General* returned home to the W&A RR over the rails of the Cincinnati, New Orleans, Texas & Pacific RR from Columbus to Chattanooga. The return trip was more eventful than the northbound trip had been. Mr. Alex Jeffrey, later a Southern Railway engineer, who handled the *General* from Somerset, Ky., to Chattanooga told an interesting story which almost resulted in disaster for the *General.*

"The *General* was much smaller than the eight wheelers we were running at the time," Alex said, "and being much older, I naturally couldn't run her as fast as we wheeled the Class A's. However, I was running about 35 miles per hour when the accident occurred just north of Emory Gap.

"Peter Gorman was my conductor, and as it was a very hot day, he elected to ride the pilot of the *General*. In those days the right-of-way wasn't kept cut as it is today, and in many places the weeds and bushes were almost like trees. When I rounded a curve, I saw over the top of some bushes, two men pumping a handcar. I couldn't see the car itself, and naturally had no idea how many men were on it, but I reached for the whistle cord as I shut off and clutched the old Johnson reverse bar. Then I saw a half dozen or more men tumble off the car and roll into the bushes, and I recognized Section Foreman Costello as I went by him with the speed of the *General* hardly checked.

"I didn't know what would happen to the little kettle when she struck the handcar, and I thought of Peter Gorman as I reversed her and gave her a shot of steam. We hit a terrible wallop. I saw parts of the handcar fly through the air as the old lady shuddered under the impact and the crushing of her long nosed pilot timbers.

"When everything stopped and I had time to look around," Alex chuckled, "I saw Peter Gorman crouching on the boiler behind the huge diamond stack, holding on for dear life as he peeped around it. No one was seriously hurt but Gorman lost ten years of his life the few minutes he was hugging the stack."

The Dalton (Ga.) Argus, Sept. 1, 1888, took note of the movement of the *General* to Columbus, Oh., and reported that the *General* "passed up the road this week" enroute to Columbus and the GAR Encampment. The writer went on to describe the *General*. "The *General* is getting somewhat aged now, and will not excite jealousy for beauty; but

while pulling the Dalton accommodation last season, she frequently picked up fifty miles an hour, for a short jump, and on one occasion took the neck off a wild turkey as nicely as if it had been done by a rifle ball. If Bennett Smith had been at the throttle, with the Andrews party, she might have got through, even if she had to swim the Tennessee River to reach the Federal lines. . . ."

During Sept. 1889, the Society of the Army of the Cumberland held their annual meeting in the city of Chattanooga. Again, the W&A RR, ever willing to join with the veterans and promote the historic "Kennesaw Route" pulled the *General* out of service and had her on display opposite the Palace Hotel for the benefit of the attending veterans.

Occasionally, an erroneous story would surface concerning the *General,* and there was a good example in 1889. *The Railroad Gazette* of Nov. 1, 1889, carried a story announcing that the historic locomotive *General* had been sold to the Empire & Dublin Railroad for use in construction work. This road was then being built from Hawkinsville to Dublin, Ga. *The Chattanooga Times* newspaper also carried the same story, and this prompted Joseph M. Brown to announce clearly in the *Kennesaw Gazette* of Dec. 1, 1889, that "This is all a mistake. The W.&A. still owns the *General* and has no idea of selling her." Another instance occurred in the *Railroad Gazette* of Jan. 19, 1894, which carried an announcement that the *General* has finally "landed at the Libby Prison War Museum in Chicago, where it will doubtless remain permanently." At that time the *General* was in storage in Nashville, Tenn.

A writer for *The Locomotive Engineer* visited the south in early 1890 and made a trip over the W&A RR. He visited the Road's shops in Atlanta which were located in the vicinity of the present day World Congress Center, and he gave an excellent description of what they were like and what was in them. He wrote: "In the roundhouse are a half dozen dismantled and rusted old hulks that have long been dead, and now seem like honored remains lying in state. In one of the stalls, undergoing repairs, was the *General*, the engine stolen from the Confederate camp at Big Shanty in 1862 by a number of daring Federal scouts, and run north in an attempt to destroy bridges on the line, and cut off the supplies of the Confederates at Chattanooga.

"One cannot look at this old engine and not feel a thrill for the brave men who fought and died over her in the great national struggle. The reason these old engines are still in service is undoubtedly caused by the fact that the lease is about to expire, and the officials of the State are unwilling to allow the lessee anything for betterment of the equipment. All the engines are named, most of them equipped with steam driving brakes, diamond stacks, and short fronts are the rule, but new engines have the extension and open stack. It looked rather strange to see several sections of every freight train with one of these little engines ahead of each section; they are rated all the way from five to twelve cars. It is a good road for engineers, as they get $4.00 per day whether they work or not, with a good rest at each end of the line."

On Dec. 27, 1890, the lease of the Western & Atlantic Railroad Company expired. A new lease was then entered into by the State of Georgia with the Nashville, Chattanooga & St. Louis Railway to operate the W&A RR, for a period of 29 years at the monthly rate of $35,001.00. There was much confusion about the transfer of property, including locomotives and rolling stock, from the former lessee to the State of Georgia and to the new lessee. A total of 44 locomotives were delivered by the former lessee and the *General*, Number 3, was included. The condition of the *General* was listed as "condemned, value $1,500.00." The total value of the locomotives and rolling stock transferred to the NC&StL Ry under the lease of December 27, 1890, was declared by the State of Georgia to be $361,041. The NC&StL Ry claimed a total value of only $260,000. This matter was finally resolved at the conclusion of the lease, December 27, 1919, when the NC&StL Ry agreed to receive all of the old locomotives and rolling stock as if actually in existence at the agreed value of $361,041. Many years later this was to become a very important agreement when ownership of the *General* was challenged by the City of Chattanooga.

On May 30, 1891, the *General*, while retired from service, was wiped off and made ready for another run to Chattanooga. This time the old engine was coupled onto the rear of the afternoon freight train for the run to Chattanooga rather than making the trip under her own steam as she had done so many times before. The purpose of this trip was to have her on hand for the festivities attendant to the unveiling of the Ohio Monument to the Andrews Raiders in the National Cemetery. This was the first of many display trips the *General* would make under the auspices of the NC&StL Ry whose

THE *GENERAL* AT VININGS, GA., WITH E. WARREN CLARK IN THE CAB. CLARK WAS RESPONSIBLE FOR THE RESTORATION OF THE ENGINE.

THE *GENERAL* AT THE NASHVILLE SHOPS OF THE NASHVILLE, CHATTANOOGA & ST. LOUIS RAILWAY AFTER BEING REBUILT IN 1892.

THE *GENERAL* AT CHICKAMAUGA, GA., IN SEPTEMBER 1892 AFTER RESTORATION. E. WARREN CLARK SITS ON THE COW-CATCHER.

management was as eager to promote the historic rail route as the W&A RR Company had been.

On Memorial Day, May 30, 1891, the day of the dedication, the *General* was fired up in place so there would be ample steam to blow her whistle. Conductor William A. Fuller was also on hand for the dedication as were surviving members of the Raiding party.

Shortly after this move, the *General,* along with two other W&A RR engines, was retired from service and stored on a siding at Vinings, Ga. There they rested pending some corporate decision as to their fate.

In early 1892, E. Warren Clark, of Columbia, Tenn., a professional photographer and lecturer, located the *General* on the siding at Vinings and came up with the idea of having the old engine rehabilitated and displayed at the World's Columbian Exposition in Chicago in 1893. He also made a historic photograph of the *General* and two other W&A engines while stored on the side track at Vinings. Clark approached Mr. John W. Thomas, President of the NC&StL Ry, about the matter, and the latter agreed. The *General* was then moved from Vinings to the NC&StL Ry Shops at West Nashville for repairs. The *General* was completely refurbished, and the diamond stack was replaced with a Radley & Hunter type balloon stack as the old engine was to be a wood burner again. . . . The *General* was then taken to Atlanta awaiting time to go to Chicago.

In the meantime there was a reunion of the veterans of the Army of the Cumberland at Chattanooga in Sept. 1892. On Sept. 13, 1892, the *General* came up from Atlanta to be on hand for this reunion. Engineer Bill Keelin was in charge, and Fireman John Hamett kept the short pine logs going into the fire box. The *General* arrived at 5:45 p.m. and was placed on a side track of the NC&StL Ry just outside the Union Depot on the side toward the Southern Hotel. Engineer Brown guarded the engine while in Chattanooga to be sure that relic hunters did not make off with any loose parts. The *General* remained for the duration of this reunion.

While on this trip the *General* stopped at Chickamauga and was there photographed by Clark. Conductor Fuller was along too, and in one of the photographs Clark is found sitting on the pilot. This photograph was later used by Clark on a brochure he had printed to pass out to visitors in Chicago. This trip brought out the problems involved in running the old engine as a wood burner,

and the decision was made to prepare her again as a coal burner. The *General* was taken to Nashville Shops where new coal grates were installed, and a new stack of the balloon type, slightly smaller than the first one, was installed with a coal funnel inside. This gave the engine the appearance of a wood burner as she was originally built, but she would burn coal easily obtained on any railroad. On Oct. 12, 1892, Clark visited the Shops in Nashville, photographed the *General*, and took her out for a trial run. Everything was found to be satisfactory, and the *General* was ready for her trip to the Fair in Chicago. However, the Fair in Chicago was not yet ready for the *General.* The World's Columbian Exposition was not scheduled to open until the spring of 1893, and Clark had to wait until then to take the *General* to Chicago.

The *General* moved to Chicago in the early spring of 1893 accompanied by Mr. Henry "Buster" Carden, a native of Rome, Ga., and a long time engineer on the NC&StL Ry. The *General* was placed on display in Section N, Post 7-11 of the Transportation Building Annex at the World's Columbian Exposition, and was one of 62 locomotives shown. The NC&StL Ry also provided Clark with a specially equipped box car which carried displays of Tennessee farm and forest products and also had living space for Clark. When the Fair ended the *General* was brought back to Nashville for storage. While it was a very interesting and well attended display at the Exposition, the whole thing was an expensive project for Clark, and he was broke when it was all over. . . .

In 1895 the *General* was brought to Atlanta for display at the Cotton States and International Exposition held that year. Conductor William A. Fuller was a frequent visitor to the engine during the Exposition and on one occasion was photographed with the *General*, complete with top hat and tails....

In 1897 the State of Tennessee commemorated her 100th year as a State with the Tennessee Centennial Exposition held in Nashville at what is today known as Centennial Park. John W. Thomas and E.C. Lewis, both officials of the NC&StL Ry, also served as officers of the Tennessee Centennial Exposition, and the railroad gave much support to the affair. This included displaying the *General*, and again the old engine was under the control of engineer Henry "Buster" Carden of Rome, Ga.

The question has often been raised as to when the *General* was placed on display in the Union Depot in Chattanooga. For some time it was

THE *GENERAL* IN ATLANTA IN 1895. WILLIAM A. FULLER STANDS ON THE GROUND BESIDE THE TENDER.

thought that the time was in late 1893 after the *General's* return from the World's Columbian Exposition in Chicago. This question arose again and became important in the case when the City of Chattanooga was trying to obtain a legal judgment to force the L&N RR to keep the *General* on display in that city. Richard M. Jahn, one of the attorneys for the City of Chattanooga, filed an affidavit, dated Jan. 31, 1969, with the court in support of a motion for a new trial. One of the points made in support of the motion for a new trial had to do with the date the *General* was placed on display in the Union Depot in Chattanooga. By careful search, Mr. Jahn found an article in the *Chattanooga News* of May 17, 1901, which carried the following account of the arrival of the *General* in Chattanooga the previous evening. "The *General* is in town. It arrived last night. This is the famous engine which the Andrews Raiders captured during the Civil War and in which fight a large number of them were killed. A handsome monument now stands to their memory in the National Cemetery in this city." Thus it was established that the *General* arrived in Chattanooga on May 16, 1901, for permanent display in the Union Depot of that city. *The Chattanooga Press* of May 31, 1901, carried a similar story as did the *Chattanooga Times* of May 27, 1901. Mr. Jahn went on to introduce several other news articles to support the

theory that there was a need for the railroads serving Chattanooga to curry favor with the citizens of Chattanooga, and that may have been the reason why it was decided to place the *General* on display as was done. If this be true, it relates to a critical time in 1967 when the *General* was again used in this manner to curry favor with the citizens of Georgia. . . .

In 1906 the GAR Annual Encampment was held in Chattanooga, and the NC&StL Ry sponsored a special reunion of the survivors of the Andrews Raid. This reunion was held from September 18 to 20 and was attended by six survivors of the Andrews Raiders and two members of the pursuing party. The group was photographed near the Ohio Monument to the Raiders in the National Cemetery and also in front of the *General* in the Union Depot. The NC&StL Ry issued a handsome pamphlet on this occasion in honor of the reunion of survivors of the Andrews Raiders. It was well that they were treated so generously for this was their last reunion as death took its toll during the following years. . . .

The year 1927 marked the 100th birthday of the Baltimore & Ohio Railroad, one of the pioneer railroads of the country. The B&O RR decided to commemorate the event with "The Fair of the Iron Horse," a Centenary Exposition of the Baltimore

THE *GENERAL* AT THE B&O
CENTENNIAL IN 1927.

& Ohio Railroad held at Halethorpe, Md., near Baltimore. Elaborate facilities were built to present the pageant and to display the many examples of locomotives and rolling stock made available for the occasion. Among the many historic locomotives on hand for the fair was the *General*. The *General* left Chattanooga on Aug. 12, 1927, and this time it did not travel under her own steam. She was loaded aboard a flat car, with her stack removed, to reduce clearance problems, and moved to Nashville in regular freight service over the NC&StL Ry, thence the L&N RR to Louisville, where it was turned over to the B&O RR for movement on to Halethorpe, Md. A few weeks later, the *General* was returned to her berth in the Union Depot in Chattanooga.

In late 1931 there was a move afoot in Atlanta to remove the *Texas* from the Cyclorama at Grant Park and allow the NC&StL Ry to recondition the engine for display at the Union Station in Atlanta. Governor Richard B. Russell agreed that this could be done as long as the *Texas* was not taken out of the boundaries of Georgia. He also agreed that it would be necessary for the railroad to obtain permission from the City of Atlanta to do this. Subsequently, the City of Atlanta refused, and the *Texas* was not moved. This action was well received by the press, and it was not long before the mayor of Chattanooga Ed Bass heard of the proposal. He came up with an even better idea. He proposed to the mayor of Atlanta James L. Key that the *Texas* and the *General* repeat the epic race of the Civil

War between Atlanta and Chattanooga. News of this proposal was distributed by the wire services, and soon Joseph W. Parrott of Lima, Oh., a grandson of two of the Andrews Raiders, was in touch with Mayor Bass of Chattanooga seeking permission to ride the *General* during this great chase. The race did not take place. A reenactment of this historic event was not to be for another 30 years, but it did make good copy for the newspapers of the time.

In 1933 the *General* was again removed from the Union Depot in Chattanooga and loaded aboard a flat car for another trip to Chicago. This time she attended the Century of Progress Exposition. Again, the balloon stack was removed for shipment, and when it was placed back on in Chicago, it was put on backwards. The famous rooster comb was to the front of the stack rather than to the rear as it should have been.

In Dec. 1938, the production of the movie *Gone With the Wind* was well under way, and the late Wilbur G. Kurtz was on the lot in California as historical advisor for the production. He lamented in his diary of Dec. 28, 1938, the fact that no plans were being made to have locomotives in the railroad yard scenes. He offered to write the NC&StL Ry to see if they could borrow the *General*, and he was told to do so. He wrote on December 29, 1938. On Jan. 3, 1939, President Fitzgerald Hall of the NC&StL Ry responded and said that he had planned to and would send the *General* to New York for the World's Fair and that it would not be available for about a year. Mr. Kurtz than wrote back

The *General* at the Chicago World's Fair in 1933.

The *General* at the 1939 New York World's Fair.

seeking to get the engine during February and March before the opening of the New York World's Fair. Mr. Hall responded in a positive way and went on to state that freight charges for hauling the *General* with tender to Los Angeles and back would be $3.00 per hundred pounds each way which would add up to considerable cost. The answer then was too much money. For the lack of a few thousand dollars, the *General* failed to appear in *Gone With the Wind*. The locomotives that did appear were wooden mock-ups made by David O. Selznick's people in the carpenter shop.

In 1939 it was New York's turn to have a World's Fair, and the old *General* was invited. She was shipped on a flat car to the Flushing Meadows site of the New York World's Fair and joined several other historic locomotives in the railroad exhibit. The Fair was extended another season in 1940, and the *General* did not return to her berth in the Union Depot in Chattanooga until the fall of 1940.

The year 1939 also saw the first of several skirmishes in the press that were to take place concerning the custody of the *General*. James V. Carmichael, then representing Cobb County in the State Legislature, authored a resolution of the General Assembly requesting that the *General* be re-moved from its place in the Union Depot in Chattanooga to the Kennesaw Mountain National Battlefield Park for permanent display. Almost immediately, descendants of Capt. William A. Fuller, in Atlanta and Chattanooga, and a host of others, came out in opposition to the move preferring that the *General* remain in Chattanooga. As has often been the case over the past one hundred years, anything to do with the *General* and the *Texas* provided the color for a series of newspaper stories. After a few weeks the matter was laid to rest and nothing was done.

In 1948 the *General* made her third trip to Chicago. The occasion was the Railroad Fair sponsored by the Nation's railroads, and the *General* was one of the many historic locomotives on display. Again, the move was made by freight car in regular freight service. While at the Fair, security was not as good as it should have been, and several oil cups were stolen and almost a cord of wood taken from the tender! Upon her return from the Fair, the *General* was again placed on display at the Union Depot, Chattanooga.

On Feb. 17, 1950, the governor of Georgia approved a Resolution of the General Assembly authorizing the posthumous presentation of a gold

THE *GENERAL* AT THE CHICAGO RAILROAD FAIR IN 1948.

medal to William A. Fuller for his services to the W&A RR and the State of Georgia in successfully pursuing the Andrews Raiders on April 12, 1862. Actually, Governor Joseph E. Brown sent a message to the General Assembly on Nov. 6, 1862, recommending that this be done. There were too many problems facing Georgia at that time to do anything about the governor's recommendation. Now the medal was to be presented to the oldest living survivor of the family of William A. Fuller. Honorable mention was made in the Resolution of those who assisted Fuller in the pursuit. The late Wilbur G. Kurtz, Atlanta artist and historian who had married a daughter of William A. Fuller and who devoted most of his life to a study of this event, was commissioned to design the medal. Unlike the design of the Ohio Memorial in the Chattanooga National Cemetery, Mr. Kurtz presented a true likeness of the *General* as she appeared in 1862, based on his many years of careful research. The medal was struck by The Williams and Anderson Company of Providence, R.I., and was presented to William A. Fuller at a public ceremony in front of the Cyclorama Building, Grant Park, Atlanta, on May 15, 1950. . . .

While the *General* rested peacefully at her place in the Union Depot in Chattanooga in 1957, a significant event took place that would have a lot to do with her future. An Aug. 30, 1957, the Nashville, Chattanooga & St. Louis Railway was merged into the Louisville & Nashville Railroad. Under the terms of the merger all assets of the NC&StL became the property of the L&N RR as did all the obligations and liabilities of the NC&StL Ry. This included the lease of the Western & Atlantic Railroad which was originally leased to the NC&StL for 29 years effective Dec. 27, 1890. Upon the expiration of that lease, a new lease for 50 years was entered into that expired on Dec. 27, 1969. In this way the L&N RR acquired custody and ownership of the *General.*

Two years later, in 1959, when the State of Georgia was in the process of developing Stone Mountain Park, the second battle for custody of the *General* took place. This time the Stone Mountain Memorial Association wanted the *General* for display at the park then being built. The Chairman of the Association Matt McWhorter called on the president of the L&N RR to release the *General* for display at Stone Mountain Park. One account indicated that the railroad had agreed and would also provide a car to display with the old engine. This later proved to be incorrect, and in spite of much publicity over a period of several months in which the governors of Georgia and Tennessee also got involved, the *General* did not come to Stone Mountain Park. So heated was the controversy that *Newsweek Magazine* carried a story about it in their National Affairs Section, March 23, 1959. The matter was finally settled in July 1959 when William H. Kendall, the L&N president, advised that the railroad would not give up possession because the locomotive was of value to the railroad "in a historic sense and for advertising purposes" and that "we do not believe that it would be to the best interest of the railroad at this time to surrender possession of this most interesting old engine." Later, On July 23, 1959, Attorney General Eugene Cook of the State of Georgia gave an official opinion to the governor advising him that the L&N RR could acquire full title to the *General* in 1969, if it chose to under the terms of the existing lease contract whether the State of Georgia through its legislature agreed or not.

After the merger of the NC&StL and the L&N railroads, several members of the public relations staff of the L&N began to day dream about firing up the old *General* and running her again, especially during the period of the forthcoming observance of the Civil War Centennial. About this time, Warren A. McNeill came to the L&N as public relations director, and when he heard of this idea he had it checked out in detail to include costs and then presented the idea to the top management. The proposal was approved, and the green light given to bringing the old locomotive to Louisville for rehabilitation in the L&N Shops there. In view of the previous bouts in the press about where the *General* should be located, L&N President Kendall directed that the engine be removed from Chattanooga at night and the explanation given later.

The decision was made to move the *General* from the Union Depot in Chattanooga on the night of June 6, 1961. Once *The Georgian* passenger train had passed through around 8:50 p.m. there would be no one around the depot, and the work could be done undetected. The key people were on hand to do the job including William A. Gaines, Manager of Mechanized Equipment and an old NC&StL man who had worked with the *General* on many previous occasions. As soon as the last visitor had left the station, the doors were locked and lights put out, and railroad police made sure that any curious passersby were steered in other directions.

ON JUNE 6, 1961, THE *GENERAL* WAS REMOVED FROM THE UNION STATION IN CHATTANOOGA, TENN., TO BE TRANSPORTED TO LOUISVILLE FOR RESTORATION.

THE *GENERAL* UNDER WRAPS AT THE SOUTH END OF THE L&N'S WAUHATCHIE YARD AT CHATTANOOGA, JUNE 7, 1961, JUST PRIOR TO DEPARTURE FOR LOUISVILLE.

The tall fence that had surrounded the *General* was first cut, and then the crew came in with cross ties and rail. A section of some 60 feet of rail was required to move the *General* out of the depot. After the temporary track was completed, a diesel switcher and two flat cars came in to hook up with the *General*. In the meantime others had oiled every bearing and moving part long stiff from disuse. The *General's* long outmoded link and pin coupler was fastened to a modern one on the flat car, and slowly the old engine began to move. She was carefully moved out on Track No. 9 of the station concourse and there covered with a heavy canvas as partial protection from the rainy weather and also to conceal it during her journey out to Craven Yard. It was then around one o'clock, and the streets of Chattanooga were deserted and no one noticed the strange movement. In Craven Yard, the *General* was loaded aboard two flat cars and switched to Wauhatchie Yard for the movement to Louisville. At 3:53 p.m., the afternoon of June 7, 1961, the *General* left Wauhatchie Yard securely loaded on one flat car with her tender on another and various parts in an accompanying box car, all secured by canvas, coupled behind a five unit diesel in a fast freight headed for Nashville. In Nashville it was shunted around the yard and coupled to another fast freight for the trip to Louisville. There she was carefully placed in the L&N's South Louisville Shops for reconditioning for her role in the reenactment of *The Great Locomotive Chase* scheduled for the following April.

While the L&N people did succeed in getting the *General* out of the depot without detection, an enterprising reporter of the *Chattanooga News Press* T. Grady Gallant found it missing the next morn-

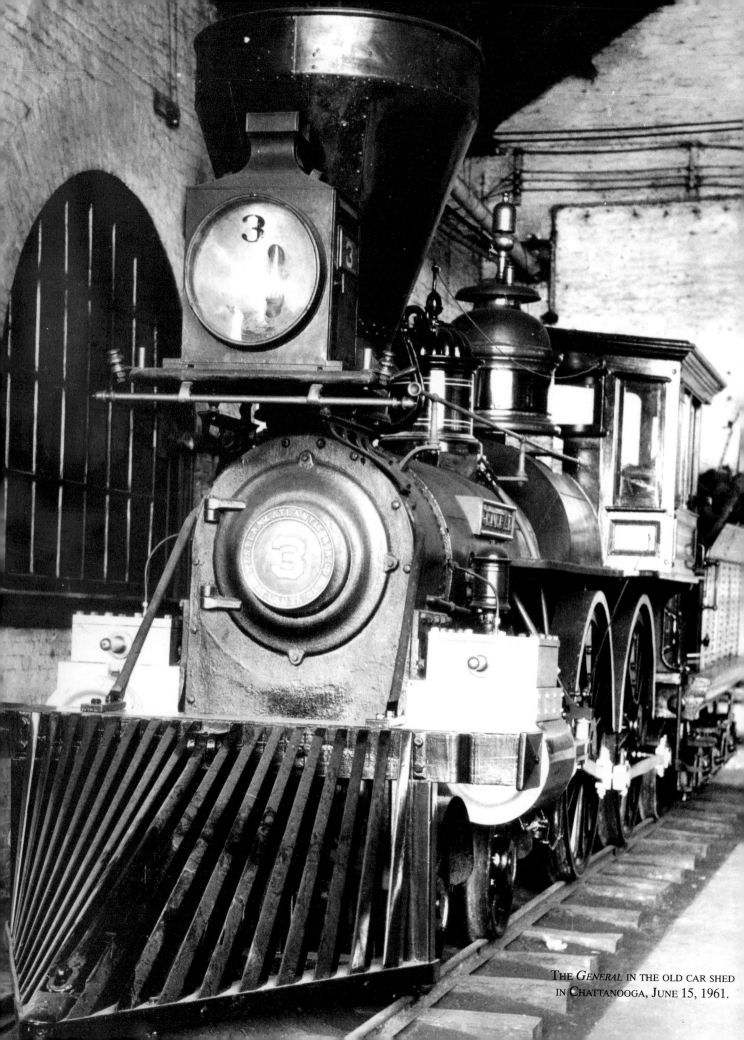

The *General* in the old car shed in Chattanooga, June 15, 1961.

ing, and much press coverage was given the second "stealing" of the *General*. This of course, was just what the L&N wanted as did all others connected with the affair.

Again, the controversy as to where the *General* should be permanently displayed played fuel for the press. This time a third party entered the bickering. The City of Paterson, N.J., where the *General* was built, let it be known that they were also interested in obtaining the *General*. While there had been thousands of locomotives built in Paterson over the years, the city had not a single one on display. They finally solved this problem by obtaining one from Panama. . . .

The overhaul was completed, and on Feb. 7, 1962, the *General* was placed under steam again and operated under her own power for the first time since 1914. Now she was an oil burner, thus making refueling easier. The job had been a labor of love for the L&N employees who did all the work, and they were extremely proud of the job they had done. The boiler had passed a hydrostatic test at 175 pounds pressure, but her working pressure was reduced to 125 pounds which was quite adequate for her mission. On that windswept winter afternoon the old *General* came steaming out of the shops with her bell ringing and her whistle blowing, and she moved about a hundred feet to the "slip track." There, on well oiled rails, she thrashed her drivers while the shop men inspected her motion work in motion and made the necessary adjustments. After this trial movement the *General* was taken back to the Shops, repainted in red, yellow and black, and made ready for the road.

On March 28, 1962, the open platform, wooden, Jim Crow type combine car No. 665, built in 1913 and painted a bright yellow, was hooked up to the *General,* and she was off for a trial run to Lebanon, Ky., with officials and press aboard.

It turned out to be quite a long trip—17 hours and 50 minutes, and many things went wrong. Still it was a successful trip; they found out what the *General* could do and how long fuel and water would last. The engine could go about 80 miles without refueling, requiring water every 25 on the average.

The trip was a dress rehearsal for the big run scheduled for April 14th. It was quite a thrill for those aboard to listen to the quiet exhaust of saturated steam as the *General* moved along. It was hard for some of the passengers to realize that they were riding behind the engine that James J. Andrews and seven others were hung for stealing in 1862 and that

it was then 1962.

On April 3, 1962, the *General* had another special run to make before her historic debut on April 14th. This time the passengers were members of the Board of Directors of the L&N RR, and the run was from Anchorage, Ky.

The big day for the *General* was April 14, 1962—bigger perhaps than April 12, 1862. This was the date for the reenactment of *The Great Locomotive Chase* on its 100th Anniversary. April 14th was chosen rather than April 12th because the 14th fell on Saturday. It was a very busy day for the W&A Division of the L&N RR. Some 100,000 spectators were expected along the line from Kennesaw, renamed Big Shanty for the day, northward. There were two special trains of 14 and 15 cars each, respectively, with 1,400 passengers following from Atlanta to Chattanooga. The passengers represented 38 states from California to New Hampshire, and Canada and West Germany. In addition there were two sections of the southbound *Georgian,* a southbound freight, the northbound *Dixie Flyer* and a light diesel following the *General* just in case—all this on a single track railroad. L&N trainmaster Vernon W. Ayers was in overall charge, and all train movements went well; the *General* reached Chattanooga within a few minutes of the eight hours scheduled.

Two train orders, Form 19, were issued by the L&N dispatcher pertaining to the movement of the *General* on April 14th. The first order, No. 868, was issued at 11:57 p.m., April 13, 1962, to Conductors and Engineers of all northbound trains. "Account Engine *General* being run under full control between Atlanta and Chattanooga looking out for vehicular and pedestrian travel on and near tracks particularly through towns." The second order, No. 501, was issued at 4:12 a.m. to Conductor and Engineer of the "Engine *General*, Western and Atlantic 3. Engine *General*, Western and Atlantic 3, run passenger extra Tilford to Chattanooga." There were no mishaps in spite of the large crowds along the way and the heavy traffic on the W&A Division.

The *General* made scheduled stops at Marietta, Kennesaw, Cartersville, Kingston, Calhoun, Dalton and Ringgold. She was not scheduled to stop at Adairsville, but the local people saw to that. As the *General* came into view, a local band and the police blocked the track. When the *General* came to a halt, town officials served warrants on Georgia Governor Ernest Vandiver and L&N President Kendall

THE *GENERAL* UNDERGOING RESTORATION, SOUTH LOUISVILLE SHOPS OF THE LOUISVILLE & NASHVILLE RAILROAD, 1962. PHOTO BY C. NORMAN BEASLEY, L&N RR

THE *GENERAL*, FIRST TIME UNDER STEAM DURING RESTORATION FEB. 7, 1962, SOUTH LOUSVILLE SHOPS SLIP TRACK, LOUISVILLE, KENTUCKY. PHOTO BY EDISON H. THOMAS, L&NRR

THE *GENERAL* AT RINGGOLD, GEORGIA, APRIL 14, 1962.

THE *GENERAL* AT THE TILFORD YARD OF THE LOUISVILLE & NASHVILLE RAILROAD, ATLANTA, GEORGIA, APRIL 12, 1962, JUST PRIOR TO RERUN ON APRIL 14, 1962.

The *General* at Big Shanty, Georgia, April 14, 1962. At left, Ernest Vandiver, Governor of Georgia, and right, William H. Kendall, President Louisville & Nashville Railroad.

The *General* at
Atlanta, Georgia,
April 12, 1962.

Ringgold, Georgia, April 14,
1962, after the *General* and
Car 665 had passed.

The *General* at Nashville,
Tennessee, July 6, 1962. photo
Martin J. Robards, L&N RR

(both on the coach) for "refusing to stop the *General* at Adairsville ...." The *General* steamed into the Union Depot in Chattanooga at 4:35 p.m. only ten minutes behind the advertised time, amidst the strains of a band playing the Star Spangled Banner and the cheers of thousands. Without question this was the *General's* biggest day.

During the ceremonies that followed, L&N President Kendall presented each crewman who had brought the *General* to Chattanooga "a day's pay in Confederate money." Such payment and the Civil War vintage attire of the crew, as well as beards, was all part of a formal agreement between the L&N RR and the several operating brotherhoods involved, signed in Atlanta on April 13, 1962. The special crew was made up of George W. Black, Conductor, of Decatur; Paul E. West, Engineer, Jack R. Barrett, Fireman, Chester L. Bozeman, Flagman, all of Kennesaw; George W. Ferguson, Trainman, and W.H. Alexander, Train Porter. Also with the *General* were Russell White and W.A. Rice, Travelling Engineers.

The *General* arrived in Atlanta on Tuesday, April 10th, aboard the special flat car that was to carry her thousands of miles over the eastern part of the United States during the next few years. The L&N RR prepared two flat cars to transport the *General* and the special sectionalized ramp that was built to permit her easy loading. Rails were placed on one flat car permanently and with the ramp, the *General* and tender were easily pushed onto the flat car. She was then tied down with special equipment, the balloon stack removed and she was ready to roll—piggyback fashion.

After the reenactment of the Chase of April 14th, 1962, the *General* began her tour as follows:

April 15-22	- Chattanooga, Tenn.
April 26-29	- Washington, D.C.
May 2-5	- Columbus, Oh.
May 8-15	- Memphis, Tenn.
May 19-20	- Fort Knox, Ky.
May 22-27	- Evansville, In.
May 28-June 2	- The *General* ran under her own steam from Evansville to Chicago—her fourth trip to the windy city—stopping at intermediate points along the way.

The trip to Washington and her stay there from April 26 to the 29th was in connection with special commemorative ceremonies honoring the Centennial of the Medal of Honor, the Nation's highest military award. . . . Special commemorative ceremonies were held on the lawn of the White House with President John F. Kennedy and his guest Prime Minister Harold Macmillan of England in attendance. Among descendants of the Andrews Raiders present was Joseph W. Parrott of West Salem, Or., a grandson of Jacob Parrott who was the first individual to receive the Medal of Honor.

The *General* remained on tour until Dec. 22, 1962, when she was returned to Chattanooga for the holidays. The old engine had performed beautifully travelling 9,000 miles under her own steam plus another 5,000 miles aboard her special flat car. She visited 120 cities in 12 states during 1962, and 640,000 visitors passed through Combine Car No. 665. It was a very successful year for the *General* and for the L&N RR. The reenactment on April 14, 1962, of *The Great Locomotive Chase* was the highlight of Georgia's Civil War Centennial observance, and a special medal, designed by sculptor Julian Harris of Atlanta was executed for the occasion. One side bears a likeness of the *General* and the other a likeness of William A. Fuller, conductor of the *General's* train on April 12, 1862.

The 1962 Georgia General Assembly passed a joint resolution expressing appreciation to the L&N RR for the restoration of the *General* and "for allowing the debut of this historically significant locomotive to take place in Georgia at the site of *The Great Locomotive Chase* for the Centennial Commemoration of the Andrews Raid." 1963 was another big year for the *General,* and she began her tour with a return visit to Big Shanty, on April 12th, then northward to Chattanooga and points in Virginia, Pennsylvania and Ohio. Well over a month was spent in touring Ohio as this was the home state for most of the Andrews Raiders, and there are many descendants living there today. At the conclusion of her travels in 1963, the *General* again returned to Chattanooga for the winter. During 1963 the *General* travelled 7,200 miles of which 2,200 was under her own steam, and 386,000 visitors passed through Combine Car No. 665. Again it was a very successful year for the *General* and for the L&N RR. The press coverage was fantastic with every state of the Union represented as well as England, Holland, Germany and France. President Kendall's statement in 1959 as to the advertising value of the *General* had certainly been confirmed.

THE *GENERAL* ON THE NORFOLK & WESTERN RR, JUNE 1963. JOHN KRAUSE PHOTO

At the conclusion of the tour in 1963, the L&N RR management felt that more people could see and enjoy the *General* if she was placed on exhibit at the New York World's Fair scheduled for 1964. Accordingly the *General* spent the summer of 1964 in New York. Actually she began her tour in 1964 at Louisville, April 26 to May 2, as one of the attractions for Derby Week. During this period, the *General* steamed along the Louisville waterfront and was photographed with the famous riverboat *Delta Queen* in the background.

Following the festivities in Louisville, the *General* took itself to the New York World's Fair. While there, the *General* again went to sea. She was transported by railroad car ferry across New York harbor, reminiscent of her trip from Philadelphia in 1855 when she sailed to Savannah. The *General* was fired up in New York and on Memorial Day, May 30th, steamed across the scenic Hell's Gate Bridge which joins the New York boroughs of Bronx and Queens. Again on June 1st she proceeded over the tracks of the Long Island Railroad under her own steam to the Fair gate. After this run she was transported to the plaza of Better Living Center at the Fair for display during the duration of the fair.

In the fall of 1964, the *General* was brought to Chattanooga to be on hand for that historic city's 150th Birthday Celebration during the week of Sept. 10 to 17th. The *General* was not under steam for this occasion.

The last time the *General* appeared under her own steam was in 1966. The occasion was the 32nd Southern Governor's Conference which was held at Kentucky Dam Village near Paducah, and the *General* was on hand to give the conferees a fine panoramic view of the dams, locks, and power plants and the lakes the dams created. The date was Sept. 17 to 21, 1966, and this time the *General* travelled over the rails of the Illinois Central Railroad whose Kentucky Division tracks go right over the top of the dams. It had been more than two years since the *General* was out under steam, and she performed like the veteran that she was.

The lease of the W&A RR, acquired by the L&N RR when they merged the NC&StL Ry into their system, expired on Dec. 27, 1969. The process for a new lease had began some two years earlier, and this time there was some competition between the L&N RR and the Southern Railway. The initial bids were thrown out for a technical reason, and a second invitation extended. During a hearing of a legislative committee on Feb. 3, 1967, at which L&N President Kendall was being ques-

ANOTHER VIEW, JUNE 1963. JOHN KRAUSE PHOTO

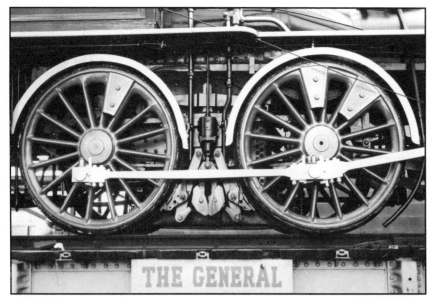

DRIVERS OF THE *GENERAL*, LOUISVILLE, KY., SEPT. 17, 1966. EDISON H. THOMAS PHOTO

tioned, he was asked when the *General* would be returned to Georgia. He replied that he would return the *General* to Georgia when it was indicated to him that the State would like to have it. He also stated that if the *General* was removed from L&N authority, they would want to be reassured that proper quarters were available for its future protection as a heritage of history. The proposition was confirmed by Mr. Kendall in a letter to the State of Georgia dated Feb. 10, 1967, and he also indicated the *General* could be returned to the State prior to the termination of the lease.

The General Assembly of the State of Georgia responded and passed a resolution which was approved by the governor on April 5, 1967, expressing the State's desire to have the famous locomotive returned to Georgia and designated Kennesaw as the site for it to be displayed.

During September 1967, the *General* was enroute to Kennesaw from Louisville via Nashville and Chattanooga. The L&N had been asked to make the *General* available for trips in the Kennesaw area during a fund-raising fair to be held Sept. 14-16, 1967, at Kennesaw and sponsored by the Big Shanty Historical Society. The *General* was enroute to Kennesaw for this purpose when stopped in Chattanooga.

Plans had been made to receive the *General* at Kennesaw on Sept. 12, 1967, and some of the invited guests were arriving before it was generally known that the *General* had been stopped at Chattanooga that morning at 1:30 AM by a party headed by Mayor Ralph Kelly of that city. Mayor Kelly thought the *General* belonged in Chattanooga, and he took this action to see that it did not go to Geor-

gia. This seizure triggered the long legal battle that ended finally when the U.S. Supreme Court made its decision on November 9, 1970.

The City of Chattanooga contended to have ownership rights in the *General* and to have a paramount right to its possession by virtue of the following: (1) that the *General* was dedicated to the City of Chattanooga and its citizens in the nature of a charitable trust which the L&N RR and its predecessor were fully empowered under the leases from the State of Georgia to do; (2) that the City of Chattanooga and its citizens had acquired a proscriptive interest in the *General;* (3) that the L&N RR and its predecessor had impliedly contracted that the L&N RR would permit the *General* to remain on permanent display in the City of Chattanooga; and (4) that the L&N RR was estopped by its conduct as alleged to permanently remove the *General* from the City of Chattanooga. The City of Chattanooga further contended that the L&N RR had undertaken to deliver the *General* to the State of Georgia in return for Georgia's renewal of its lease of the W&A RR to the L&N RR and that the L&N RR had acted adversely to the trust imposed upon it and should be removed as trustee of the *General.*

The *General* remained in Chattanooga at Wauhatchie Yard until Dec. 16, 1967, when it was returned to the South Louisville Shops of the L&N RR for safekeeping. This move was approved by Frank W. Wilson, U.S. District Judge at Chattanooga in an order filed on Dec. 18, 1967.

In 1969 the Waterville, Ohio Historical Society became interested in placing a more suitable monument on the grave of Mark Wood, one of the Andrews Raiders, who is buried in Forest Cemetery, Toledo, Oh. In due course, negotiations were completed, and an imposing monument was created by Universal Memorial Company of Elberton, Ga., made from Georgia blue granite and based on the drawing created by Wilbur G. Kurtz showing the *General* as she appeared in 1862. The monument also has data about Mark Wood and his part in *The Great Locomotive Chase.*

In the meantime, the legal process had begun, and on Jan. 4, 1969, Judge Frank W. Wilson, U.S. District Judge at Chattanooga, ruled that the L&N RR did own the *General* and could dispose of it as they wished. In his conclusion, in July 1969, Judge Wilson noted that the issue before his court was "not the appropriateness or inappropriateness of the display of the *General* either in Chattanooga, Tennessee, or Kennesaw, Georgia. Nor is it for this court to decide where or how the *General* might be most appropriately displayed. A suggestion having merit in the eyes of the Court is that the Chickamauga Battle Field National Monument, Chickamauga, Georgia., would be an appropriate placement for the display of the *General.*" A resolution to this effect was introduced in the Georgia General Assembly, but it did not pass.

The City of Chattanooga appealed this ruling, and the case was referred to the U.S. Court of Appeals for the Sixth District. This Court, on May 21, 1970, upheld Judge Frank W. Wilson's ruling. Again, the City of Chattanooga appealed the ruling, and the case was referred to the U.S. Supreme Court.

While this legal action was taking place the *General* remained in Louisville for safe keeping. On Nov. 17 and 18, 1971, the *General* was moved into the historic Louisville Union Station and shared the place of honor with a new Seaboard Coast Line Railroad diesel locomotive No. 1776, the "Spirit of '76," brightly colored in red, white and blue paint for the forthcoming Bicentennial of the United States. Over 4,500 persons viewed the two locomotives, and this was the last occasion for such use by the L&N RR.

The United States Supreme Court refused to hear the appeal of the City of Chattanooga on Nov. 9, 1970, and the ruling of the U.S. Court of Appeals for the Sixth District, at Cincinnati, was upheld. This meant that Judge Wilson's initial decision was final and the L&N RR could do with the *General* as they wished.

While the matter of who got the *General* and where was involved with the judiciary, the Georgia General Assembly in its 1969 session attempted to start all over again. Even though the General Assembly had already indicated that Kennesaw was to be the future home of the *General,* an attempt was made in the House to have the locomotive enshrined in Chickamauga National Battle Field Park. Concurrently, a move was started in the Senate to place the *General* in a new state historical museum to be located in Underground Atlanta near the historic Zero Mile Post of the W&A RR. This proposal envisaged the *Texas* being removed from the Cyclorama and placed on display with the *General.* Neither effort was successful, and when the legislature adjourned, Kennesaw was still designated as the future home for the *General.*

The action of the U.S. Supreme Court settled the matter, and the people of Kennesaw, thus reassured, went about preparing a home for the *General.* Like most cities and towns of today, Kennesaw needed help to provide a suitable building to house and display the locomotive. Help came from several sources, and one of the most important was Steve Frey and his family of Kennesaw. The Frey family owned a rather sizeable building near the depot in Kennesaw that had formerly housed a cotton gin and which was vacant. It is located a few yards from the tracks of the W&A RR where the *General* was stolen by James J. Andrews and his party that rainy morning of April 12, 1862.

The Frey family offered the building to the City of Kennesaw. The City accepted. Gill Tapp, architect, had the vision and the capability to design modifications and additions that have made the building a very suitable home for the locomotive, and it is now known as the Kennesaw Civil War Museum.

As preparations were being made to welcome the *General* to Kennesaw and Cobb County, the Cobb County Chamber of Commerce produced a commemorative medal honoring the *General.* The design featured a drawing of the *General* on the front side and the Great Seal of the Confederacy was placed on the back.

By the first of February 1972, all was in readiness at Kennesaw, and Mayor Louis E. Watts of that city so informed Governor Jimmy Carter. Governor Carter then informed President Kendall of the L&N RR and requested the return of the *General* to Georgia. Those who had been involved in the long legal battle hastened to point out that movement of the locomotive could be challenged as before and recommended a secret move to Georgia. This was agreed upon by all concerned. The *General* was made ready for shipment and loaded aboard its special flat car and covered with tarpaulins to conceal it. On Feb. 15, 1972, the *General* was added to the consist of L&N Freight No. 29 southbound for Atlanta—but not via Chattanooga. The route from DeCoursey was through Knoxville and Cartersville to Atlanta, and no publicity was given to the fact that the *General* was being moved. The *General* arrived safely in Atlanta that evening and was placed in the NC&StL Ry roundhouse that still stands at Tilford Yard. A guard was assigned to be sure the locomotive was protected, and no mention was made that it was there in spite of an earlier leak to the press.

Friday, Feb. 18, 1972, was the date announced for the presentation of the *General* to the people of Georgia. At 10:30 a.m. in a light drizzling rain, several hundred people gathered at the passenger station of the Georgia Railroad across the street from

the State Capitol in Atlanta. President Kendall of the L&N, accompanied by several officials of the railroad, standing in front of the *General,* formally presented the locomotive to Governor Jimmy Carter and the people of Georgia.

The Deed of Gift, dated Feb. 18, 1972, made by the L&N RR Company to the State of Georgia, conveyed to the State of Georgia the steam locomotive *General* "in consideration of the State of Georgia's agreement to use the said locomotive for public exhibition purposes only and to adequately protect and preserve this historical artifact." The Deed further provided that should the State of Georgia use the *General* for any other purpose, title thereto would revert to the L&N RR Company or its successor.

News of this event was transmitted over the press wire services and was picked up by newspapers from coast to coast and several foreign countries. It is doubtful if a corporate entity has ever

GOV. JIMMY CARTER ACCEPTING THE *GENERAL* AT THE ATLANTA RAILROAD STATION, FEB. 18, 1972.

before given up so easily an object of such great advertising and promotional value.

Following this ceremony, the *General,* still aboard its special flat car, was moved in local freight service to Kennesaw around 6:00 p.m., and several hundred citizens were on hand to welcome the *General.* Their long wait was over. It had been almost five years since Sept. 12, 1967, when they had turned out to greet the *General* only to learn that it had been stopped in Chattanooga. Now the *General* was home, and a police guard was placed around it until the following day when the locomotive would be placed in the Big Shanty Museum.

Saturday, Feb. 19, 1972, was a cold, raw day in Kennesaw with a chill factor of about zero. It began with clouds and snow flurries which by mid-afternoon gave way to sunshine. At 9:00 a.m. work began on the movement of the *General* from the house track at Kennesaw to the Big Shanty Museum, some 150 yards away. W. Albert Rice, Superintendent of Locomotive Operations for the L&N RR and who had travelled many miles with the *General* while on tour in 1962 and 1963, was on hand to supervise the operation. Normally, the *General* was unloaded from its special flat car by use of the portable ramp designed for that purpose and with a switch engine and an idler car. This time

it would not be so easy. A tractor was used to pull the *General* off the special flat car. The decision had been made to haul the locomotive and tender by truck from the house track to the rails of the Museum. The only rails available were those on the special flat car on which the *General* had arrived. They had to be taken off and installed on the low bed truck-trailer. After this was done, the ramp was used to run the *General* up onto the trailer, and the tractor provided the power. First the tender and then the engine were moved to the Museum building. Thus the old engine went to its final resting place in a very undignified way. At 5:00 p.m. the *General* was safely in the Big Shanty Museum, and Mayor Louis E. Watts had a crew on hand immediately to cut the rails and begin closing the north wall of the building. The north end of the building had been left open for this purpose. The *General* was safely and securely at home at last!

April 12, 1972, one hundred and ten years after *The Great Locomotive Chase* on the W&A RR in Georgia, the Big Shanty Museum at Kennesaw was officially opened to the public. During the four day festival that followed over 4,000 visitors observed the *General* in its new home. . . .

THE *GENERAL* AT KENNESAW, GEORGIA., PRIOR TO UNLOADING OPERATION, FEBRUARY 1972.

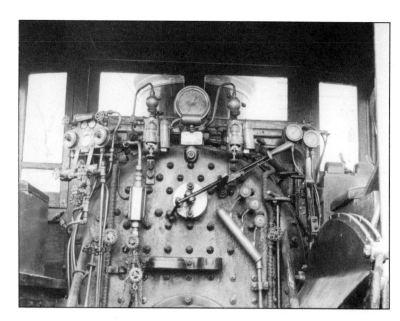

VIEW OF THE CAB
OF THE *General*.

MOVING DAY INTO THE KENNESAW
MUSEUM, FEBRUARY 19, 1972.

The Locomotive *Texas*

The locomotive *Texas*, like the *General*, was built in Paterson, New Jersey, but not by the same builder. The *Texas* was built by Danforth, Cooke & Company and placed in service on the Western & Atlantic Railroad in October 1856. The original cost of the *Texas* was $9,050. At the time the gauge of the Western & Atlantic RR was five feet and the *Texas* was built to that gauge. The drivers were 60 inches in diameter, and there were four together with four leading truck wheels making the locomotive of the well known American type with a 4-4-0 wheel arrangement. Her cylinders were 15 inches in diameter, and the stroke was 22 inches. The *Texas* was of the same power and approximately the same size as the *General.* The engine was shipped from New Jersey by water to Savannah and there put on the rails of the Central Railway of Georgia to Macon and thence over the rails of the Macon & Western RR to Atlanta. One of the first modifications made to the engine in the shops of the Western & Atlantic RR in Atlanta was to replace the pilot or cow catcher with one of horizontal pieces of strap iron. This type cow catcher was a mark of engines of the Western & Atlantic RR in those days, and all pilots were of this type. The man who made them was Richard A. "Uncle Dick" Saye who died in 1910.

During the Civil War period, it was customary to assign a locomotive to an engineer and to a special run. In April 1862, the *Texas* was assigned to Peter James Bracken engineer, and his fireman was Henry P. Haney. Bracken was a man of 28 years while Haney was a mere lad of 15 years. They were assigned to a regular freight run between Dalton and Atlanta. At Dalton, the Western & Atlantic RR connected with the East Tennessee & Georgia Railroad which served east Tennessee and had connections to the north and east. On April 11, 1862, the *Texas* ran north leaving Atlanta about 10:00 a.m., and arriving at Dalton around 6:00 p.m. On the morning of April 12, 1862, Bracken left Dalton with the *Texas* and 21 loaded cars bound for Atlanta. About two miles south of Adairsville, he was flagged by Conductor William A. Fuller and Anthony Murphy, foremen of Machinery and Motive Power at the State Road Shops in Atlanta. These two were afoot at this point seeking to overcome their train pulled by the *General* which had been stolen that

PETER JAMES BRACKEN

HENRY P. HANEY

morning by the Union raiding party led by James J. Andrews, spy and contraband merchant. Bracken knew both Fuller and Murphy, and he stopped his train and took them aboard. They proceeded to tell Bracken what had happened, and Bracken backed his train to Adairsville. Just a few minutes before, the *General* with its three cars had passed him at Adairsville, and he was curious then about the train speeding through with no one aboard who was familiar to him. They reached Adairsville within a few minutes, and the 21 cars were set aside on the fly. Then "The Great Locomotive Chase" was on more even terms, even though the *Texas* was running in reverse....

The pursuit of the *General* by the *Texas* continued northward for some 51 miles before the *General* was abandoned by the Andrews Raiders about two miles north of Ringgold. Certainly the *Texas* was the hero of this run, but through the years the *General* has received most of the credit and the notoriety. Captain Fuller was inclined towards the *Texas,* as he stated in an interview in 1895. "The question as to whether the *General* or the *Texas* should have the honors has been discussed. I am rather inclined to the *Texas,* but at the same time I never could have availed myself of the service of the *Texas* if I had not succeeded in getting the *William R. Smith,* at Kingston, nor could I have got to the *Smith* if the *Yonah* had been out of reach at Etowah. And if I had not had the use of the old handcar from Moon's Station to Etowah, I never could have reached the *Yonah* in time. So all of these came in for a share." Along with the *Texas* should be honored those men who were running her. At top of the list is Peter James Bracken, the engineer, Henry P. Haney, the fireman, Alonzo Martin, wood passer, and Fleming Cox, brakeman, together with Conductor William A. Fuller, and foreman Anthony Murphy.

As the chase ended and the raiders abandoned the *General* and fled to the woods, each man for himself, Bracken eased the *Texas* to within a few feet of the *General.* He then directed young Haney to go aboard and see if anything was wrong. Haney found the firebox door open and very little fire in the firebox. He then tried the water cocks and found little or no water in the boiler. After a wait of 20 or 30 minutes, the *Texas* took the *General* in tow and moved her back to Ringgold. Here the *General* was left, and Bracken and Haney with the *Texas* went on down to Adairsville where they picked up their freight cars and proceeded to Atlanta just as though nothing had happened.

In October 1895 Peter J. Bracken summed up his experience in running the *Texas* on April 12, 1862, in a letter to William A. Fuller, as follows: "I was running the *Texas* on the day that Andrews stole the *General.* If I had not been running myself, I would not have rode on her with anyone else running as I would not (have) taken the chances or run the risk we run that day with any one else handling the engine. It makes me nervous now when I think of the X-ties on the track. I do not want any unnecessary notoriety about the chase and would not answer or pay any attention to those questions from any one else but on account of old times and old friendship, I will answer them to the best of my recollection and ability. My recollections are that no one else touched the throttle of my engine from the time I saw you coming down the hill east of Adairsville until we run up on the *General* about three miles above Ringgold."

Bracken continued as a railroader but left the Western & Atlantic Railroad soon after the War. He died in his 76th year in Macon, Georgia, on May 26, 1909, and was buried on Holly Ridge in Rose Hill Cemetery. In 1971, through the efforts of Jim Bogle, his grave was marked with an appropriate memorial bearing the likeness of the *Texas* in its war time character as researched and drawn by the late Wilbur G. Kurtz. Henry P. Haney left railroad service shortly after the War and became a fireman rising to the position of Assistant Chief of the Atlanta Fire Department before his death. He is buried in Casey's Hill Cemetery in Atlanta.

GRAVE OF PETER JAMES BRACKEN, ROSE HILL CEMETERY, MACON, GA, WITH THREE GRAND-DAUGHTERS, LEFT TO RIGHT, MRS. JOHN A. PENNINGTON, MISS LOUISE SMITH AND MRS. MILDRED MILLER, SEPT. 25, 1971.

GRAVE OF HENRY P. HANEY (1846-1923) AT CASEY'S HILL CEMETERY, ATLANTA.

The *Texas* continued in service for the remainder of the War. The next accounting to be found of the *Texas* appears in a handwritten report rendered by John H. Flynn, Master Mechanic of the W&R RR, to Superintendent Robert Baugh of the Road. Flynn wrote: "The engine *Texas*, in Virginia, is expected in a short time, as a messenger has been despatched for her." This report, dated October 21, 1865, gave a listing of the engines owned by the Western & Atlantic RR together with a statement of their condition. A total of 47 engines were listed with only two of them reported as being in "good order" — the remainder requiring repairs of one kind or another. Such was the condition of the motive power of the state-owned railroad after the Civil War. A year later, on September 30, 1866, Master Mechanic Flynn reported the engine *Texas* as being under repair, the total cost of which was $2,898.94.

Why was the engine *Texas* in Virginia in the fall of 1865 almost 200 miles north of the end of the rails of the Western & Atlantic RR which terminated at Chattanooga? What had happened to this engine that had performed so well on April 12, 1862, with Engineer Peter Bracken at the throttle and Conductor William A. Fuller and his party aboard, in the famous chase of the *General?*

Early in 1862 Governor Joseph E. Brown was very much concerned over the scarcity of salt for the people of Georgia. Salt was a necessary item for the curing and preserving of food, and as the supply dwindled it was soon subjected to unprincipled speculation. A minor source of salt was the dirt floor of the smokehouse where the meat was hung to cure. The dirt was taken up and boiled in water to reclaim the salt that had accumulated. Governor Brown sought to overcome this shortage. Since he was the Chief Executive Officer of the State owned Western & Atlantic RR he had an instrument by which he could act quickly, and he directed the Superintendent of the Road to enter into a contract for the purchase and delivery of salt. The nearest source of salt was in the western part of Virginia at a place known as Saltville about 30 miles east of Bristol and some eight miles off the main line of the Virginia & Tennessee Railroad. There was a branch line that connected Saltville with the Virginia & Tennessee RR. Saltville was surrounded by a series of salt domes, and the salt was within 200 feet of the surface of the ground. The salt was brought to the surface as a brine which was then evaporated by cooking in open vessels. Aside from the cooking vessels and some piping, fuel was the main thing needed in order to keep the fires going, and wood was used for this purpose.

Governor Brown, having contracted for the production and delivery of salt from Saltville, soon ran into problems of transportation. He could and did exercise reasonable control over the railroads in Georgia, but beyond Chattanooga he had to rely on the East Tennessee & Georgia RR to Knoxville and the East Tennessee & Virginia RR beyond. These two railroads were short of equipment, and Governor Brown agreed to loan some from the Western & Atlantic RR. Accordingly, early in 1863, the engine *Texas* with nine box cars and a few platform cars were moved northward to the East Tennessee & Virginia RR for the purpose of hauling wood to Saltville for use as fuel, and the salt out for distribution to the needy people of Georgia. This equipment remained in Virginia until after the end of the War when Master Mechanic Flynn arranged for its return to the home rails of the Western & Atlantic RR.

It is not known why the *Texas* was chosen for this special duty. The requirement was initially stated for a good engine capable of heavy duty. Perhaps the role of the *Texas* as the real hero of "The Great Locomotive Chase" caused it to be selected for this important duty. Most likely it was because of the overall condition of the *Texas* which was good.

VIEW OF SALTVILLE, VIRGINIA.

THE *TEXAS* UNDER STEAM NEAR EMERSON, GA, IN SEPTEMBER 1903, THE LAST KNOWN INSTANCE OF THE ENGINE BEING PHOTOGRAPHED IN USE.

The locomotives of the Western & Atlantic RR were not given numbers until after the Civil War in 1866. Prior to this time they were named as were the *Texas* and the *General*. The numbering system assigned in 1866 was quite simple. It started with Number 1 and continued generally based on the date the engine was placed in service on the State Road. The *Texas* was the 49th locomotive to be acquired, and it was assigned that number. About 1880, the locomotives were renumbered, and the *Texas* was assigned the Number 12 and named the *Cincinnati*. Again, the numbers were assigned, based on date of acquisition, to those locomotives remaining on the roster. The *Texas* carried Number 12 until 1890, following the lease of the Western & Atlantic RR by the Nashville, Chattanooga & St. Louis Railway, when it was assigned road Number 212 and continued with the name *Cincinnati*. It remained Number 212 until taken out of service after 1903.

Little is known of the *Texas* during the period from 1866 to 1900. It was in continuous service during this period and likely went through one or more major overhauls. It was converted to a coal burning locomotive in the early 1870s, and the balloon type Radley & Hunter stack was replaced with the more efficient diamond stack. Boilers did not

last more than 15 or 20 years, and it is likely that the *Texas* had at least two replacement boilers. Prior to and during the Civil War period, annual reports of the Western & Atlantic RR reflected considerable data on the operation and performance of locomotives. The year 1861, for example, was a good year for the *Texas*. At a total cost of $79.20 for repairs, the *Texas* ran 21,054 miles (equal to 76 round trip from Atlanta to Chattanooga) for an average of 30.3 miles per cord of wood consumed, and pulling 1,705 loaded cars and 991 empty cars. The engine must have been a good steamer for the average of 30.3 miles per cord of wood consumed was pretty close to a record for locomotives on the Western & Atlantic RR.

On May 31 and June 1, 1886, the gauge of the full length of the Western & Atlantic RR was changed from five feet to four feet nine inches, the standard gauge of the railroads of the United States. This was necessary in order to provide for the interchange of cars from one railroad to the other. Most of the railroads of the south were involved for they had been constructed of the broader gauge. At this time, the gauge of the *Texas* was also changed. At some time during this period, new drivers of a smaller size were put on the engine. Originally the drivers were 60 inches in diameter, and they were changed to 56 inches in diameter.

By 1903, the *Texas* had been shunted to a small branch line at Emerson, Georgia, which served some mines in the area. We are indebted to the late Wilbur G. Kurtz who arranged to have the engine photographed near Emerson in September 1903, and this is the last known instance of the engine being photographed under steam and while still in service. Soon after, the *Texas* was retired from active service and moved to the Western & Atlantic RR yards in Atlanta, where it suffered from exposure and lack of care.

For a while it appeared as though the old engine would go to the scrap heap. In 1907 a campaign began that was to save the *Texas*. On August 3, 1907, the *Atlanta Georgian* ran a story on the front page under a bold headline that read: "Shall This Be The Fate of the Gallant Old *Texas*?" The writer put it bluntly when he wrote: "It was the *Texas* that ran down the *General* and the *Texas* was manned by good Georgians too! Conductor William A. Fuller, who died in Atlanta two years ago, was in charge that day, and Anthony Murphy, Peter Bracken, Henry Haney, Fleming Cox and Alonzo Martin, were the men who stood by him. Should the vanquished be crowned with laurels while the victor is torn to pieces and cast aside? Place her upon a stone base in some prominent spot. The Capitol ground would be perhaps the best place for the engine means something to all Georgians."

With this article, the *Georgian* began a campaign to raise funds by individual subscription from its readers for the purpose of buying the *Texas* and arranging for her display. Subsequently, then President John W. Thomas, of the Nashville, Chattanooga & St. Louis Railway, indicated that he would be willing to present the *Texas* to the State of Georgia. Three more years lapsed, and the *Texas* continued to deteriorate in the Western & Atlantic RR yards in Atlanta.

In August 1910 the Western & Atlantic Railroad Committee of the House of Representatives of the Georgia General Assembly became interested and initiated some action. A Resolution in

ATLANTA, GA., 1909

"relation to the preservation of the State's engine *Texas*" was passed by both houses of the General Assembly. Note here that the General Assembly felt that the *Texas* was then owned by the State of Georgia. The Resolution was approved by Governor Joseph E. Brown on August 9, 1910. (Joseph M. Brown was a son of Joseph E. Brown, Governor of Georgia during the Civil War period and who had sent the *Texas* north to Virginia in 1863.) It was resolved, by the Senate and the House of Representatives, "that the Governor of the State take such steps as may be necessary to preserve the *Texas* and have such repairs made as will prevent its decay." A joint committee was also appointed to report to the next General Assembly "A proper place for keeping on exhibition of both the *Texas* and the *General* and for the preservation of the same."

In spite of this action by the General Assembly, nothing was done immediately. This was a period when a sort of unfriendly attitude existed between the State government and the railroads. Neither was willing to take the lead and do something about the *Texas*. Again, the Atlanta newspapers came to the rescue.... Wilbur G. Kurtz wrote several articles for the *Atlanta Constitution* advocating preservation of the *Texas*. In the Spring of 1911, the city of Atlanta, through its mayor, Courtland S. Winn, let it be known that the city was interested in preserving the *Texas* at least until the State could take final action. Governor Joseph M. Brown confirmed this action in a letter to Mayor Winn on April 12, 1911. The Governor ordered "that the engine known as *Texas* be turned over to the authorities of the said City of Atlanta to be by them temporarily protected and housed until final disposition is made of the same by the General Assembly...." By letter dated May 13, 1911, Mayor Winn acknowledged this order and took charge of the *Texas* and gave his official receipt for same.

A few days earlier on May 10, 1911, the *Texas* was moved to Grant Park in the area of Fort Walker. Movement of the engine was accomplished by towing it around the belt line railroad to South Boule-vard where it was hauled over a tramway by a steam-roller to Fort Walker. The tramway was laid in sections, and as soon as the locomotive was hauled over a section, the crossties and rails over which it had passed were taken up and relaid in front. It took about ten hours to make the trip from the Boulevard crossing to the park, a distance of about one-half mile with a considerable grade.

Once in Grant Park, nothing was done to restore or preserve the engine, but it was saved from the scrapper's torch. It was still exposed to the elements and to souvenir hunters. Interest in the old engine continued, and the 50th anniversary of the Andrews Raid in 1912 was the occasion for several comprehensive articles in the Atlanta papers. At this time it was strongly urged that the *Texas* be restored to its war time appearance. During the subsequent years many exterior changes had been made for operating reasons, and the engine did not look as it did during the Civil War period. Two of the most obvious changes were reflected in the stack and the pilot or cow catcher. The latter had been removed, and a wide step placed across the front of the engine for the benefit of railroad men for the engine was also used in switching service. The bal-

THE *TEXAS* AFTER BEING MOVED TO GRANT PARK IN 1911.

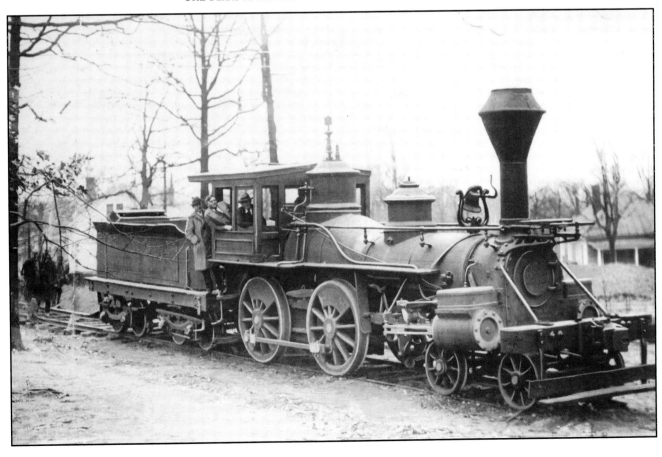

TA HITS GEORGIA FLOGGINGS

Crash Mars Texas' Last Run

The "Texas," the old pride of the W. & A., which lived out its term of usefulness in another era, filled out its round of experience Thursday night when it figured in an auto crash while being moved to its final home in the cyclorama building at Grant Park. These two views show the extent of the damage. The man is H. G. Bradley, who fired the engine in the eighties.

THE *ATLANTA JOURNAL* OR *ATLANTA CONSTITUTION* MARCH 15, 1920.

THE *TEXAS* WAS STORED IN THE BASE-MENT OF THE OLD CYCLORAMA BUILDING BUT NOT RESTORED TO ITS WARTIME LOOK.

loon shaped stack, symbolic of the wood burning days, had been replaced with a more functional diamond stack designed for the burning of coal.

The next important date for the *Texas* in this part of her history was March 15, 1927. It was on this date that the engine was moved indoors to the basement of the new Cyclorama Building in Grant Park. At long last a home was provided that protected the engine from the elements and also from souvenir hunters. The final move was a relatively easy one yet a mishap did occur. The engine was involved in an accident with an automobile! The feat could hardly have happened to the *Texas* in her days of active service.

In 1931 the *Texas* was in the news again. On October 28, 1931, the *Atlanta Journal* carried a news article reporting that Governor Richard B. Russell (the late Senator Richard B. Russell of Georgia)

had granted the Nashville, Chattanooga & St. Louis Railway authority to recondition the *Texas* and place the locomotive on one of the tracks at the Union Station in Atlanta for display. Then the NC&StL Ry, lessee of the State-owned Western & Atlantic RR, would have the *Texas* on display at one end and the *General* on display at the other end, Chattanooga. In spite of the fact that this was a time of reduced earnings for the railroad, Mr. James B. Hill, then president of the railroad, was willing to stand the expense, estimated at $600, to remove the *Texas* from the Cyclorama at Grant Park to the Union Station, in downtown Atlanta, and put the locomotive in good condition again. Notwithstanding Governor Russell's generosity, the Atlanta City Council refused to surrender possession of the *Texas*, and the locomotive remained in the basement of the Cyclorama Building.

While protected in its new home in the Cyclorama Building, it was not until 1936 that action was taken to restore the engine to its character of the 1850s and 1860s. It was indeed fortunate that the man who had spent so much effort in learning how the engine did appear in those historic times and who was skillfully able to transfer this information to canvas with pen and brush, the late Wilbur G. Kurtz, was placed in charge of the restoration. Today, the *Texas* looks pretty much as it did in 1856 when placed in service on the State Road, the wood burning stack is in place, the headlight on horizontal iron bars has been provided, the cab and running board replaced, the boiler covered with Russia iron, the cylinders and steam chests encased in brass, bands of the same metal placed around her boiler, a nameplate on each side of the boiler with the name *Texas* in bold letters, and the overall color dark brown with blue and yellow trimming. Thus the *Texas* stands in silent tribute to those heroes who manned her on that eventful day in 1862, Bracken, Haney, Fuller, Murphy, Martin and Cox.

The *Texas* on display in the Cyclorama building in 1971, its home since 1927.

Little imagination is required today, as one stands near the old engine, to picture those gallant men in the cab and on the tender as they pursued the Andrews Raiders aboard the *General.*

During the Civil War Centennial observance in 1961, after it became known that the Louisville & Nashville RR was refurbishing the locomotive *General* to run under its own steam again, an effort was made by a wealthy Texan to do the same with the *Texas.* He did not receive a favorable response and nothing came of the matter.

On February 15, 1973, the Georgia Historical Commission, recognizing the historical importance and significance of the *Texas,* forwarded a nomination for the inclusion of the engine in the National Register of Historic Places. On June 19, 1973, the Director of the National Park Service advised that the nomination had been accepted and the *Texas* had been entered in the National Register of Historic Places.

The *Texas* remained in the basement of the Cyclorama Building, a place where its preservation has been assured, yet a place which did not afford the viewer an opportunity to really see the old engine because of the lack of space. A small panel did little more than explain why the *Texas* was saved and placed on display. Plans were made in 1972 to build a new modern structure for the Battle of Atlanta painting, the Cyclorama. These plans included the *Texas* and more room was planned to display the locomotive and explain its history.

In 1975 no action had been taken to build the new building for the Cyclorama painting. Concerned citizens began expressing their views about the condition of the painting and the need for a new building to house it. Nothing was said about the *Texas.*

In 1979 with still no action taken to restore and preserve the Cyclorama painting and the *Texas,* legislation was introduced in the Georgia General Assembly to move both to the Stone Mountain Memorial Park a few mile east of Atlanta. The legislation did not pass.

In 1981 the Cyclorama Building was upgraded and the *Texas* is now more visible to the public.

The *Texas* was removed from the basement of the Cyclorama building on April 22, 1981.

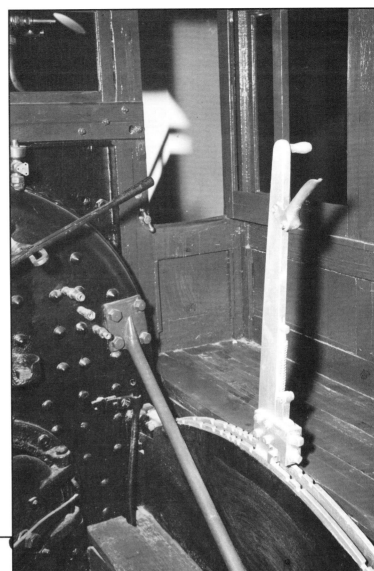

AT RIGHT: THROTTLE AND
JOHNSON BAR OF THE RESTORED
TEXAS. BELOW: RESTORED
FIREBOX.

THE FULLY RESTORED *Texas* HAS BEEN ON
DISPLAY IN THE ATLANTA CYCLORAMA BUILD-
ING AT GRANT PARK SINCE SEPTEMBER 1981.

By Elinor Hillyer

Famous Engine That Captured the General is Moved From Shelter on Hilltop to the Cyclorama Building at Grant Park. Once Ran a Mile a Minute, but Takes a Week to do Half a Mile on Its Last Trip.

There was no rush of steam or familiar locomotive chug-chug as the smoke poured from the stack of the "Texas" when it began its recent journey from the top of the hill in Grant park to the Cyclorama building. Only the roar of a caterpillar tractor and creak of ropes and pulleys echoed through the park as the Texas crept rheumatically from its thirty-year-old moorings.

It was backwards that the intrepid old war engine chased the stolen General in the Andrews raid, and it was backwards that the Texas made its last trip out the southwest entrance of the park, down South Boulevard to the central entrance, and from there along the roadway to the Cyclorama.

The Texas is the famous engine which captured the General, after it had been stolen by a group of Federal soldiers in disguise, at Big Shanty, near Marietta, Ga. The Western and Atlantic railroad between Atlanta and Chattanooga was the backbone of the Confederate armies at that time, over which supplies were transported. The Andrews raiders, by capturing the General, hoped to burn bridges and tear up track, thus cutting the Confederate troops off from their food bases. The Texas, picked up at Kingston, raced after the General, and finally overtook it.

Dead Monster

Moving the Texas was a big job, almost as big a job as the race from Kingston to Ringgold, sixty-five years ago. It would have been easy if the Texas could have been given a little shove and sent trundling down the wooded hillsides. In fact, taking it down that way was discussed, but the grade was decided to be too steep. You can't coast sixty-five year old engine down a roadway as if it were a bicycle.

On that famous day in April the old engine made as much as a mile a minute, but its last journey was a slow one, more than a week for a half-mile run.

For, in spite of the brave "firing up" and the clouds of smoke, the old monster is quite dead. The firebox door will open only halfway, the piston rings are rusted in the cylinders, and driving rods, which were disconnected to allow the wheels to turn when the engine was brought here, have never been put back in place.

But even in death the Texas presented a picturesque aspect, as it slid down the improvised track, while groups of onlookers gathered to watch the opening lap of the journey.

The first thing done by the city construction department, which handled the undertaking for the park department, was to tear the shed away which covered the locomotive, and make an examination to ascertain whether it could stand the trip.

Exit Backwards

J.Y. Donaldson, foreman on the job, who has been with the city for twenty-three years, says that the Texas was brought to the hilltop in exactly the same manner in which it left, only, of course, it came in forward and went out backward.

Besides himself, seven workmen, two truck drivers and a tractor driver were required to move the Texas. The tender, or fuel car, was disconnected from the engine and preceeded it down the runway.

Two hundred feet of track, the rails spiked to the crossties, had been laid from the embankment to the Boulevard, over a heavy platform known as a trailer, usually used by the department to move steam rollers and concrete mixers. The tender, held back by cables attached to trees, reached the street in about three-quarters of an hour.

Once on the paved street, the caterpiller tractor was attached to the comparatively light tender and set off dragging it towards the other entrance without any rails. When the entrance was reached, the final grade began. Cables were again brought into play to keep the tender from slipping down hill too fast, and trucks headed in the opposite direction held it back.

Finally, after a few hours' time, the tender was drawn across the back of the Cyclorama to the north entrance, where dirt had already been dug away to allow a smooth and level space to lay the rails.

Then the big work, the moving of the Texas itself began. The engine had already been moved over to the very brink of the grade, and soon followed the tender over the top. As fast as the Texas passed over one section of rails they were picked up and placed in front. In this way a half-mile run was made on 200 feet of track.

When the Texas reached South Boulevard, moving along the level was not the simple thing that pulling the tender had proved. The caterpiller engine again supplied the power, but every fifty feet a halt had to be ordered to pick up the track traveled over and lay it in front. In spite of delays, several days later the Texas stood at the doors on the north side of the Cyclorama, with its rear end toward the entrance.

The room in the basement of the Cyclorama building where the Texas now stands, was constructed especially for the locomotive when the structure was planned. There are two large doors on the north side, which some day

[will] be filled with glass. A wide stairway leads down from the main entrance to the showroom. The engine is standing facing the doors, which explains why it had to be backed in. There it will be painted and shined so as to be quite as dashing looking as its famous rival, the General, which stands in the Western and Atlantic railroad station in Chattanooga.

Though the Texas has managed to maintain its personality, age and time have made inroads upon it. The big balloon smokestack is not the same that puffed sparks and vapors during the Andrews raid. The old chimney was nearly twice as big. That was the only way enough draught could be secured on the old wood-burning engines. The Texas did not go into retirement after its famous exploit of rendering futile the Andrews raid, but it was active at the Battle of Atlanta and was used after the war by a mining company in Bartow county. It was during this period of its career that the present smokestack came into being.

Echoes From the 60's

At the same time the old-fashioned link and pin coupler was removed and a newer one put on. Fortunately the old coupling pins remain, and it is the intention of the city to replace the present couplers with models of the original sort.

Some of the old wood on the engine which has been there ever since it was constructed has decayed. These pieces will be replaced, and the connecting rods will be put in place for the first time since the engine was given to the city of Atlanta.

But much remains the same about the Texas. The same bell and the same whistle that sounded through the Georgia hills sixty-five years ago are still there. The same levers that felt the fingers of the excited engineer, the same steam gauge that Captain Fuller watched anxiously, and the same old-fashioned tallow cups which oiled the cylinders during that faraway crisis--all these are in the cab yet.

In front of the smoke stack there is still the platform for the big oil headlight, and underneath one can still see the old style of big weight on the reverse, where springs are used on modern locomotives. The pilot, with its rudimentary cowcatcher, is the same that hurtled over the crossties at the rate of fifty-five miles an hour.

If the Texas has had many adventures, its final haven is reached. The Texas has made its last run, and now, as a museum relic, takes up it eternal rest under glass.

REMOVAL OF THE *TEXAS*
FROM THE CYCLORAMA,
APRIL 22, 1981.

MOVING THE *TEXAS* BACK IN
SEPTEMBER 1981 AFTER THE
CYCLORAMA RENOVATION.

The Andrews Raid-A Sequel

All of the raiders were captured within a period of 12 days and placed in confinement in the little Swims Jail in Chattanooga, Tenn., located at the corner of 5th and Lookout streets. That is, all who actually got as far south as Marietta, for some who volunteered and started did not make it all the way.

THE SWIMS JAIL LOCATED AT THE CORNER OF 5TH AND LOOKOUT STREETS, CHATTANOOGA, TENN. DRAWING BY WILBUR G. KURTZ

On Monday night, April 7, 1862, it is reasonably certain that there were 23 men who met with James J. Andrews on the outskirts of Shelbyville, Tenn., to learn of their assignments and duties. There may have been another but his identity has never been established. This group included one civilian besides Andrews, William Campbell, and the remaining 22 were soldiers from Gen. Ormsby M. Mitchel's Third Division. Their meeting place was a pretty knoll on the Holland farm a little less than two miles east of Shelbyville and not far from the banks of Tennessee's Duck River. This location is identified today on Tennessee Highway Number 64.

Four of these 24 men did not get to participate in the actual chase of the locomotives for, before a week had passed, they found themselves in the Confederate Army. This was their instructions if things went wrong.

Two members of the party, Corp. Samuel Llewellyn, Company I, 33rd Ohio Volunteer Infantry, and Pvt. James Smith, Company I, 2nd Ohio Volunteer Infantry, had not reached Chattanooga

before they came under suspicion and they joined a Confederate artillery unit to avoid the issue. This occurred near Jasper, Tenn. Smith was actually confined in the Swims Jail for a short time but was never identified as a member of the raiders. Some weeks later they made good their escape and returned to their own lines. In subsequent years, Smith was placed on the same footing as other members of the party. Pvt. John Porter and Cpl. Martin Hawkins, who had failed to catch the train as it left Marietta, according to instructions, joined the Confederate Army and soon found themselves at Camp McDonald at Big Shanty. It was only a matter of time before their identity was established as being of the raiding party and from then on their fate was tied to those who had made the run.

By the night of April 24 Andrews and all 21 members of his party were Confederate prisoners and were soon in jail in Chattanooga. Later, on Saturday, May 31, 12 of them were taken from the Swims Jail and started for Knoxville for court-martial on the charge of being spies. Andrews had been quickly tried in Chattanooga and on the same day, he was notified that he would be hanged as a spy one week later.

June 6, 1862, was a fateful day for Chattanooga as preparations were being made for the hanging of Andrews, for on that day the city came under bombardment from Union forces across the river.

Brig. Gen. James J. Negley, leading units of Gen. Mitchel's Third Division, bombarded the city briefly using 4 1/2-inch Parrott guns. With this happening, the Confederate authorities thought it more prudent to move Andrews and the eight members of his party still confined in the Swims Jail down to Atlanta. The reason there were only nine of the party then in confinement in Chattanooga is that John Wollam was at large. He and Andrews had escaped from the Swims Jail on Sunday, June 1, and Wednesday, June 4, Andrews had been recaptured and placed back in the jail. Wollam was not recaptured until the end of June and he rejoined his comrades, then in jail in Atlanta.

Andrews and the eight men were escorted under guard to an early morning train for Atlanta on June 7. They arrived at the old brick car shed about 11:00 a.m. The party detrained and was turned over to a squad of the city provost guards who conducted them to the barracks, a three story building known as the "Concert Hall." This edifice stood on the site of the First National Bank building, previously the site of the Peachtree Arcade, at the northwestern intersection of Peachtree Street and the railroad.

Andrews did not remain in confinement in the Concert Hall very long. Within an hour he was on his way to his execution at the point near the intersection of present day Juniper and Third streets, N.E. The route taken by modern designation, was from Peachtree Street at Five Points to Baker, West Peachtree from Baker to Alexander, and right into Alexander. In front of the present St. Luke's Church, a left turn was made into Peachtree Street, then northward on Peachtree to North Avenue, where a right turn was made to Juniper, and then left, or northward, to the intersection of Juniper and Third Streets. Here James J. Andrews was hanged and buried, and his remains rested there until 1887. Col. Oliver H. Jones was the Provost Marshal of the Military Post of Atlanta and was in overall charge of execution.

The *Southern Confederacy* on June 8, 1862, recorded the event as follows:

EXECUTION OF ANDREWS, THE ENGINE THIEF

Yesterday evening's train from Chattanooga brought to this place, to be executed, Andrews, the leader of the Engine Thieves, under sentence of death, *convicted by court-martial of being a spy. He was carried out Peachtree Street road, accompanied by three clergymen, and escorted by a guard. A considerable crowd followed to witness the execution.*

He was a native of Hancock County, Va., born in 1829, brought up by pious Presbyterian parents, who now reside in South-west Missouri. A good portion of his life had been spent in Fleming County, Ky. He had no family but was engaged to be married this month.

He said he was induced to attempt stealing of the engine under promise of a large reward by the fed'ls, and the privilege of smuggling through from the north, $5,000 worth of goods per month; that he did not intend to burn the bridges, but to take the engine to the federals; and that he was not an enemy to the Confederate government or people.

He seemed to be very penitent—was composed till he came on to the scaffold, when a slight tremor was perceptible.

These statements were made by Rev. W.J. Scott, at his request. Rev. Mr. Conyers offered up a feeling prayer. Rev. Mr. Connor administered a few seasonable words of counsel. The three then took leave of him and he was launched into eternity.

Thus ended the life of this daring adventurer, who, according to his own confession, was playing into the hands of both parties in this war to make gain—always, however, in the confidence of the enemy; but he was convicted of being a spy.

Mr. Scott believes he was not a man of much ability—had but little cultivation, and was victimized by shrewder men than himself.

Following the execution of Andrews, the jailed party was removed to the Fulton County jail, located at the corner of Fraser and Fair streets (now Memorial Drive). Several days later, the 12 who had been taken to Knoxville for court-martial were removed to Atlanta and confined with the others. Because of exigencies of the service, courts-martial for only seven of the group had been completed. The Confederate authorities now felt it best to remove them from the area of Knoxville and get them deeper behind Confederate lines.

In the columns of the *Southern Confederacy* for Thursday, June 19, 1862, was the following:

HUNG

Yesterday afternoon seven more of the Engine

EXECUTION OF THE SEVEN ANDREWS RAIDERS NEAR OAKLAND CEMETERY, ATLANTA, JUNE 18, 1862. GEORGE D. WILSON IS HOLDING HIS RIGHT HAND UP AND MAKING A SPEECH. DRAWING FROM "CAPTURING A LOCOMOTIVE" BY WILLIAM PITTENGER.

thieves were hung near this city. They were a portion of the twenty-four that arrived here in strings a few days ago. They are all Ohioans. We have not learned their names.

With these 41 words, seven men met their fate on the afternoon of June 18, 1862, at the southeast corner of Fair Street and South Park Avenue, across from Oakland Cemetery. On this same date, the Post of Atlanta acquired a new Provost Marshal. Col. Jones was relieved by Capt. Green J. Foracre, and one of his first jobs was to handle this execution.

Many years later, Wilbur G. Kurtz sought the precise place where these seven men had been hanged. It was in 1906, on one of his early visits to Atlanta, and he had interviewed several eyewitnesses. Their accounts were carefully noted, but still there was doubt. James Bell, a long time Atlanta resident, was assisting Mr. Kurtz in his research, and he was not satisfied at this point either. Then Bell remembered James McClellan, who was present at the execution and who had lived and worked in the neighborhood afterwards and consequently would be familiar with the environs.

James McClellan was located and taken to the area. With no hesitation at all, McClellan walked to a spot in low ground, in the southeast angle of Fair Street and South Park Avenue. In 1906 this lot had not filled in as it is now. The original grade was considerably lower than either street, and the trace of a stream bed was still visible. McClellan stated that the sevenfold execution took place on a scaffold which paralleled the little stream, and that the seven men, when aligned on the trap, all faced southeast. McClellan then pointed out the spot nearby where the seven men had been buried:

Sergeant Major Marion A. Ross,
    2d Ohio Volunteer Infantry
Private George D. Wilson,
    Company B, 2d Ohio Volunteer Infantry
Private Charles P. Shadrach,
    Company K, 2d Ohio Volunteer Infantry
Sergeant John M. Scott,
    Company F, 21st Ohio Volunteer Infantry
Private Samuel Slavens,
    Company E, 33rd Ohio Volunteer Infantry
Private Samuel Robertson,
    Company G, 33rd Ohio Volunteer Infantry
William Campbell, civilian

For the remaining 14, now confined in the old Fulton County Jail, the summer was rather quiet and restful. The local Confederate authorities were not so contented, however, and were seeking information as to the disposition of their prisoners. By October the evidence was increasing to the raiders, that something was in the wind that boded no good for them. They saw an escape as their best course of action. Accordingly, plans were made, and on October 16, when the evening meal was being served to them, they went into action. Eight of them were successful. Generally, six of them went northward overland, traveling by night and hiding by day, until they were safe behind Union lines. Two of them, Alf Wilson and Mark Wood, made their way southward via the Chattahoochee River and to the Gulf and were picked up by the U.S. Gunboat *Somerset* of the East Gulf Blockading Squadron then operating in the Gulf of Mexico.

Those who succeeded in escaping were:
Private John Alf Wilson,
    Company C, 21st Ohio Volunteer Infantry
Private Mark Wood,
    Company C, 21st Ohio Volunteer Infantry
Private John Reed Porter,
    Company F, 21st Ohio Volunteer Infantry
Private Wilson W. Brown,
    Company F, 21st Ohio Volunteer Infantry
Corporal Daniel A. Dorsey,
    Company H, 33rd Ohio Volunteer Infantry
Corporal Martin J. Hawkins,
    Company A, 33rd Ohio Volunteer Infantry
Private John Wollam,
    Company C, 33rd Ohio Volunteer Infantry
Private William J. Knight
    Company E, 21st Ohio Volunteer Infantry

The remaining six spent the winter of 1862-63 in the Fulton County Jail. By March 1863 arrangements had been concluded for their exchange as prisoners of war via City Point, Va., and on March 17, 1863, they were once again free men. This group included:
Corporal William Pittenger,
    Company G, 2d Ohio Volunteer Infantry
Private Jacob Parrott,
    Company K, 33rd Ohio Volunteer Infantry
Corporal William H. Reddick,
    Company B, 33rd Ohio Volunteer Infantry
Private Robert Buffum,
    Company H, 21st Ohio Volunteer Infantry
Private William Bensinger,
    Company G, 21st Ohio Volunteer Infantry
Sergeant Elihu Mason,
    Company K, 21st Ohio Volunteer Infantry

Following their exchange and prior to visiting their homes, these six men were brought to Washington, D.C. There they were interviewed by Secretary of War Edwin M. Stanton who presented each the newly authorized Medal of Honor and a gift of $100 cash. Jacob Parrott was the recipient of the first of these medals. Later, the men were presented to President Lincoln and subsequently were minutely interrogated by Judge Advocate General Joseph Holt as to their experiences behind the Confederate lines and while in prison. From this testimony Holt made his official report to the Secretary of War dated March 27, 1863. This resulted in publication of the Holt Report, a most complete document in itself concerning the Andrews Raid and the first publication of an official nature. A portion of this report found its way into the Official Records of the War of the Rebellion. After completion of

FULTON COUNTY'S FIRST JAIL ERECTED IN 1855 AND DESTROYED BY GENERAL SHERMAN'S FORCES IN 1864. THE BUILDING STOOD AT THE CORNER OF FRASER AND FAIR STREETS (NOW MEMORIAL DRIVE). ALL OF THE ANDREWS RAIDERS, EXCEPT ANDREWS, WERE CONFINED IN THIS JAIL FROM JUNE TO OCTOBER 1862. DRAWING BY WILBUR G. KURTZ

into the Official Records of the War of the Rebellion. After completion of furloughs at home, these men rejoined their units in the vicinity of Murfreesburo, Tenn.

On August 14, 1863, William Pittenger was discharged from the Army on account of physical disability. By October 1863 he had ready his first booklength account of the Andrews Raid—*Daring and Suffering, a History of the Great Railroad Adventure.* Just prior to its publication, seven more of the survivors of the raid had been awarded the Medal of Honor in September 1863, Brown, Dorsey, Hawkins, Knight, Porter, Wilson and Wood, and to the families of Robertson and Ross posthumous awards were made.

The Civil War continued. With the exception of William Pittenger, all of the survivors of the Andrews raiding party were still in service at the end of 1863. Several had taken part in the Battle of Chickamauga and had gone through the adventure of a second capture and imprisonment by the Confederates. A few would serve until 1865, but during the months of 1864 many of them left the service, some for disabilities and others for expiration of terms of enlistment. On July 6, 1864, the Medal of Honor was awarded to James Smith and two weeks later, on July 20, a medal was awarded to John Wollam. Thus 17 of the participants (or their families) had been recognized.

Mark Wood, one of the eight who had made good his escape from the Fulton County Jail in October 1862, and who survived service during the rest of the war, died a short time later, on July 11, 1866, at Toledo, Ohio. A month later, on August 4, 1866, the Medal of Honor was awarded to John M. Scott, posthumously, and sent to his family near Findlay, Ohio. In July 1883, a Medal of Honor was awarded to Samuel Slavens, posthumously, and forwarded to his family. This was the last Medal of Honor to be awarded the members of the Andrews raiding party—19 in all. It appears in the records that no application was made by anyone for Medals of Honor for George D. Wilson, Samuel Llewellyn and Charles P. Shadrach, and medals were never awarded. Andrews and Campbell, as civilians, were not eligible for the award.

In 1865 the Civil War ended, and with the end came many tasks, not the least of which was to care for the honored dead. Neither the Union Army nor the Confederate Army had trained graves registration service personnel found in the modern army of today. Consequently, most of the dead were left to lie where they had fallen with what little care and attention could be spared by their fellow soldiers or concerned civilians in the area. In and around Atlanta there were several thousand who remained where they had fallen, both Confederate and Union dead. Now the job was to locate and remove their remains to a more honored final resting place. In the case of the Union dead, this job fell to the Military Departments then still active in the Confederate States.

Thus in the Spring of 1866, Mr. Jonas Drury was sent to Atlanta on a disagreeable assignment. He had executed his assignment and returned to Chattanooga where he sat down and wrote the following letter:

Chattanooga, Tenn., April 20th, 1866
Capt. W.A. Wainwright
   Asst. Qr. Mr.
   Captain—
   Persuant to instructions from Bvt. Maj. Thos. J. Carlile, A.Q.M. dated April 11th, I proceeded to Atlanta, Ga., and commenced a search and general enquiry for the bodies of seven Ohio soldiers hung by Rebels in the woods near Atlanta on or about the 22d of June 1862. From eye witnesses I learned that they were all hung at one time and on one pole. When they dropped, two of the ropes broke and let the soldiers down, where they remained until the other five were dead when they were cut down and their ropes applied to those who had broken theirs, they were rehung until they were dead—

   They were all buried in coffins and in one hole six lay side by side the seventh lay across at their feet. The place of burial is about twelve rods from where they were executed. The spot selected for their interment is now the bed of a small creek, but probably when buried, the place was dry. In taking them up I first took the body buried on the right and marked the new coffin in which I deposited the body No. 1, the second No. 2, and so on to No. 7.

(Here Drury listed the description of each body and then he went on with the following)

   I was informed that the execution of the order for hanging, was given to a Capt. Barnes (who is since dead). That no chaplain was present at the execution but that Capt. Barnes made a prayer before execution. Capt. Andrews of same crew was executed by himself on the day of his arrival in Atlanta. He was hung about one mile from the city near Peach Tree Street, Northeast from the Depot. I do not know that his remains have been removed. I was informed that there are many soldiers bones yet unburied.

   The coffins containing the remains of the seven soldiers are now in the Georgia Depot awaiting your orders.

   The above report is respectfully submitted.
                         Jonas Drury

When George Davenport Wilson enlisted in the Union Army at Franklin, Ohio, on Aug. 31, 1861, he had two children, a son and a daughter. The daughter died shortly after her father enlisted in the Union Army. The son lived on and we now skip the years till 1904, when that young man from Greencastle, Ind., Wilbur G. Kurtz, was getting into his lifelong study of the Andrews Raid and the men who participated in it. Wilbur Kurtz was in the company of William J. Knight, one of the engineers on the expedition on April 25, 1904, and they were discussing various aspects of the affair. In the course of this conversation, Knight told a rather curious story relating to George D. Wilson.

During the 1880s and 1890s, Knight had toured Ohio and Indiana with an illustrated lecture on the Andrews Raid. The illustrations were not the stereopticon of the period, but a long roll of canvas on which some not very talented artist had painted a series of pictures designed to visualize the narrative as delivered by the engineer who held the throttle of the locomotive *General*. The canvas was attached to two rolls, one of which was motivated by a crank, both rolls being supported by an assembled framework. The apparatus, when knocked down, was packed in an oblong box with large lettering painted thereon, notifying all beholders that it was the property of William J. Knight, Engineer of the Andrews Raid.

One day in the early eighties, Knight boarded a Baltimore & Ohio Railroad train at Belleville, Ohio, and on the car platform was accosted by a uniformed man with a baggage master's badge on his cap who asked if his name was Knight. Being assured that it was, the man asked him to come forward to the baggage coach as he wished to talk with him. Going forward, Knight was given a chair while the baggageman checked up his cargo. Later he addressed Knight and inquired if he was one of the Andrews Raiders. Admitting that he was, the baggage man then introduced himself as David Davenport Wilson, son of George D. Wilson, one of the seven men hanged in Atlanta. Young Wilson, who appeared to be about 20, then remarked that he had seen Knight's box—label and all—come aboard the car, and had spotted the owner because of the Medal of Honor pinned to his coat.

Knight was then asked if he recalled that George D. Wilson had any jewelry on his person while a prisoner. Knight did recall as much, stating that there were two articles, one a large gold ring

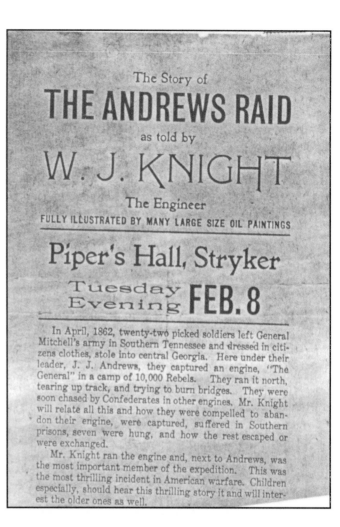

The Story of
THE ANDREWS RAID
as told by
W. J. KNIGHT
The Engineer
FULLY ILLUSTRATED BY MANY LARGE SIZE OIL PAINTINGS

Piper's Hall, Stryker
Tuesday Evening FEB. 8

In April, 1862, twenty-two picked soldiers left General Mitchell's army in Southern Tennessee and dressed in citizens clothes, stole into central Georgia. Here under their leader, J. J. Andrews, they captured an engine, "The General," in a camp of 10,000 Rebels. They ran it north, tearing up track, and trying to burn bridges. They were soon chased by Confederates in other engines. Mr. Knight will relate all this and how they were compelled to abandon their engine, were captured, suffered in Southern prisons, seven were hung, and how the rest escaped or were exchanged.

Mr. Knight ran the engine and, next to Andrews, was the most important member of the expedition. This was the most thrilling incident in American warfare. Children especially, should hear this thrilling story it and will interest the older ones as well.

with a massive seal, and the other, an oval frame about the size of a quarter in which was emplaced a photograph of his wife. He even recalled that when Wilson returned to his cell after hearing his death warrant read in the room across the hall (on the second floor of the Fulton County Jail), he told the officer in charge that he wished the two articles buried with him; the ring being a present from his wife, and the oval portrait worn as a pin, being a portrait of the donor. After this explanation, he removed the portrait from the lapel of his coat and affixed it to the inside of his coat. Several years later, Knight continued, the bodies were removed from the sevenfold grave of Atlanta for reinterment in the National Cemetery at Chattanooga. At this time, the ring and the pin were found and sent to the War Department at Washington, he thought.

"Would you know the ring if you saw it?" young Davenport asked Knight.

"Yes," replied Knight, "I think I would."

There on the extended hand of David Davenport Wilson was the gold band with the large square seal. He went on to explain that the articles had been sent to Columbus, Ohio, from the War Department, were advertised, and so came into the possession of George D. Wilson's son.

A tragic sequel to this story, is that on the first day of the National Grand Army of the Republic Encampment at Columbus, Ohio, in August 1888, where Capt. William A. Fuller and the celebrated locomotive the *General* were honored guests, the press announced a train wreck at Ankneytown, Knox County, Ohio, in which the baggage man David Davenport Wilson had lost his life.

At the close of 1866, there remained alive 15 of the original raiding party and all of the major participants on the Confederate side. On July 20, 1871, Robert Buffum cut his throat and died by his own

hand while in a mental institution at Auburn, N.Y. He, like Mark Wood, had escaped a Confederate noose and many enemy bullets. In 1886 Martin J. Hawkins died at Quincy, Ill. In 1896 another died and was buried at Pemberville, Ohio, with the following words inscribed on his tombstone: "A Soldier slumbers here. Captain Elihu H. Mason, Mitchel Raider."

In 1886 and 1887 the American Press Association published a very complete serialized story of the Andrews Raid. Fred J. Cook was manager of their Atlanta office and, as such, gave his personal attention to local connections with the event. Cook was urged by his headquarters to make a concerted effort to locate the remains of James J. Andrews as

The Locomotive General - with ten of the eleven surviving Andrews Raiders and Capt. William A. Fuller, at the G.A.R. Encampment - Columbus, Ohio — August 1888
J. Alfred Wilson - Wilson W. Brown - William J. Knight   William Bensinger
                                                                Jacob Parrott
Elihu H. Mason - William H. Reddick
John Wollam - Daniel A. Dorsey - William Pittenger   Capt. William A. Fuller

In August 1888 the Grand Army of the Republic (GAR) held their annual encampment at Columbus, Ohio. Ten of the Andrews Raiders attended as did William A. Fuller. On the tender is J. Alfred Wilson, in the cab are Wilson W. Brown and William J. Knight, standing at left are Elihu H. Mason and William H. Reddick, sitting in front are John Wollam, Daniel A. Dorsey and William Pittenger, standing by the cow catcher are William Bensinger and Jacob Parrott and resting on the post is William A. Fuller. This is one of three photographs made of the men assembled by the famous engine, the *General*, brought up under its own steam from the Western & Atlantic Railroad in Georgia. Fuller gave a talk on the raid and mentioned the great potential military value of it, had it succeeded. He closed with a stirring tribute to the intrepid raiders. The impetus for placing a monument to the event was suggested here.

a grand sequel to their publication. Cook made inquiry and located John H. Mashburne who had lived all those years near the spot where Andrews was executed and who assured Cook he could locate the grave. Final arrangements were made and on April 11, 1887, Cook, with Mashburne as guide, Maj. E.J. Kirke of the United States Army stationed in Atlanta, Dr. C.L. Wilson, President of the National Surgical Institute of Atlanta, and a Black laborer armed with pick and shovel, started out to find the remains. Mashburne led them to the present day intersection of 3rd and Juniper streets, N.E. About 20 steps southeast of the intersection, they stopped near a large rock beneath a pine tree where a tangled mass of blackberry bushes grew in a depression in the ground. Here under the direction of Mashburne, the laborers began to dig, and at the depth of about three feet they discovered a portion of a human skeleton. As the bones were exhumed and laid aside it soon became apparent they were of a large man and were later declared to be the remains of James J. Andrews.

Maj. Kirke initiated action to have them transferred to Chattanooga and there interred in the National Cemetery. This was done, for records of the Chattanooga National Cemetery indicate that the remains of James J. Andrews were shipped from Atlanta, Ga., on Oct. 7, 1887, via the Western & Atlantic Railroad. The exact date of interment is not known, but it is thought to be the following day, October 8. Andrews was buried in the semi-circle formed by the graves of the seven who had been executed. The arrangements for his reburial were handled by Post No. 45 of the G.A.R. in Chattanooga.

Out of this service grew an active movement to build a suitable memorial to the Andrews Raiders. Within Post 45, a committee of five was appointed as a standing "Andrews Monument Committee." Maj. C.W. Norwood was chairman of this committee, and his efforts culminated in action by the General Assembly of the State of Ohio about three years later. That body, on March 20, 1889, passed a law authorizing the expenditure of $5,000 for a monument to the Andrews Raiders to be erected in the National Cemetery at Chattanooga. The design finally chosen called for a miniature of the *General* to be cast in bronze to surmount a Vermont marble pedestal nine feet six inches long, five feet three inches wide, and seven feet six inches high, the whole to be 12 feet from the ground. The monument was unveiled on Memorial Day, May 30, 1891,

and the speaker for the occasion was J.R. Foraker, former Governor of Ohio and later Senator from that State.

Another interesting coincidence comes to light here. Governor Foraker was a first cousin of Capt. Green J. Foreacre, C.S.A., who was Provost Marshal of the Military Post of Atlanta in June 1862 and who had been in charge of the execution of the seven raiders. The two cousins did not see eye to eye on many things including the spelling of the family name!

The likeness of the *General* which stands atop this beautiful monument is not that of the 1860's when the balloon stack prevailed and wood was the fuel. Rather the likeness is of the 1880's when that most colorful part of the steam locomotive had been replaced by a functional straight diamond shaped stack more suitable for the burning of coal.

Inscribed on the sides of this monument are the names of the raiders and the organizations in which they served. The names of two are missing—James Smith and Samuel Llewellyn.

The year 1897 recorded the death of the first major participant on the Confederate side, Jeff Cain, the engineer of the train from which the *General* was stolen. He lies buried in Oakland Cemetery in Atlanta. His tombstone bears the following inscription, indicating that someone failed to get the facts of the raid straight before undertaking such a lasting task.

Jeff Cain

The historic engineer of the W.&A.R.R. manned the famous "General" on the thrilling war time run. It was he who drove the locomotive in the historic chase of the Andrews raiders, May 12, 1862.

In 1903 William H. Reddick died in Letts County, Iowa, and his tombstone states he was a "Member of the Andrews Raiders." In 1904, at Fallbrook, Calif., William Pittenger died and was buried with this notation on his gravestone, "One of the Andrews Raiders." He was the man who had done so much to record the actions of the raiders and who had gone on to lead a very successful life in the ministry.

The year 1905 took its toll from both sides—John A. Wilson died and was buried in Union Hill Cemetery, Wood County, Ohio, and his gravestone makes no reference to the Andrews Raid. In

Atlanta death claimed William Allen Fuller and his gravestone in Oakland Cemetery bears the following record:

On April 12, 1862, Captain Fuller pursued and after a race of 90 miles from Big Shanty northward on the Western & Atlantic Railroad, recaptured the historic war-engine 'General' which had been seized by 22 Federal soldiers in disguise, thereby preventing destruction of the bridges of the railroad and the consequent dismemberment of the Confederacy.

After the war, Capt. Fuller continued with the Western & Atlantic Railroad in the capacity of conductor and later served as General Freight and Passenger Agent for the Macon & Western Railroad. He engaged in the mercantile business and later in real estate. He was very active in civic affairs and was one of the founders of the Pioneer Citizens Society of Atlanta.

During the week of Sept. 17, 1906, the survivors of the Andrews Raid held their final reunion in Chattanooga. Those present at this last muster were: Daniel A. Dorsey, John R. Porter, Jacob Parrott, William J. Knight and William Bensinger. Still living but unable to be present were Wilson W. Brown and Samuel Llewellyn. Also present were Anthony Murphy and William A. Fuller of Atlanta. The latter represented his father who had passed away a few months earlier. One of the highlights of this occasion was the making of a photograph of the group in front on the old locomotive *General* under the vaulted roof of the Union Station where the engine stood on display for so many years.

In 1908 Jacob Parrott died and was buried in Kenton, Ohio. An inscription on his gravestone reads as follows; "Lieut. Parrott was honored by Congress with the first medal issued for distinguished bravery." In the following year, 1909, Anthony Murphy died in Atlanta and was buried in Oakland Cemetery. Murphy was a native of Ireland and was only nine years of age when his parents emigrated to this country. They lived in Pennsylvania and New Jersey, and it was there that young Murphy received his education and learned the machinist trade. It was this training that brought him to Atlanta to work for the Western & Atlantic Railroad. After the war he served for several terms on the City Council and is credited with inaugurating the waterworks movement in Atlanta.

The year 1909 also claimed Peter J. Bracken, who had been the engineer of the *Texas* during her famous run backwards on April 12. He was buried in Macon, Ga.

Samuel Llewellyn, one of the least known of the raiders and one to whom the Medal of Honor was never awarded, died in 1915 while living at the Ohio Soldiers and Sailors Home at Sandusky. He was buried at Coalton, Ohio. The year 1916 was a critical one in that it took both of the engineers of the raiding party and was also the year that the examining board of review of past awards of the Medal of Honor reported their actions. This board carefully examined the 2,625 awards of the medal made to that time. It found 911 past awards which it regarded as failing to meet the newly established requirements. Accordingly, these 911 names were struck from the Country's Medal of Honor Roll. Fortunately for the Andrews Raiders, their claims to the Medal were found valid and their names remained on the official Roll.

William J. Knight and Wilson W. Brown, both engineers on the raid, died in 1916. Brown was buried in New Belleville Ridge Cemetery, Wood County, Ohio, and Knight was buried at Stryker, Ohio. On Knight's gravestone this line is inscribed: "Engineer of Andrews Raid in Georgia, Apr 12, 1862."

In 1918 two more of the raiders passed on. Daniel A. Dorsey died at the Veteran's Home in Wadsworth, Kansas, and was buried in the cemetery there. William Bensinger died and was buried at McComb, Ohio.

John Reed Porter was the last survivor of the raiding party. He died in 1923 and was buried at McComb, Ohio. In that same year, another participant in the great locomotive chase died, Henry P. Haney. He had left the service of the railroad following the war and spent many years with the Atlanta Fire Department. He was buried in Atlanta at Casey's Hill Cemetery. Haney, though not quite 16 years of age at the time of the raid, served as Bracken's fireman on the *Texas* during the pursuit of the *General.*

IN MID-SEPTEMBER 1906 THE LAST REUNION OF PARTICIPANTS IN THE ANDREWS RAID WAS HELD IN CHATTANOOGA, TENN. IT WAS SPONSORED BY THE NASHVILLE, CHATTANOOGA & ST. LOUIS RAILWAY AND HELD IN CONJUNCTION WITH THE REUNION OF THE SOCIETY OF ARMY OF THE CUMBERLAND. THIS PHOTO WAS TAKEN ON SEPTEMBER 19 AT 9:15 A.M. IN FRONT OF THE OHIO MEMORIAL TO THE ANDREWS RAIDERS. FROM LEFT IN FRONT: JOHN R. PORTER (WHO OVERSLEPT AND MISSED THE ENTIRE EVENT), MRS. KNIGHT, WILLIAM J. KNIGHT, JACOB PARROTT, MRS. PARROTT, DANIEL A. DORSEY AND HENRY HANEY (AS A 15-YEAR-OLD BOY SERVED ON THE CREW OF THE *TEXAS* AS A FIREMAN). IN THE BACK ARE WILLIAM BENSINGER, WILLIAM A. FULLER, CHARLES BENSINGER AND ANTHONY J. MURPHY (ONE OF THE PURSUERS). FULLER HAD DIED THE YEAR BEFORE AND WILSON W. BROWN AND PETER BRACKEN WERE STILL LIVING AT THE TIME BUT DID NOT ATTEND. PORTER WAS THE LAST SURVIVOR OF THE RAID, DYING IN 1923. HANEY WAS THE LAST CONFEDERATE SURVIVOR, ALSO DYING IN 1923.

WILLIAM J. KNIGHT, STANDING NEAR STACK. LEFT TO RIGHT: PORTER, UNKNOWN, UNKNOWN, PARROTT, MRS. KNIGHT, MRS. PARROTT, CHARLES H. BENSINGER, BENSINGER, MURPHY AND DANIEL A. DORSEY, PHOTOGRAPHED IN THE CHATTANOOGA CAR BARN.

AT LEFT: WILLIAM A. FULLER ABOUT 1890.

AT RIGHT: CAPT. WILLIAM J. WHITSETT, 1904, WHO WITH OTHER MEMBERS OF THE 1ST GEORGIA JOINED THE CHASE AT CALHOUN, ABOARD ANOTHER LOCOMOTIVE, THE *CATOOSA*, THAT UN-COUPLED ITS CARS AND SPED OFF BACKWARDS BEHIND THE *TEXAS* AFTER A HASTY EXPLANA-TION HAD BEEN SHOUTED FROM FULLER. AT RINGGOLD, WHITSITT SPREAD THE ALARM AND AN IMPROVISED POSSE ON HORSEBACK AND AFOOT HELPED ROUND UP THE FLEEING RAIDERS.

THE WESTERN & ATLANTIC RAILROAD WAS OPERATED BY THE STATE OF GEOR-GIA UNTIL 1870 WHEN IT WAS LEASED TO THE WESTERN & ATLANTIC RAILROAD COMPANY, A PRIVATE CORPORATION. AT THE END OF THAT LEASE IN 1890, IT WAS LEASED TO THE NASHVILLE, CHATTA-NOOGA & ST. LOUIS RAILWAY. IN 1957 THE LOUISVILLE & NASHVILLE RAIL-ROAD ABSORBED THE NC&ST.L. TODAY THE ROUTE IS LEASED BY CSX.

THE *SOUTHERN INTELLIGENCER*, ATLANTA, GA., MAY 8, 1862

SUCCEEDING PAGES:
THE KENNESAW GAZETTE

THIS WAS A COMPANY PUBLICATION OF THE WESTERN & ATLANTIC RR COMPANY THAT LEASED THE W&A RR FROM THE STATE OF GEORGIA FROM 1870 TO 1890. THE PRESIDENT WAS THE FORMER GOVERNOR JOSEPH E. BROWN AND HIS TRAFFIC MANAGER WAS HIS SON JOSEPH M. BROWN, ALSO LATER A GOVERNOR OF GEORGIA. "LITTLE JOE" AS HE WAS CALLED WAS THE EDITOR OF *THE KENNESAW GAZETTE*.

GOVERNOR BROWN AGREED TO LET THE *GENERAL* ATTEND THE 1888 REUNION OF THE GAR AND THE ANDREWS RAIDERS IN COLUMBUS, OHIO. "LITTLE JOE" THEN PUT TOGETHER THIS SPECIAL EDITION OF THE *GAZETTE* TO BE PASSED OUT TO THE GAR MEMBERS AT COLUMBUS.

THIS ACCOUNT WAS LATER PICKED UP BY THE NASHVILLE, CHATTANOOGA & ST. LOUIS RAILWAY AROUND 1903 AND BECAME THE ACCOUNT THEY PUBLISHED IN BOOKLET FORM FOR MANY YEARS UNTIL AFTER THE LOUISVILLE & NASHVILLE RAILROAD TOOK OVER IN 1957 AND THE HISTORICAL BOOKLET WAS REWRITTEN.

NOTE THE PARAGRAPH AT THE BOTTOM OF PAGE 3. THE *GENERAL* WAS NOT INVOLVED IN ANY SUCH MOVEMENT. THE *GENERAL* WAS INVOLVED IN THE MASS DESTRUCTION BY GENERAL HOOD ON THE NIGHT OF SEPT. 1, 1864.

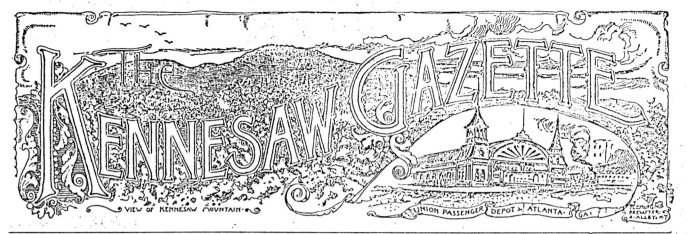

VIEW OF KENNESAW MOUNTAIN. *UNION PASSENGER DEPOT, ATLANTA, GA.*

Extra Number, Complimentary to The Grand Army of The Republic.

National Encampment, Columbus, Ohio, September 11, '88.

Vol. III.   ATLANTA, GA., SEPTEMBER 7, 1888.   NO. "Extra."

The Capture of a Locomotive.

A Brilliant Exploit of the War.

"Twenty minutes for breakfast."

Nothing particularly interesting about the old familiar cry, but when on a bright April day, in 1862, the train man sang out:

"Big Shanty, twenty minutes for breakfast," the hearts of a score of brave men beat faster, as they knew the hour had come for the beginning of one of the grandest exploits in history.

The men, from their dress were citizens and had boarded the northbound train at Marietta, a pretty little Georgia town twenty miles north of Atlanta. They paid their fare to different points, and from the conversation it was learned that "they were refugees from the Yankees," but in reality were disguised soldiers of the U. S. Army, under command of General Mitchell, then in middle Tennessee, bound south.

They were volunteers to do a dangerous work, and were to get through the country as best they could, to Marietta, their board a train bound for Chattanooga, and, at Big Shanty, seven miles away, while the train crew and passengers were at breakfast, detach the engine, run north, obstruct the track, cut the wires and burn bridges, of which there were fifteen between Big Shanty and Chattanooga; this was the brilliant scheme; how well it was carried out may be found in the words of the conductor's story.

On the morning of the 12th of April, 1862, Capt. W. A. Fuller left Atlanta at 6 o'clock, in charge of the passenger train, having three empty freight cars next to the engine, which were intended to bring commissary

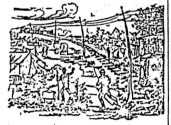

THE START.

stores from Chattanooga to Atlanta. When he reached Marietta, twenty miles distant from Atlanta, a considerable party of strangers, dressed in citizen's clothes, got on board and paid their fare, some to one point, and some to another. They all claimed to be refugees from within the Yankee, desirous of joining the Confederate army.

Seven miles from Marietta, at Big Shanty, the train stopped for breakfast. Big Shanty has been noted for the last twenty years as a place to get a superb meal. Most of the passengers and train's crew went to the breakfast house, which was situated some forty feet from the track. At this time Big Shanty was the location of a camp of instruction, called

CAMP McDONALD,

and there were about 3,000 Confederate recruits there at the time, being drilled, ready to send to the front for active service. The passengers had taken seats at the table, Capt. Fuller was sitting on the opposite side of the table from the railroad, and facing the train. He saw through the window some of the strangers who got on at Marietta get on the engine in an excited manner and

START OFF RAPIDLY,

with the three freight cars detached from the passenger train. He remarked to his engineer, Mr. Jeff Cain, and Mr. Anthony Murphy, who was present, the then foreman of the Western & Atlantic Railroad shop:

"Some one who has no right to do so has gone off with our train."

All three arose up and hurried out

The "General."

Some deserters had been reported as having left Camp McDonald, and the commanding officer had requested Captain Fuller to look out for them and arrest any soldiers who attempted to get on his train without a passport. No one had any idea that the parties in possession of the engine were Federals, but supposed it had been taken by parties desiring to desert Camp McDonald, and who would run off a short distance and abandon it.

Captain Fuller, Murphy and Cain left Big Shanty with a clear and well defined motive and a fixed determination to recapture the engine, no matter who the parties were. They started out

ON FOOT AND ALONE,

nothing daunted in putting muscle in competition with steam. Captain Fuller outran his companions, and soon reached Moon's station, two miles from Big Shanty. Here he learned from the trackmen that the men with the engine stopped and took from them by force their tools. They reported that on the engine and in the freight cars there were some twenty-four or twenty-five men. While stopping here some of the men gathered the tools, and others climbed the telegraph poles and cut the wires in two places, carrying away about one hundred yards of the wire. This statement satisfied Captain Fuller that these men were Federals in disguise. This added new stimulus to his resolve. The determination then was not only to capture his engine but the Federals.

With the assistance of the track hands, he placed on the track a hand-

car, such as is used to haul cross-ties and tools, and pushed back for his engineer, when he soon met Messrs. Murphy and Cain.

Knowing the schedules, grades, stations and distances so well, he was confident that by using great effort he could reach Etowah river by the time the fugitives could reach Kingston. At Kingston he knew they would have to contend with a number of freight trains, which would necessarily detain them several minutes.

As soon as he got Mr. Murphy and Mr. Cain on board, he told them his plan was to push on to Etowah as quickly as possible, for there he hoped to get old "Yonah," an engine used at Cooper's Iron Works, and his plan proved successful. No men, or set of men ever worked harder, using greater diligence, or were in more danger than they were, as the sequel will show. In the "rapid transit" by hand-car, Capt. Fuller, Mr. Murphy and Mr. Cain took turns in pushing,

TWO RUNNING ON FOOT

and pushing, while the other rested; one mile from Moon's station they found a large pile of cross-ties on the track—placed there by the fugitives to obstruct pursuit. The obstructions were removed and they pushed on to Acworth. Here they pressed into service such guns as they could find, and were joined by two citizens, Mr. Smith, who lives in Jonesboro, and Mr. Steve Stokely of Cobb county, who rendered valuable service in the subsequent pursuit. Resuming their journey they found no obstructions until they reached a short curve two miles from Etowah. Here two rails from the outside of the curve had been taken up. The result was the hand-car was ditched. In a few seconds Capt. Fuller and his men had the car on the track.

BEYOND THE BREAK,

and with renewed energy and determination they pushed on to Etowah,

THEY CUT THE WIRES.

wh... to their great joy,
t... found the engine as
t... supposed they would.
A... et it appeared a slim
chance. The engine was
standing on the side-track,
with the tender on the turn-
table. The tender was
turned around and pushed
to the engine and coupled
up and a coal car attached.
Some six or eight Confederate soldiers volunteered in
the chase and took passage
in the coal car. From Etowah to Kingston, Captain
Fuller ran at the rate of

SIXTY MILES PER HOUR

and found the fugitives had
passed by. A large num-
ber of freight trains had
pulled by the station so as
to let the fugitives out at
the further end of the track.
The agent informed Captain
Fuller that the leader of the
fugitives claimed to be a
Confederate officer who had
impressed the train at Big
Shanty, and the three cars
were loaded with fixed ammunition for General Beauregard at Corinth. Captain
Fuller, he said, was behind
with the regular passenger
train. He insisted that the
agent should let him have a
switch key and instruct the
conductors of the down
trains to pull by and get out
of his way, as it was important for him to go on to
Chattanooga and Corinth as
rapidly as possible.

So authoritative was he
in his demand, and so plausible in speech, that the
agent, a patriotic man, be-
lieving his story, carried out
his request, and so the fugitives, by the finesse of their
leader, passed by one great
obstruction. The freight
trains were gathered here,
and so heavy to move, that
had Captain Fuller stopped
to get them out of his way
to pass, his delay would
have been too long. Find-
ing he could not pass with old Yonah,
he abandoned it. The
Rome engine was on the Y, headed for Chattanooga,
with one car attached. He immedi-
ately took possession of it and continued the chase with all who would volunteer to go with him. He had not
proceeded far before he found cross-
ties on the track every 200 or 300
yards.

After passing Kingston, the fugitives punched out the end of the rear
car, which enabled them to drop out
ties without slacking up. Captain Fuller was forced to lose time in stopping
to remove these obstructions. Labor-
ing under these disadvantages, the pursuers redoubled their energy and proceeded to Adairsville. When he
reached a point four miles from
Adairsville he found sixty yards of
track torn up, and

SET OUT ON FOOT,

calling on his men to follow. When
he had gone half a mile, he looked
back and saw none but Anthony Murphy following him. He made two
miles as

QUICKLY AS HE COULD RUN,

and met the express freight. Having
a gun and knowing the signal, the engineer recognized Capt. Fuller and
stopped the train immediately. Knowing that Mr. Murphy was only a short
distance behind, the train was detained
until he came up. He the took a po-

sition at the rear end of the train,
twenty car lengths from the engine,
and

STARTED BACKWARD

in the direction of Adairsville, without
taking time to explain matters to the
engineer or conductor.
When he got within 200 yards of
the switch at Adairsville, Capt. Fuller
jumped off the train, ran ahead and
changed the switch, so as to throw the
cars on the side-track. He accomplished this, changed the switch to the
main track, and jumped on the engine
which had been uncoupled from the
train. The feat was accomplished so
quickly that the train and engine

RAN SIDE BY SIDE

for fully 300 yards. He now had only
the engine with the following crew :
A. Murphy ; Peter Bracken, the engineer ; Fleming Cox, the fireman, and
Alonzo Martin, wood passer. He resumed the chase, making Calhoun, 10
miles distant, in 12 minutes. As he
approached Calhoun, Capt. Fuller recognized the telegraph operator from
Dalton, a lad twelve years old. The
operator recognized Capt. Fuller, and
as the engine passed by at the rate of

FIFTEEN MILES PER HOUR,

grasped Capt. Fuller's hand, held out
to him, and was safely landed on the
engine. The operator having discovered that the wire had been cut, made
his way down to Calhoun, looking for

the break.
As they sped along rapidly as an engine, with five feet ten-inch wheels,
going backward, and 165 pounds of
steam, could possibly run, he then
wrote out the following telegram to
Gen. Leadbetter, then in command at
Chattanooga :
"My train was captured this A. M.
at Big Shanty, evidently by Federal
soldiers in disguise. They are making
rapidly for Chattanooga, possibly with
an idea of burning the railroad bridges
in their rear. If I do not capture them
in the meantime, see that they do not
pass Chattanooga."
Capt. Fuller's desire now was to
reach Dalton and send the telegram
before the fugitives could cut the wire
beyond Dalton.
Two miles beyond Calhoun

THE FUGITIVES WERE SIGHTED FOR THE

FIRST TIME,

and from their movements they were
evidently greatly excited ; they detached one of their freight cars and left
it at the point where they were discovered. They had partially taken up
a rail, but that or the car did not detain Capt. Fuller. He coupled the car
to the engine without stopping, got on
top of the freight car and gave signals
to the engineer by which he could run ;
as the car in front obscured his view.
Two and a half miles farther Capt.
Fuller came across another freight car

which the fugitives had
detached.
As before, he coupled
this on without stopping,
and pushed on to Resaca,
where he switched the
two cars off on the siding.
Again he started out with
an engine only. Two
miles north of Resaca,
while standing on the rear
end of the tender, he discovered in a short curve a
T rail diagonally

ACROSS THE TRACK,

and being too close to stop,
the engine went over it at
the rate of 55 miles per
hour.
After this, until they
reached Dalton, only oc-
casionally were obstruc-
tions met with.
At Dalton he dropped
the telegraph operator,
with instructions to put
through the telegram at
all hazards, and contin-
ued the chase. Two miles
beyond he overtook the
fugitives

TEARING UP THE TRACK,

in plain view of Col. Jesse
A. Glenn's regiment
camped near by. They
cut the telegraph wire just
after the Dalton operator
had flashed Capt. Fuller's
telegram over it, preventing him receiving the usual acknowledgement of
"O. K." from Chattanoo-
ga.
The fugitives resumed
their flight, and never
perhaps did two engines
with five feet ten-inch
wheels make faster time
than the pursued and the
pursuer. The fugitives
had the ...age in the
fact that ... General," a
"Rogers,"... headed for
Chattanooga, while the
"Texas," a "Danforth &
Cook" engine, was run-
ning backward. The 15
miles to Ringgold and
three miles beyond was
made in less time than Capt. Fuller
ever made the same distance in twenty-
two years' experience as a conductor.
Half way between Ringgold and Graysville he got within one quarter of a
mile of the fugitives, who, being so
closely pressed, set their only remaining

FREIGHT CAR ON FIRE

with a view of cutting it loose on the
next bridge. The smoke of the "General" plainly evidenced that she was
sagging. The fugitives abandoned the
engine and took to the woods in a west-
erly direction. Capt. Fuller now ran
up and coupled on to the burning car.
The fire was extinguished and the car
sent back to Ringgold in charge of the
engineer. As Capt. Fuller passed
Ringgold he noticed some fifty or sev-
enty-five militia mustering, and sent
word back to the commanding officer
to put all his

MILITIA ON HORSEBACK

and send them into the woods in pursuit of the fugitives as quickly as possible. This was about half past one
o'clock p. m.
Although jaded and fatigued, Capt.
Fuller, Anthony Murphy, Fleming
Cox and Alonzo Martin took to the
woods in pursuit.
When the fugitives abandoned the
engine, Andrews, their leader, said :

"EVERY ONE TAKE CARE OF HIMSELF," and they left in squads of three or four. Four of them were run down in the fork of the river at Graysville and one was forcibly persuaded to tell who they were.

The militia, mounted on fresh horses, scoured the woods that afternoon, and by the next day the last of the fugitives were captured.

Later there was a trial by military court and eight of the number were executed. Six were exchanged, but before the sentence of the court was carried out eight escaped.

Thus ended one of the most daring exploits on record.

THE CHASE.

Notes.

Accounts have been published before, but in local papers only: though one of the band published a work called "Capturing a Locomotive," J. B. Lippencott & Co., of Philadelphia.

The leader's name was J. J. Andrews, a Kentuckian; he was one of the executed.

The *Southern Confederacy*, a paper published at Atlanta at the time, says:

"The fugitives, not expecting pursuit, quietly took in wood and water at Cass Station, and borrowed a schedule from the tank-tender upon the plausible pretext that they were running a pressed train, loaded with powder for Beauregard. The tank-tender was named William Russell, who said he would give the shirt off his back for Beauregard if it had been asked for."

In the book referred to, Mr. Pittenger, who was on the flying engine, says:

"We obstructed the track as well as we could by laying on cross-ties at different places. We also cut the wires between every station. * * Finally, when we were nearly to the station where we expected to meet the last train, we stopped to take up a rail. We had no instruments but a crowbar, and instead of pulling out the spikes as we could have done with the pinch bars used for that purpose by railroad men, we had to batter them out. * * Just as we were going to relinquish the effort the whistle of an engine in pursuit sounded in our ears. * * With one convulsive effort we broke the rail in two, took up our precious half rail and left.

"We were scarcely out of sight of the place where we had taken up the half rail, before the other train met us. This was safely passed. When our pursuers came to the place where the broken rail was taken up, they abandoned their engine, and ran on foot till they met the freight train and turned it back after us. * * We adopted every expedient we could think of to delay pursuit; but as we were cutting the wire near Calhoun they came in sight of us. * * We instantly put our engine to full speed, and in a moment the wheels were striking fire from the rails in their rapid revolutions. The car in which we rode, rocked furiously and threw us from one side to the other like peas rattled in a gourd. I then proposed to Andrews to let our engineer take the engine out of sight while we hid in a curve after putting a cross-tie on the track; when they checked to remove the obstructions, we could rush on them, shoot every person on the engine, reverse it and let it drive backward at will."

The article in the *Southern Confederacy*, says of the fugitive Federals:

"They had on the engine a red handkerchief, indicating that the regular passenger train would be along presently. They stopped at Adairsville and said that Fuller, with the regular passenger train was behind, and would wait at Kingston for the freight train, and told the conductor to push ahead and meet him at that point. (This was done to produce a collision with Capt Fuller's train.) * * When the morning freight reached Big Shanty, Lieut. Cols. R. F. Maddox and C. D. Phillips took the engine, and with fifty picked men followed on as rapidly as possible. (Capt. Fuller, on his return, met them at Tunnel Hill and turned them back.) Peter Bracken, the engineer on the down freight train, ran his engine 50½ miles—two of them backing the whole freight train up to Adairsville—made twelve stops, coupled the two cars dropped by the fugitives, and switched them off on sidings, in one hour and five minutes." (Captain Fuller fully corroborates the invaluable services rendered by the veteran Bracken.)

Judge Hall, of Georgia, remarked that "in the daring of its conception, it had the wildness of a romance; while in the gigantic and overwhelming results it sought and was likely to accomplish, it was absolutely sublime."

In his evidence at the trial, Pittenger stated that during the chase, Andrews' men came near open mutiny. They proposed to stop the engine in a short curve,

AMBUSCADE AND KILL FULLER

and his men as they came up, but Andrews would not agree to it. Capt. Fuller was not aware of this danger; but he pressed his pursuit so hotly that they had little time to take on wood and water. When the "General" gave out, the fugitives were burning oil cans, the tool box and planks ripped off the freight car. As they abandoned the engine they reversed her in order to bring on a collision with Capt. Fuller's engine, but in their excitement they left the brake on the tender, and the steam had not sufficient

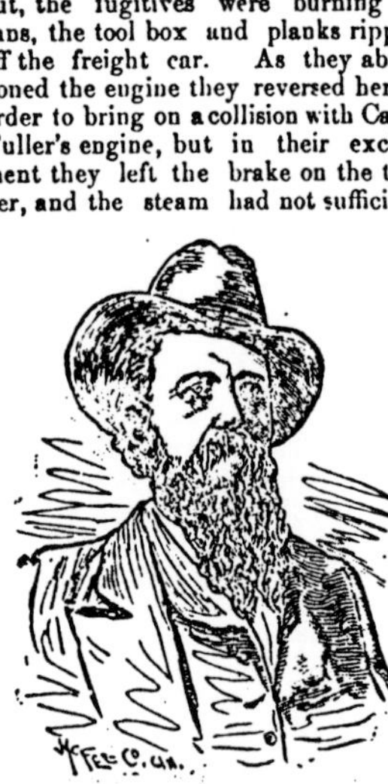

CONDUCTOR W. A. FULLER.

force to back the engine.

There were twenty-two men engaged in the enterprise; twenty of them were from Ohio and two from Kentucky.

They were to receive $60,000 in the event of success. For the brilliancy of the effort they should have been paid anyhow, even in addition to the gold medals subsequently voted them by Congress.

Of the *dramatis personæ* of the pursuers, Capt. Fuller and Mr. Murphy, are citizens of Atlanta, Ga., Jeff Cain, the engineer, is still in the service of the Western & Atlantic Railroad, running the switch engine at Cartersville. Mr. Bracken is running a saw mill in south Georgia, and Mr. Fleming Cox is running a locomotive south of Macon.

The engines have been long in service since the chase. The "General" is now on the road pulling one of the accommodation trains. The "Texas" is also on the road pulling a freight train. For some unknown reason the present master machinist's predecessor changed her name to the "Cincinnati," and under this name she runs. It ought to be changed back to that under which she became known to fame by overhauling the "General."

The "Yonah" was dismantled and used as a stationary engine in the Atlanta shops.

The "General."

Apropos of the illustrated article in this paper, headed *The Capture of a Locomotive*, we reproduce the following article, which appeared in the KENNESAW GAZETTE of March, 1886, and shows that the old "General" has had an eventful life:

THE "GENERAL."

This famous locomotive is still on the Western & Atlantic Railroad pulling a train. She is one of the "old issue;" but is retained in service, although her capacity is rather limited when compared with the big "ten-wheelers" and other more modern locomotives which the ever wide-awake Western & Atlantic Railroad company now possess.

It is a matter of national knowledge that the "General" was captured by 22 Federal soldiers, in disguise, April 12, 1862, at Big Shanty, and the attempt was made by them to escape with her and burn the bridges on the W. & A. R. R., etc. Their chase from Big Shanty to a point near Ringgold and the capture of the entire party, are well known facts.

It is not known, however, that the "General" was almost under fire of the Federal batteries at the great battle of Kennesaw Mountain, June 27, 1864. When the battle began during the early morning General Johnston sent up a train load of ammunition, etc., to the Confederate lines at the east base of Kennesaw Mountain. The ammunition, etc., was unloaded and carried to the front as quickly as possible, but the engine and train were detained at that point, by order of General Johnston, to carry back the wounded at the close of the battle. During the entire morning the "General" and her train stood at the point where is now the station, Elizabeth, and some of the Federal bombshells, flying over the Confederate entrenchments, exploded almost in her neighborhood. In the afternoon the wounded soldiers from Featherston's division and others in that portion of the field were placed aboard the train, and the "General" brought them down to Marietta and thence on to Atlanta.

The "General" was also the last W. & A. R. R. engine to leave Atlanta when Hood's army evacuated it, and it was thought just before she left that it would be impossible to take her away, but they managed to get her safely out, and she went southward with a train load of refugees, war material, etc.

The W. & A. R. R. runs sixteen passenger trains daily.

The Western & Atlantic Railroad.

No railroad in the United States has as much historic interest as this. Almost every mile of it, from Chattanooga to Atlanta, from the Mountain City on the north to the Queen City on the south, is replete with associations connected with the civil war, and especially with Sherman's "Atlanta campaign." Setting out from the foot of Lookout mountain the traveler is whirled past

MISSIONARY RIDGE,

ever to be associated with the names of Grant, Sherman, Sheridan, McPherson, Hooker, and others, on to Chickamauga—"river of death." By this prophetic name did not the Indians unwittingly foreshadow the terrible slaughter along the banks of this stream on those three memorable days in September, 1863? Graysville recalls two battles of lesser note.

Passing

RINGGOLD

we pass through the deep cut where Gen. Cleburne bravely stayed Hooker's victorious progress November 27, 1863, and look up the steep sides of the ridge, down which the Confederates rolled huge rocks that inflicted great loss upon their assailants and threw them into confusion.

We look out at

TUNNEL HILL

to see two battle grounds, one on either side of the track, and passing through the tunnel and then along the foot of Rocky Face mountain to Mill Creek gap, we fly through the gorge which Gen. Sherman found impassible.

DALTON

also has its battle record, while a few miles to the southwest are Snake Creek gap and Dug gap, which played such an important part in that skillful flank movement of Sherman's, which compelled Johnston to fall back from Mill Creek gap, evacuate Dalton and retire to Resaca. Westward from the road, just north from this latter point, we see the ridge, on the western slope of which Johnston so skillfully disposed his forces during that four-days' battle, and the loss of nearly 1,800 men failed to dislodge them, but from which the Confederate General wisely withdrew, when again he was likely to be flanked and cut off from his base of supplies by Sherman's movement, across the Oostanaula at Lay's ferry.

CASS STATION

reminds one of the artillery duel between the two armies on May 24, 1864, at Cassville, a few miles north of the station.

And here is

ALLATOONA

and its pass, from which, also, Sherman compelled Johnston to fall back and which he afterwards fortified and made his base of supplies. This, also, was the scene of that struggle which occasioned that communication by signal "through the sky" and over the heads of the enemy from the top of Kennesaw Mountain, that suggested that stirring religious hymn, "Hold the Fort."

BIG SHANTY

is a little place, but is memorable as the station at which the locomotive, known as the "General," was boldly captured by a few Federal soldiers with the intention of burning the bridges on the Western & Atlantic Road, which was then in possession of the Confederates and the right arm of their strength.

And now behold

KENNESAW MOUNTAIN,

that looked down upon the most protracted and bloody struggle in all this campaign. There it is in advance of us, and now at our right, towering up 700 feet above the surrounding region, a mighty and indestructible monument to the soldiers who gave their lives for their country on its declivities and are buried in the cemetery at Marietta, only a short distance from its foot.

On we go and soon cross the historic

CHATTAHOOCHEE,

and the plains beyond, which were so long the home of war and bloodshed, and at last enter Atlanta, not unworthily called the Queen City of the south—the city so thoroughly destroyed twenty-five years ago and now so thoroughly and beautifully rebuilt.

It will please you to know that among the newest and finest of these buildings is that of the Atlanta Y. M. C. A. This is the headquarters of another army also composed of young men who are engaged in another Atlanta campaign. They would take that city for Christ as you would fain take Peoria, and both them and you may be well inspired for that better conflict by the examples of courage, fortitude and endurance set by those who fought for their country.
—*The Transcript, Peoria, Ill.*

The Medal of Honor

Today, people think of the Medal of Honor as an award given for action involving actual conflict with an enemy, distinguished by gallantry and bravery at the risk of life above and beyond the call of duty; and in recent times a great number of awards were made posthumously. This is not the way it was in the beginning, during the Civil War.

The correct name is the Medal of Honor and not the Congressional Medal of Honor. While the Medal, like so many other things in life today, is given by authority of the United States Congress, the proper name is the MEDAL OF HONOR.

The Medal dates back to the early days of the Civil War when it soon became evident that a lot of effort would be required in the areas of training, direction, and inspiring example in order to produce armies equal to the task ahead. Inspiring example was thought to be one of the most important of these three and that it provided the best way to lead the peculiar breed of men raised in the early days of our nation. Union Secretary of the Navy Gideon Welles, perhaps more clearly than others, recognized that when all other forms of a government's defenses are down, its survival rests with the bravery of the men who wear their country's uniform. Welles thought that a medal might be helpful in inspiring men of the Navy to the heights of John Paul Jones and Commodore Perry. This would allow a valorous individual to be recognized for his heroism without being put in the uncomfortable position of boasting of his exploits. About the same time, Lt. Col. (later Maj. Gen.) Edward D. Townsend, Assistant Adjutant General of the Union Army, had the same thoughts and felt that the Army, too, needed a medal for the recognition of gallantry and bravery.

The Navy beat the Army in the race for a medal. On Dec. 8, 1861, Senator James W. Grimes of Iowa, introduced a bill in the Senate to further promote the efficiency of the Navy. Included was a provision for the issuance of a medal of honor. This bill was passed and signed into law Dec. 21, 1861. The pertinent language was: "The Secretary of the Navy, be, and is hereby, authorized to cause 200 medals of honor to be prepared with suitable emblematic devices, which shall be bestowed upon such petty officers, seamen, landsmen, and marines, as shall most distinguish themselves by their gallantry in action and other seamanlike qualities during the present war." Seven months later additional legislation provided that the Navy's medal was to be awarded to those "distinguishing themselves in battle or by extraordinary heroism in the line of their profession." In this way the award was extended beyond the Civil War and noncombat heroism in the line of their profession was clarified. Commissioned officers were excluded—their heroism apparently being assumed. It was not until 1915 that Congress enacted legislation authorizing the award of the Navy Medal of Honor to commissioned officers.

On July 12, 1862, a bill was signed into law which created the Army's Medal of Honor. This bill provided that the president could present medals of honor "to such noncommissioned officers, and privates as shall most distinguish themselves by their gallantry in action and other soldier-like qualities, during the present insurrection." On March 3, 1863, the Army altered its legislation to provide medals to those who "most distinguish themselves, or may hereafter, most distinguish themselves, in action." No noncombat awards would be allowed, officers would become eligible, and the award would extend beyond the Civil War.

The Civil War's Medal of Honor was designed by William Wilson & Son Company of Philadelphia, a silversmith firm located there. They submitted a design to Secretary Welles through James Pollock, Director of the U.S. Mint. Welles approved the design, and when the Army's medal was authorized, Secretary of War Edwin M. Stanton accepted Pollock's suggestion that the Army adopt the same basic design, altering only the suspension devices. Pollock described the piece this way: "A five pointed star, one point down. On the obverse the foul spirit of Secession and Rebellion is represented by a male figure in crouching attitude holding in his hands, serpents, which with forked tongues are striking at a large female figure, representing the Union or Genius of our country, who holds in her right hand a shield, and in her left, the fasces. Around these figures, are thirty-four stars, indicating the number of states in the Union." The reverse of the medal was left blank, allowing for engraving of the recipient's name, unit, date and place of the cited action.

Both medals would be suspended with a ribbon consisting of a blue horizontal top bar with alternating vertical stripes of red and white—seven red and six white, as on the U.S. Flag. The Navy's medal would connect to the ribbon with a rope-fouled anchor, while the Army's design consisted of an eagle, wings spread, astride crossed cannons and cannonball stacks.

Both services possessed the medals by early March 1863; all they had to do was find recipients worthy of the decoration.

Despite the fact the Navy medal came first, the Army made the first awards.

In April 1862, James J. Andrews, a civilian scout for the Union Army led a band of 20 enlisted men and one other civilian from various Ohio regiments deep into Confederate territory. There were two other enlisted men who started with the group but who did not get into Georgia with the remainder. Their plan was to board a train headed north out of Atlanta for Chattanooga, capture the train and continue steaming north, stopping frequently to cut telegraph lines and burn bridges, thereby disrupting Confederate lines of communication and aiding the Union Army's drive on Chattanooga.

Unfortunately, the plan went awry, and all the men were captured. Eight, including their civilian leader, were executed in June 1862, in Atlanta. Eight more escaped from jail in Atlanta in October of that year. Then on March 17, 1863, nearly a year after their adventure began, the remaining six raiders were exchanged via City Point, Va. When they arrived in Washington on March 25, 1863, Secretary Stanton sent word that he would like to see them. He was particularly impressed by Jacob Parrott, at age 19, the youngest of the group. Parrott calmly recited the major details of the raid, then related the story of the brutal beatings he had suffered at the hands of his captors. After listening to their hair-raising tale, Stanton praised Parrott's devotion to duty, then turning to an aide, selected a black morocco leather case. "Congress has by a recent law, ordered medals to be prepared on this model and your party shall have the first; they are the first that have been given to private soldiers in this War," he said as he pinned the medal to the left breast of Parrott's uniform. The remaining five men were also presented medals as of March 25, 1863.

Eventually 19 of these men were awarded the Medal of Honor. The official citation for their award is: "Nineteen of twenty-two men (including two civilians) who, by direction of General Mitchell (or Buell), penetrated nearly 200 miles south into the enemy's territory and captured a railroad train at Big Shanty, Ga., in an attempt to destroy the bridges and track between Chattanooga and Atlanta."

To illustrate how disorganized and routine the system for awarding the Medal of Honor was in the beginning, one can look at the awards to these 19 men. Six got them on March 25, 1863. Eight more medals were awarded in September 1863, but only one of these is recorded on a specific date—September 17th. Two were awarded in July 1864, one of them to Pvt. James Smith after his father had requested of Secretary Stanton that the same be done. One more was awarded on Aug. 4, 1866, and the last one on July 28, 1883. One also wonders why it was not known whether it was General Mitchel or General Buell who sent the Raiders out and also why it was not known in Washington how to correctly spell General Ormsby McKnight Mitchel's name—with one "l" rather than two. Since eight men were executed in Atlanta in 1862, one might assume that all the military men of that group got the Medal of Honor. Not so; two of them—Perry G. Shadrach and George D. Wilson never were awarded the Medal. James Smith, who did not participate in the raid but who tried and later was imprisoned for some time as a result, was awarded the Medal of Honor after his father requested that he be placed on the same footing as those who had been so recognized. As an example of how well-appreciated and regarded the Medal was, this letter was written by James Smith after he had received the Medal:

Parkersburg, Oct. 15th/64
Sir: I was made happy yesterday by the receipt of the medal which the secretary of war was pleased to award to me for services rendered and which I hope to wear long and honorably.

I am doubly happy to have received this mark of distinguished appreciation during the administration of that gentleman, scholar and patriot A. Lincoln: long may he wave.

Very Respectfully
Your Obt. Servt.
James Smith.
E.D. Townsend, Asst. Adjt. Genl.
Washington, D.C.

James Smith had enlisted under an assumed name in the 2d Ohio Inf. in 1861 at the age of 16.

He later got into Georgia with the 2d Ohio throughout the Atlanta Campaign. He died on Jan. 28, 1868, at the age of 23.

There have been few awards of the Medal of Honor, perhaps none, that attracted so much attention over the years as those awarded to the Andrews Raiders.

The first sailor to earn the Medal of Honor was "captain of the maintop" John Williams of the *USS Pawnee.* During the attack on Mathias Point, Va., on June 26, 1861, Williams, although severely wounded in the thigh by a musket ball, retained command of his assault boat. When the flagstaff was shot away, he held the stump of it that secured the flag in his hand and rallied his men. That qualified as his medal-winning deed.

Corp. John Mackie was the first U.S. Marine to earn the nation's highest award. While aboard the *USS Galena* in the attack on Fort Darling on the James River in Virginia on May 15, 1862, Mackie ignored the heavy volume of enemy fire raining down on his ship and maintained his musket fire against the rifle pits on the shore. Later, when ordered to fill vacancies at guns caused by casualties, he manned the weapons with skill and courage, and brought the attention to himself that secured the award for him.

Among those first individual awards of the Medal of Honor, the deed of Sailor Williams spoke most clearly of the significance the flag held for the men of the Civil War. To both sides it was more than a piece of cloth. It symbolized their beliefs and the cause for which they shed their blood. Because of this, and the fact that flags were used as reference and rallying points during a battle, the desire to keep the flag flying and well-protected provided a source of inspiration to the soldiers. Also because of this, the capture of a unit's standard was a tremendous embarrassment and affront to the unit involved. For the man who seized the flag, the act spoke most highly of his heroism in capturing the trophy. Subsequently, many of the Medals of Honor earned by soldiers involved flags. Citation after citation reads: "capture of enemy flag," or "recapture of regiment's colors," or "planting national colors on the enemy's works," or "gallantry as a color bearer."

Not all recipients of the Medal of Honor were men, at least not in age. Many of these distinguished heroes were in their teens, and at least one was only 12 years old.

The first Medal of Honor awarded after the original presentation ceremony for the Andrews Raiders in March 1863, went to Musician Willie Johnston, Company D, 3rd Vermont Infantry. Willie was born in 1850. When his father enlisted in December 1861, young Willie begged to go with him. The commanding officer agreed to let Willie join up, and he was enlisted as a drummer boy on Dec. 11, 1861.

Willie's first fight was at Lee's Mills, Virginia, on April 16, 1862. During his next campaign, the Seven Days fighting and the Peninsula Campaign from June 25 to July 1, 1862, Willie was cited for the Medal of Honor. It was during the disastrous retreat from that campaign, when strong men threw away all their equipment so they would have less weight to carry, that young Willie Johnston retained his drum and brought it safely to Harrison's Landing. There, he had the honor of drumming for the division parade, he being the only drummer to bring his instrument off the battlefields.

Young Johnston's division commander noted these facts and included them in his report. Somehow, President Lincoln heard the story and wrote Secretary Stanton suggesting the youth be given a medal. Stanton agreed, and Willie Johnston was presented his Medal of Honor Sept. 16, 1863, at the age of 13, for a deed performed when he was but 12 years of age.

The Army had no monopoly on youthful heroes. Two of the youngest recipients of the Navy Medal of Honor were Cabin Boy John Angling of the *USS Pontoosuc* and Second Class Boy Oscar Peck of the *USS Varuna.* Both were 14 years old when they earned their decorations.

Entire regiments fought through terrible battles time after time, with none of their members being recognized by the awarding of this high honor. Considering that, it would seem impossible for any man to be so brave as to earn two Medals of Honor, but it happened, not just once but three times during the Civil War.

The sole Army recipient to have this distinction bears a name familiar to nearly every American, but this man's heroism was almost completely overshadowed by his brother's flamboyance. Second Lt. Thomas W. Custer, Company B, 6th Michigan Cavalry, earned his first Medal of Honor on May 10, 1863, at Namozine Church, Va., when he captured an enemy flag. He was 18 at the time.

Two years later, on April 6, 1865, young Custer leaped his horse over the enemy's line of works and fearlessly dashed up to the Confederate color guard.

When close to the colorbearer, Custer took a shot in the face which nearly knocked him off his horse, but he remained upright in the saddle and fired at the Confederate holding the flag, hitting him and causing him to reel. Frenzied, Custer reached out and clutched the flag, then spurred his horse and dashed back to Union lines, his trophy held high.

Riding up to his brother Brevet Maj. Gen. George A. Custer, the lieutenant told him, "The Rebels shot me, but I have their flag." He turned to return to the fight, but the general, realizing the severity of Tom's wounds, ordered him to the rear. His brother refused, so the young major general placed him under arrest and had him escorted to the aid station.

Lt. Custer recovered from those wounds and proudly wore his two Medals of Honor, much to his brother's chagrin. Tom would die at the general's side at the Little Big Horn Battle in 1876.

Another two-time medal winner Coxswain John Cooper earned his first Medal of Honor during the Battle of Mobile Bay on Aug. 5, 1864. Aboard the *USS Brooklyn* he worked his gun with skill and courage throughout the savage battle and was cited for his heroic conduct. Then again at Mobile, on April 16, 1865, Cooper was detailed as quartermaster on the staff of Rear Admiral Thatcher. On that day there was a tremendous fire in Mobile, and, at the risk of being blown apart by exploding ammunition, Cooper advanced through the holocaust and rescued a young comrade from almost certain death. That compassionate act brought him the rare second award.

Boatswain's Mate Patrick Mullen also received his two Medals of Honor for combat and noncombat deeds. While serving aboard the *USS Don,* Mullen led a boat expedition up the Maddow Creek in Virginia. Attacked by Confederate forces, Mullen lay on his back under the gunwales of his boat and worked his artillery piece from that position. Despite his awkward posture, his fire was so accurate that many Confederates were killed or wounded and forced to retreat from the fight. That bit of tenacity brought him his first ribbon and five-pointed star. Then on May 1, 1865, he rescued an officer of the *Don* from drowning and received not only another Medal of Honor, but the lifelong gratitude of the officer involved.

Several other Civil War awards are worth mentioning. The only instance in history of two brothers being awarded the Medal of Honor occurred at the Battle of Five Forks, Va., April 1, 1865, when Pvts. Allen and James Thompson, Company K, 4th New York Heavy Artillery, were cited for a hazardous reconnaissance in front of their line. Arthur and Douglas McArthur represent a father-son award, again the only example. Lt. Arthur McArthur, at the age of 18 and a 1st Lt. and Adjutant of the 24th Wisconsin Regiment, won the Medal of Honor at the Battle of Missionary Ridge on Nov. 25, 1863. A year later, at 19, he was promoted to the rank of Colonel and the command of the 24th Wisconsin, the youngest officer to hold that rank in the Union Army. His son Gen. Douglas McArthur was awarded the Medal of Honor for his leadership, gallantry, heroic conduct and utter disregard of personal danger, inspiring his troops and galvanizing the spirit of resistance of the Filipino people during the Battle of Bataan in the Philippines at the beginning of World War II.

The only woman to receive the Medal of Honor was Dr. Mary Edwards Walker, a graduate of Syracuse Medical College and one of the first women physicians in this country. She was an ardent advocate of women's rights, and she often delivered lectures on the subject. She also preferred men's attire to dresses and skirts at a time when this was not quite acceptable. At the outbreak of the Civil War, Dr. Walker, then 29 years of age, applied for a commission as a Union Army Surgeon. She was turned down because of her sex. She served as a volunteer surgeon for two years in the Virginia Campaigns and then at Chattanooga and Chickamauga. Finally, George H. Thomas appointed her to replace an assistant surgeon of the 52d Ohio Infantry Regiment. A month later she was captured and sent to a Confederate prison in Richmond. After four months there, she was exchanged for a Confederate officer. This pleased her no end as she was swapped as man for man. She then served as a contract surgeon with the Union forces but saw no more combat duty. After the war, she lobbied for a rank of major. After several angry letters from Dr. Walker, President Johnson asked Secretary Stanton if there was some way to recognize her service. Stanton ordered a Medal of Honor for her, and it was awarded in January 1866. She wore it every day for the rest of her life. In 1916, the Army Review Board rescinded Dr. Walker's Medal of Honor because "her service did not appear to have been distinguished in action or otherwise." She continued to wear her medal, though then illegally, until her death Feb. 21, 1919, at the age of 86. In 1978 President Carter restored Dr. Walker's Medal of Honor.

A good example of an improper award of the Medal of Honor on a wholesale basis occurred when the medal was issued to members of the 27th Maine Infantry Regiment. The 27th Maine was a nine-months regiment, organized at Portland on Sept. 30, 1862. Almost its entire service was garrison duty in the defense of Washington City. On June 26, 1863, with only four days of their enlistment left, the members of the regiment were ordered to leave their position and prepare to be mustered out of the service. This was at the same time that General Lee was leaving Virginia for the North and the Battle of Gettysburg. All of the Union forces that could be spared were sent to General Meade, and this left the defense of Washington rather bare. President Lincoln and Secretary of War Stanton appealed to the 25th and the 27th Maine to extend their service to see the capital through the emergency. The men of the 25th refused and walked off to a man. The 27th, after an appeal by their commander Col. Mark Wentworth, did a little better. About 300 stepped forward and volunteered to remain. Stanton was overjoyed, and on June 29 directed that every man who had volunteered to remain be issued the Medal of Honor. The wording of his order was such that it could apply to anyone who volunteered to defend the capital after their service had expired. Only four days of service were performed by the 27th Maine, and the unit played no roll in the Battle of Gettysburg. The echoes of Stanton's order or promise, however, could be heard from Washington to Maine. No accurate listing of the volunteers had been made, and due to a bureaucratic mix-up an order was issued resulting in all 864 men of the 27th Maine being entitled to get the Medal of Honor. By then the men had all returned to civilian life, so the Medals were sent to the Governor of Maine in January 1865 for distribution. The Governor called on Colonel Wentworth for help. Wentworth had continued to serve with another Maine regiment and fought through some heavy battles with General Grant to the end of the war. He knew what heroism was all about and knew not one member of his new regiment earned the Medal of Honor. One can imagine how he felt about the men of the 27th Maine. He decided that he would try and follow Stanton's intent and give the medals only to those who had volunteered to remain. He stored the remaining medals, some 560, in his barn. Later this word got to some who had not been issued the medal, and they broke into the barn and took many of the medals. Later, after

Wentworth's death, those remaining disappeared entirely.

Finally, in 1916, as a result of a provision in the National Defense Act of June 3, 1916, the Secretary of the Army was directed to appoint a board of five retired Army generals "for the purpose of investigating and reporting upon past awards or issue of the so-called Congressional Medal of Honor by or through the War Department; this with a view to ascertain what Medals of Honor, if any, had been awarded or issued for any cause other than distinguished conduct by an officer or enlisted man in action involving actual conflict with an enemy." The medals given to the Andrews Raiders survived this review. Those given to the members of the 27th Maine did not, however, every one being revoked. This board was headed by Lt. Gen. Nelson Miles, himself a Civil War Medal of Honor recipient and later commander of the United States Army with more than 42 years of active service, including campaigns against the Indians in the West following the Civil War and in the Spanish-American War. This board rescinded the awards of 911 Medals of Honor. Stricken were the 27th Maine, the 29 officers and men who had accompanied the remains of President Lincoln from Washinton to Springfield, Ill., in April 1865, Dr. Mary Edwards Walker and another very colorful hero of the Indian Wars, William F. "Wild Bill" Cody. Cody, like James J. Andrew, had been a civilian guide or scout and thus was not eligible for the award. The most ridiculous award that was rescinded was one that had been issued to a Lt. Colonel Gardiner in 1872 by Secretary of War Belknap upon Gardiner's application. Gardiner wrote, "I understand there are a number of bronze medals for distribution to soldiers of the late War, and request I be allowed one as a souvenir of memorable times past."

With this action in 1916, the total awarded for the Civil War came to 1,520 of which 1,196 were Army, 307 Navy and 17 Marines.

Then came the Indian Campaigns during the latter part of the 19th century and during this period the Army made 423 awards of the Medal of Honor.

Next came the expansion period which included the Spanish-American War, the Boxer Rebellion, the entry into Korea, the Philippines, etc. During this period, a total of 342 awards were made which included 104 for the Army, 153 for the Navy and 85 for the Marines.

One of the great ironies of the so-called era of

American Expansion from 1871 to 1933 is that its most enduring figure was recommended for a Medal of Honor but was denied the award. This man was Theodore Roosevelt – Rough Rider, Governor of New York, and President of the United States. After the Rough Riders' charge up San Juan Hill on July 1, 1898, Lt. Colonel Roosevelt came home a hero, and he was recommended for the Medal of Honor. In the fall of 1898, the War Decorations Board rejected the award for lack of eyewitness statements vouching for Roosevelt's actions. By then he was Governor of New York, and he wrote his friend Sen. Henry Cabot Lodge of Massachusetts to intervene for him. Lodge reported that the War Department had offered a retroactive brevet promotion rather than the Medal of Honor. This did not satisfy Roosevelt, and he went for more help. With this effort, the Secretary of War Russell A. Alger became angry at all the pressure and refused to approve the award of the Medal. He even had the nerve to announce that Roosevelt would not receive the Medal of Honor at a formal White House dinner attended by both Roosevelt and Lodge. Roosevelt then gave up on his quest for "that infernal Medal of Honor."

While he did not get his medal, Roosevelt did a lot for the Medal of Honor. During his presidency, the standards for the award were raised, and a new design approved and patented for the first time. Roosevelt directed that henceforth the Medal be awarded "with formal and impressive ceremonial by the president, if possible."

Theodore Roosevelt did not get the Medal of Honor, but his name is on the rolls since his son Brig. Gen. Theodore Roosevelt Jr. was awarded the medal posthumously for courage and leadership in the 1944 D-Day Landings in France during World War II.

The original Civil War design of the Medal of Honor lasted until 1896 when the Army made a minor change in the ribbon from which the Medal was suspended. In 1904 a major change was made in the Army Medal of Honor, and this change was brought on by the many imitations being made and issued by various veterans groups such as the Grand Army of the Republic. The new design retained the five-pointed star with a profile of Minerva in the center, surrounded by a green enameled laurel wreath suspended from a bar with the word "Valor" inscribed and the Army eagle resting above. The Navy has made very minor changes over the years, and today the Navy Medal of Honor is about the same as it was in the beginning. In 1919, the Navy did create a new medal for actual combat only, and this was often referred to as the Tiffany Cross. Only a handful were awarded by the Navy, and it was eliminated by Congress in 1942. During World War II, another change was made for both medals where they were attached to a ribbon that is draped around the neck.

The Unification Act of 1947, which created the National Military establishment, made the U.S. Air Force a separate and equal service. It also created the National Security Council and gave official life to the Central Intelligence Agency. While the Air Force became independent in 1947, an Air Force Medal of Honor was not created until 1963. The Air Force awards during the Vietnam conflict are the only awards of the Air Force Medal of Honor. Those awarded during the Korean War were Army Medals of Honor.

Relatively few Medals of Honor were awarded for service in World War I. A total of 123 of which 95 were Army, 21 Navy and 7 Marines. Perhaps the most famous of these was to the Tennessee Mountain boy Alvin C. York.

World War II included 433 awards of the Medal of Honor with 294 by the Army, 57 by the Navy, 81 by the Marines and one by the Coast Guard. In the long history of the Medal, only one member of the Coast Guard had been awarded the Medal of Honor. Douglas A. Munro, Signalman First Class, was serving with the Navy on Sept. 27, 1942, and in charge of a group of Higgins boats attempting to evacuate a battalion of Marines from the Point Cruz area of Guadalcanal. While Munro lost his life, his actions with his buddies resulted in the safe evacuation of some 500 Marines.

There were some peacetime awards of the Medal of Honor that should be mentioned. These are different from the 180 noncombat awards of the Navy Medal of Honor which practice was ended in 1942. Nine awards have been made to Unknown Soldiers of the several wars, the last being done by President Reagan in 1984 when the Unknown Soldier of the Vietnam War was so honored. Special legislation resulted in awards to Adm. Richard E. Byrd and his machinist Floyd Bennett for the Arctic explorations; Col. Charles A. Lindbergh for his heroic flight across the Atlantic; Maj. Gen. Adolphus W. Greely whose name is probably forgotten by most Americans, whose citation referred to his lifetime of service to our Nation; and lastly, Col. Billy Mitchell, an early advocate of Air Power, who was awarded a Medal of Honor the design of which does not resemble the Medal of Honor but whose name is included in the Official Congressional compilations.

The Korean War accounts for 131 Medals of Honor—Army 78, Air Force 14, Navy 7 and Marines 42.

Vietnam included 238 awards—Army 155, Air Force 12, Navy 14 and Marines 57.

From the Civil War through the Vietnam conflict 3,394 awards have been made. This represents 3,394 heroes out of more than 38 million men and women who have served in the Armed Forces of the United States during that period, a very elite and small group who answered the call to duty and then served above and beyond.

LEGION OF VALOR

The Legion of Valor is an association of those whose valor has been recognized by the award of the nation's two highest decorations—the Medal of Honor of the Army, Navy or Air Force; and the Army Distinguished Service Cross, Navy Cross or Air Force Cross.

Organized on April 23, 1890, the association is the nation's service veterans organization. It was chartered by public law 224, an Act of Congress, and approved by the President on August 4, 1955.

Its national museum is located in the Fresno Veterans Memorial Auditorium at 2425 Fresno Street, Fresno, Calif.

The principals of the Legion of Valor are: Patriotic allegiance to the United States of America, fidelity to its constitution and laws, the security of civil liberty and the perpetuation of free institutions.

National Medal of Honor Museum of Military History

The museum was established in 1990 and is dedicated to preserving the history of events and heroes of every uniformed service from the Revolutionary War to the present.

It is located at 400 Georgia Avenue, Chattanooga, Tennessee.

MEDAL OF HONOR MUSEUM PATRIOTS POINT MARITIME MUSEUM MOUNT PLEASANT, SOUTH CAROLINA

The new Medal of Honor Museum is located on the hangar deck of the *USS Yorktown* near the main entrance of the ship and features displays representing the eight eras for which the medal has been awarded. Exhibits also include several Medals of Honor, artifacts and memorabilia related to recipients, original paintings by Patriots Point Artist in Residence, David A. Clark, original black and white renderings by the late Joe Cason, and citations describing the actions for which the coveted medals were awarded. In addition to numerous paper items related to recipients, artifacts of interest include an ashtray from the sunken submarine *Squalus* (SS-192) from which 33 of 59 crewmembers were rescued in 1939 thanks to the heroic actions of several Medal of Honor recipients, uniforms, weapons, a bible and other personal items carried in combat by recipients.

The Medal of Honor Society maintains their national office in a suite immediately beside the exhibit, and assists with solicitation of memorabilia for the exhibit. Design for the interior of the exhibit and the financing for its construction was provided by Patriots Point. The exhibits serve to educate visitors of the contributions and sacrifices made in defense of the United States and consequent "above and beyond" individual awards. The eight display consoles along the interior curved wall represent the Civil War, Indian Campaigns, Wars of American Expansion, Peacetime, World War I, World War II, Korea and Vietnam. Each console displays photographs and engraved citations for selected recipients.

At the top of each console, the number of recipients for each war or era is noted. Of the total 3,399 recipients (as of October 1993: two awards have since been made for Somalia and seven black soldiers who served in World War II were added 13 January 1997, plus others are under review), the Civil War ranks highest with 1,520. Only 123 were added during World War I. The total number of medals awarded to date is 3,418 as 19 recipients received the medal twice. Names of the recipients are listed by war or era both inside the exhibit and on exterior panels. Landside, the Medal of Honor Society has assisted youth groups with tree plantings in honor of recipients.

FRONT AND BACK VIEWS OF THE JEWELER'S MODEL OF THE FIRST MEDAL
OF HONOR WHICH WAS PRESENTED TO PRIVATE JACOB PARROTT.

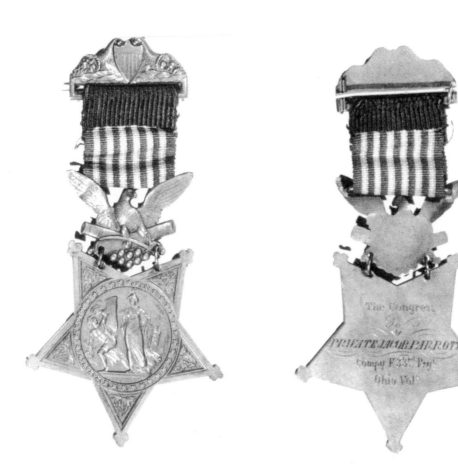

PRESENT-DAY MEDALS OF HONOR

NAVY   AIR FORCE   ARMY

The Raiders Go To Hollywood

Two major movies have been made depicting the raid to some degree—Buster Keaton's *The General* and Walt Disney's *The Great Locomotive Chase*.

A silent one-reeler entitled *The Railroad Raiders of '62* was released in 1911 by Kalem Studios. It had no historical ties to the real event but followed a story line similar to the 1862 raid. A federal soldier, dressed as a woman, stands on the track and flags down a train. A chase ensues between the captured train and the Confederates on another engine. When the captured train runs out of fuel, the captors flee but are hunted down and captured or shot.

Kalem Studios re-released the film in 1915 with five extra minutes added and it became part of the "Hazards of Helen" series.

Buster Keaton in *The General*

As the movies matured from their infant storytelling days of the turn of the century, producers began to find formulas that were successful. One of the most popular was the comedy, an extension of the vaudevillian style of entertainment that produced so many of the screen's great comedians. Comedies dominated the film world throughout the silent days with names such as Chaplin, Laurel, Langdon, Roach, Sennett, and Arbuckle.

From this group of comedian/filmmakers came a young man named Buster Keaton. Buster grew up in show business and performed with his parents in their vaudeville act when he was only three years old. In their skits, Buster performed many acrobatic stunts so that he was able to learn to use his body with agility and grace. At one time during his young career, his father used Buster as a human mop and literally mopped the stage with him.

Buster traveled to Hollywood in 1916 and struck up an acquaintance with Roscoe "Fatty" Arbuckle, in whose films he soon began working. By 1920, he wanted to branch out on his own and he became a

IN A POSED GAG SHOT, BUSTER APPEARS TO BE LISTENING FOR THE DISTANT BOOMING OF CANNON. THE MORTAR SEQUENCE BECAME ONE OF THE FILM'S FUNNIEST MOMENTS AS JOHNNIE ATTEMPTS TO AIM AND FIRE THE WEAPON AT THE FLEEING UNION SPIES, BUT NOT BEFORE HE, TOO, FINDS HIMSELF AT THE MERCY OF THE SELF-THINKING MORTAR.

very successful director as well as a star of his own comedy shorts. He developed a character in his films that was a very determined individual, never overwhelmed by the situations he got himself into, no matter how exotic they were. He became well-known for his hair-raising stunts, which often employed the use of such mechanical devices as boats, automobiles and locomotives.

Buster's success with short films led him into features. In 1924 he made *The Navigator*, his biggest money-maker. In 1926 he signed a deal with United Artists and began to look around for another story idea. His partner and co-writer, Clyde Bruckman, suggested an idea about filming a picture based on the Andrews' Raid from the Civil War.

The raid was recorded for posterity by one of the survivors, William Pittenger, when he wrote the book *Daring and Suffering: A History of the Great Railway Adventure*. Buster's decision to film this work and turn it into a comedy resulted in what many film historians consider the last of the silent era's great comedies, *The General*.

Buster's first order of business was to change the sympathies of the story. Because the raid was not considered a complete success, Buster felt the ending had to be changed to better suit a comedy. He structured the film around the locomotive's fictional engineer, Johnnie Gray, so that the audience would sympathize with him upon the loss of his locomotive. As Buster went on to explain:

> You can always make villains out of the Northerners,
> but you cannot make a villain out of the South.
> You can't do that with a motion picture audience ...
> The South lost the war anyhow so the audience resents it ...
> When the story ended, the South was winning ...
> All this took place in 1862, and the South lost in 1864.

After assembling a story outline (in the silent days comedians didn't film from scripts, they used outlines and built comedic situations as they were filming), Buster needed a location and Civil War period American-style locomotives. Buster wanted authenticity and arranged with the Nashville, Chattanooga & St. Louis Ry for the loan of the *General* as well as some trackage on a branch line near Cowan, Tenn., and portions of the main line between Atlanta and Chattanooga. Later, when Buster and his staff arrived in Chattanooga to get started on the movie, he indicated during an interview that he was a comedian and the film would be

BALANCED PRECARIOUSLY UPON THE COWCATCHER OF THE *TEXAS*, BUSTER KEATON PREPARES TO FEND OFF DISASTER AS HE CONTINUES PURSUIT OF *THE GENERAL*. IN ANOTHER MEMORABLE SCENE FROM THIS CLASSIC PICTURE, BUSTER IS PREPARING TO THROW THE RAILROAD TIE AND DISLODGE ANOTHER TIE LYING ACROSS THE RAILS. HIS TIMING HAS TO BE PERFECT; IF NOT, THE TIE LYING ACROSS HIS PATH COULD SPELL TROUBLE FOR BOTH HIM AND THE COASTING *TEXAS*.

shot as a comedy. This did not sit well with the Confederate Veterans of the south, and soon the pressure became so intense that the NC&St.L withdrew its permission to use the *General* and Buster went west.

He found what he was looking for outside Cottage Grove, Oregon. It was called the Oregon, Pacific & Eastern Railroad, a small lumber railroad, that had everything he needed: beautiful scenery, weed-covered trackage, covered bridges, rivers, and a very rustic look. In its stable of motive power the OP&E also had two vintage 4-4-0 American-style locomotives, which matched the design of the original Civil War locomotives. Buster was also able to acquire another American locomotive from a nearby lumber railroad. That gave him a total of three for his picture. Since all three were built after the Civil War, the movie crew backdated the locomotives to match those of the period for the story.

A complete train was constructed to go along with the locomotives including passenger cars and box cars. The train was completely functional, too. Every morning the entire film crew would leave the Cottage Grove Hotel and board the train for the hour-long ride out to location, and every evening ride it back.

The movie begins with the Western and Atlantic Flyer, pulled by the *General,* steaming into Marietta, Georgia. It is established at this point that its engineer, Johnnie Gray, has two loves in his life: the *General* and his girl, Annabelle Lee. Upon arrival he goes to pay a call on her and presents her with a photograph of himself, with his locomotive displayed very prominently in the background. During the visit, news comes that the South has fired upon Fort Sumter and immediately Annabelle's father and brother leave for the enlistment office. However, Johnnie isn't interested until he realizes that Annabelle expects him to go and become a soldier. With a gallant flourish, he leaves for the enlistment office.

Upon arrival, Johnnie jumps to the front of the line only to be told that the army can't use him. What he isn't told is that he is more valuable to the South as an engineer. He tries several times to enlist, but is finally kicked out the back door without discovering the reason for his rejection. He slowly walks to the front of the building, where Annabelle's father and brother are waiting to go inside. Not knowing that Johnnie has already attempted to enlist, they urge him to join them in line. Sadly, he shakes his head and walks off. Annabelle, upon learning from them that Johnnie didn't enlist, tells him that she does not want to speak to him again until he is in uniform. Feeling totally rejected, Johnnie goes to his only love, the *General.* In one of the most effective gags in the film, he sits for-

A RAILROAD ENGINEER OF THE 1860s WAS A REVERED MEMBER OF THE COMMUNITY, AND EVERY BOY IN TOWN WANTED TO EMULATE HIM. JOHNNIE GRAY PREPARES TO OIL AND POLISH HIS BELOVED *GENERAL* UNDER THE WATCHFUL EYES OF THIS SMALL INSPECTION COMMITTEE. KEATON ACTUALLY HAD TO LEARN HOW TO OPERATE THESE ANCIENT LOCOMOTIVES, AND HE CONSIDERED THEM A GREAT COMEDY PROP.

BUSTER'S *GENERAL* WAS BUILT IN 1886 AND WAS IN LUMBER HAULING OPERATIONS WHEN HE HIRED IT TO PORTRAY ITS FAMOUS ANCESTOR. CHANGES IN THE LOCOMOTIVE PRIOR TO FILMING INCLUDED THE ADDITION OF THE BIG BOX HEADLIGHT, A BACKDATED WHISTLE, A FALSE PLATE BETWEEN THE DRIVE WHEELS TO HIDE THE MODERN AIR BRAKES, AND THE APPROPRIATE NAME BOARDS.

THE OTHER LOCOMOTIVE STAR OF *THE GENERAL* WAS THE *TEXAS*, HERE RESTING BETWEEN SCENES. PURCHASED AS A BACKUP, THIS PARTICULAR LOCOMOTIVE, BUILT IN 1892, WAS DESTINED TO CROSS THE BURNING BRIDGE AT THE END OF THE FILM, BUT UPON INSPECTION IT WAS DISCOVERED THAT IT WAS IN BETTER CONDITION THAN THE LOCOMOTIVE ORIGINALLY ASSIGNED TO PLAY THE *TEXAS*. THE TWO LOCOMOTIVES WERE THEN SWITCHED, AND THIS ONE ENDED ITS DAYS HAULING LUMBER THROUGH THE PINE FORESTS OF OREGON.

lornly on the drive-rod—sad, dejected, lonely—oblivious to everything. As he sits motionless, a hogger enters the cab and steams the *General* into the engine house, with Johnnie rising up and down on the side rod all the way inside!

A year later in a Yankee encampment outside Chattanooga, Union General Thatcher meets with his chief spy, Captain Anderson. Anderson is proposing to steal a train on the Western & Atlantic Railroad and steam north with it, tearing up rails and burning bridges all the way to Chattanooga and disrupting the Confederate supply line to the city.

On the day of the raid, Anderson and twenty volunteers board Johnnie's train in Marietta. Also boarding the train is Annabelle, who is on her way to visit her wounded father. Although she sees Johnnie at the depot prior to departure, she does not speak to him.

When the train pulls into Big Shanty for breakfast, all the passengers and crew disembark to eat. Anderson and his men uncouple the passenger cars, board the *General* and its boxcars, and kidnap Annabelle who has returned to the train and spotted them. Johnnie, seeing his locomotive steam

Upon hearing the news that Fort Sumter has been fired upon, Johnnie rushes to the enlistment office, only to be rejected by the army. The set for this scene was built in Cottage Grove, Oregon, and was complete to the smallest detail but one: it had no roof. The film stock used in pictures at the time of *The General* required much light for exposure, and many of the interiors were actually exteriors, relying on the sun to provide illumination.

Upon learning that Johnnie did not enlist, a stern-faced Annabelle confronts him about his cowardice. Neither of them realize that Johnnie is far more valuable to the South as an engineer than as a soldier.

THE CAMERA CREW, MOUNTED ATOP THE BOXCAR, PREPARES TO FILM THE *TEXAS* AS JOHNNIE CONTINUES THE PURSUIT OF HIS STOLEN *GENERAL*. DURING THE ORIGINAL CHASE IN 1862, THE *TEXAS* OPERATED IN REVERSE, AND BOTH LOCOMOTIVES AT ONE TIME OR ANOTHER REACHED THE THEN UNHEARD OF SPEED OF 60 MILES AN HOUR!

away down the track, begins to chase it on foot. Although the raiders gain a large lead at first, they lose time tearing up trackage. Johnnie continues on foot for several miles until he spies a handcar. He continues the pursuit on the car until he hits a section of missing rail and is derailed. He tries an old wooden bicycle that proves inadequate. Finally, he comes across another locomotive, the *Texas*, and he continues the pursuit.

Johnnie comes across a flatcar with a mortar mounted to it. He couples it behind the *Texas* and begins to gain ground on the raiders. In one of the great scenes of film comedy Johnnie tries to fire the mortar in an effort to stop the raiders who are now just a short distance ahead. Using too little powder for his first shot, the mortar fires the cannonball into the cab of the *Texas*, landing at Johnnie's feet. Surprised, he rolls it out of the cab and onto the roadbed, then goes back to the mortar. As he prepares to load it, the first cannonball explodes on the roadbed behind him. Realizing that he needs more powder, Johnnie uses a whole cannister, loads the cannonball, and lights the fuse. He quickly moves to the *Texas*, but his foot becomes tangled in the coupler between the flatcar and locomotive. He shakes it off, allowing the coupler to fall below the flatcar's wheels, uncoupling it from

the locomotive. The vibration from the dragging coupler causes the mortar to slowly tilt downward, aiming right for Johnnie! With the fuse getting shorter and shorter, Johnnie can only think of getting away. Climbing up the back of the tender, his foot becomes tangled with a chain as the mortar takes deadly aim. As he struggles with it, the fuse gets shorter and shorter. He gets loose, climbs over the woodpile in the tender, and, in desperation, throws a piece of wood at the mortar, hitting it squarely on the front (an excellent shot, considering that he is balancing himself on a moving locomotive, and the mortar is coasting along behind him thirty feet away). He continues to scramble along the *Texas*, finding refuge by cowering on the cowcatcher. Ahead, across a small valley, steams the *General* and the raiders. The *Texas* steams around a curve, and as the flatcar coasts behind it into the curve, the mortar fires—the shot just narrowly missing the last boxcar in the raiders' train.

The raiders now believe that they are being chased by a large number of Confederates. They try to derail the *Texas* by dropping anything they can onto the rails. Even when they leave boxcars sitting on the tracks, Johnnie overcomes all obstacles with comedic determination. However, the chase does continue to draw Johnnie closer to

BUSTER DISCUSSES A BIT OF BUSINESS BETWEEN SCENES. BUSTER WORKED HARD ON HIS PICTURES, AND HE ACCEPTED ADVICE AND SUGGESTIONS FROM BOTH CAST AND CREW. IF SOMEONE HAD AN IDEA THAT MIGHT BE FUNNY, THEY WOULD TRY IT AND SEE IF IT WORKED. THERE WERE ALSO DAYS ON LOCATION WHEN BUSTER, AN AVID BASEBALL FAN, WOULD SEE A NICE FIELD NEAR THE TRACKS AND HE AND THE CREW WOULD STOP FILMING AND PLAY AN IMPROMPTU BASEBALL GAME.

Union lines. When he realizes that he is in enemy country, he stops the *Texas* and jumps off into the woods.

Lost in the woods, Johnnie spies a house that night. He enters it only to discover that it is the Union Army headquarters. He goes inside to get food just as General Thatcher, his staff, and Captain Anderson enter. Johnnie takes refuge under a table and from that vantage point overhears their plans for an upcoming attack the next day on the Rock River Bridge. He also discovers that Annabelle has been taken prisoner and is in the house.

When the staff meeting ends, Johnnie sneaks out and steals a uniform. He uses it to gain access to Annabelle's room where he wakes her and leads her to safety. Annabelle is overjoyed that Johnnie has risked his life to enter the enemy country to save her. Johnnie, realizing that he should hide the real reason for his trip north, accepts her gratitude,

and they spend a sleepless night out in the woods.

Next morning, Johnnie wakes up to find the *General* and the *Texas* being prepared with supply trains for support of the upcoming attack. He stuffs Annabelle into a sack to get her on board then climbs into the cab of the *General* and starts it down the track. The Union commander orders the *Texas* to follow with a third train following it.

The chase is now on again, only in reverse. Johnnie tries everything he can to stop the pursuing Yankees, all with great humorous consequences. Upon arrival at the Rock River Bridge, Johnnie sets it afire so that the Yankees cannot cross it. He then steams into the local town and alerts the Confederate garrison stationed there of the impeding attack. They rally to the colors and take position around the bridge.

The Union Army arrives with the trains. The commander looks over the burning bridge and decides that it is not damaged enough to stop them.

BUSILY HURRYING HIMSELF WITH THE TASK OF PROVIDING THE *TEXAS* WITH FIREWOOD, JOHNNIE IS NOT AWARE OF THE DANGER AS HE CROSSES THE LINES INTO UNION TERRITORY. IN ADDITION TO THE ASSISTANCE OF THE OREGON NATIONAL GUARD FOR THE TROOP SEQUENCES, BUSTER ALSO WAS ABLE TO ACQUIRE UP TO 125 HORSES FOR THE CAVALRY SCENES. BUSTER SUMMARIZED HIS FILMING OF THE CIVIL WAR THIS WAY: "I'D PUT 'EM IN BLUE UNIFORMS AND BRING 'EM GOIN' FROM RIGHT TO LEFT, AND TAKE 'EM OUT; THEN I'D PUT 'EM IN GRAY UNIFORMS AND BRING 'EM GOING' FROM LEFT TO RIGHT,... AND FOUGHT THE WAR."

BUSTER AND HIS FILM CREW TAKE A MOMENT TO POSE UNDER THE WARM OREGON SUMMER SUN FOR THIS PHOTO TAKEN IN JULY 1926. NOTICE THE AUTOMOBILE CHASSIS LASHED TO THE DECK OF THE FLATCAR. THIS PROVIDED A STABLE CAMERA PLATFORM FOR THE THREE CAMERAS THAT CAN BE SEEN MOUNTED ON TOP. WHEN THE FILM COMPANY LEFT LOS ANGELES FOR COTTAGE GROVE, IT FILLED 17 RAILROAD CARS WITH EQUIPMENT, COSTUMES, AND PROPS FOR THE PICTURE.

With steely determination, he orders the Texas across while the infantry fords the river in support. With a hiss of steam and a belch of smoke, the *Texas* starts across, and upon reaching the midpoint the bridge begins to sag, then weaken, and finally collapses, sending the helpless *Texas* into the river, fifty feet below.

The attack is ordered to continue as the Confederates open fire on the infantry fording the river. With the battle at its fiercest, Johnnie mans one of the artillery cannon, and with natural inability, fires it straight into the air. The cannonball lands be-

hind an upstream dam and explodes, sending a cascading torrent of water into the Federal troops. The Yankees retreat, and the Confederates march home in victory. For his bravery, Johnnie is given a commission as lieutenant, and he and Annabelle stroll off together to be alone with the *General*.

Buster spared no expense to make his comedy the most authentic he could. He was able to enlist the Oregon National Guard as extras for the soldiers in the battle scenes. The cost of filming the Texas plunging into the river was reported to be $42,000, a princely sum in 1926. The locomotive

JOHNNIE UNWITTINGLY FINDS HIMSELF TRAPPED IN THE UNION HEADQUARTERS OF GENERAL THATCHER WHERE HE OVERHEARS PLANS FOR THE ATTACK AGAINST THE CONFEDERATE ARMY AT ROCK RIVER BRIDGE. IT IS ALSO HERE THAT JOHNNIE FINDS OUT THAT ANNABELLE HAS BEEN TAKEN PRISONER. PLAYING GENERAL THATCHER (CENTER) IS JIM FARLEY; TO HIS LEFT IS GLEN CAVENDER AS CAPTAIN ANDERSON, THE ROLE BASED ON JAMES J. ANDREWS, THE UNION SPY WHO COMMANDED THE ORIGINAL 1862 RAID. THE BEARDED UNION GENERAL SEATED ON THE RIGHT IS JOSEPH KEATON, BUSTER'S FATHER.

remained in the Row River for years and was quite a popular tourist attraction until it was pulled out for its scrap value during World War II. Buster stated later that a railroad was "a great prop. You can do some awful crazy things with railroads."

Unfortunately, upon its release *The General* did not find favor among the critics of the day. Many felt that it was too long and tedious. The *New York Daily Telegraph* said it was a "trite and stodgy piece of screenfare, a rehash, pretentiously garnered of any old two-reel chase comedy ... disappointing." And the audiences did not flock to see it. The film's domestic gross was a measly $474,264.

In his biography of Keaton, author Tom Dardis reasoned why the film failed at the box office:

> It failed because (of) the sheer richness it offers—it was just too good. A great many things happen with great rapidity in *The General*, so many things that the audiences of 1927 may have found it too difficult to follow and told their friends to stay away from it ... .

In recent years, however, *The General* has enjoyed a rebirth, being elevated by recent critics to the sta-tus of a classic. In a poll sponsored by the American Film Institute in recent years, Buster's film placed among the top fifty motion pictures of all time, and one of only three silent films on the list.

One of the points that has been brought up about the film is the fact that it looks very much like a Civil War film should look. In fact, many critics have made the comment that it is photographed in such a way that you get the feeling you are looking at photographs taken by Matthew Brady, the noted Civil War photographer. One critic has gone so far as to state that *The General* is the Civil War, for few films have ever come as close to rendering the physical look of a period of history. Buster's longtime friend and business manager, Raymond Rohauer, explained the reason for this when he said, "Buster was not educated enough to be awed by history, and so avoided the trap of pompous solemnity; he was not sophisticated enough to be above it all, and so avoided the trap of patronizing superiority. To him, the historic event was simply an interesting experience."

HAVING RESCUED ANNABELLE AND COMMANDEERED THE *GENERAL*, JOHNNIE HEADS FOR THE SOUTHERN LINES TO WARN THE CONFEDERATE ARMY OF THE UPCOMING ATTACK. A BIT OF BUSINESS THAT WAS IMPROVISED ON THE SET HAD TO DO WITH THE KNOTTED PIECE OF WOOD THAT BUSTER IS HOLDING. THE *GENERAL* IS STARVING FOR FUEL, AND ANNABELLE (WHO IS NOT TOO BRIGHT) STARTS PICKING UP SCRAPS OF WOOD FROM THE TENDER TO FEED THE FIRE. SHE PICKS UP THE PIECE WITH THE KNOTHOLE AND, REALIZING THAT SUCH WOOD IS NO GOOD FOR ANYTHING, PROMPTLY THROWS IT OUT OF THE CAB, MUCH TO JOHNNIE'S CHAGRIN. AT THE TIME OF FILMING, A MEMBER OF THE CREW HAD SUGGESTED IT TO MARION MACK, SO SHE TRIED IT. BUT SHE ADDED TO THE GAG WITH SOMETHING OF HER OWN; HER CHARACTER THEN FINDS A SMALLER PIECE AND THROWS THAT INTO THE FIREBOX. BUSTER, THEN ADDS TO THE GAG BY FINDING AN EVEN *SMALLER* PIECE AND HANDS IT TO ANNABELLE TO SEE IF SHE IS DUMB ENOUGH TO THROW THAT IN. SHE DOES, AND BUSTER PROMPTLY PRETENDS TO CHOKE HER. THE SCENE ENDS AS HE GIVES HER A SMALL KISS AND GOES BACK TO RUNNING THE ENGINE. MARION MACK SAID ONCE THAT THE KISS WAS BUSTER'S WAY OF THANKING HER FOR COMING UP WITH THE GAG.

UNION CAVALRY SWIFTLY APPROACHES THE ROCK RIVER BRIDGE IN SUPPORT OF FEDERAL INFANTRY IN THE ATTACK AGAINST THE CONFEDERATES.

THE *TEXAS* CRASHES INTO OREGON'S ROW RIVER FOR HOLLYWOOD'S CAMERAS. THIS WAS THE MOST COMPLICATED AND EXPENSIVE SHOT IN THE WHOLE FILM, AND BUSTER SHOT IT WITH AT LEAST THREE DIFFERENT CAMERAS TO BE SURE HE GOT IT RIGHT. THE BRIDGE WAS CAREFULLY PREPARED BY REMOVING THE TWO CENTER BENTS, WHICH ALLOWED THE BRIDGE TO BEND IN THE MIDDLE. IN ADDITION, THERE WERE CABLES ATTACHED TO RELEASE POINTS THAT REMOVED PINS AT THE RIGHT MOMENT TO BE ASSURED THE BRIDGE WOULD COLLAPSE ON CUE.

BUSTER AND THE *TEXAS* AFTER HIS FILM CREW HAD STRIPPED THE LOCOMOTIVE OF ITS SALVAGEABLE ITEMS SUCH AS THE STACK, BELL, AND WHISTLE. PRIOR TO THE CRASH, THIS LOCOMOTIVE ALSO DOUBLED AS A UNION ENGINE IN THE FILM. NOTE THE FADED W&A RR. ON THE TENDER. THE LOCOMOTIVE REMAINED IN THIS SPOT FOR 15 YEARS UNTIL WORLD WAR II, WHEN IT WAS HAULED OUT OF THE RIVER AND SOLD FOR SCRAP.

FIFTY YEARS AFTER THE DEMISE OF THE *TEXAS*, IN 1976, A SMALL SECTION OF BUSTER'S ROCK RIVER BRIDGE STILL EXISTED, HEADING OUT OVER THE ROW RIVER TO INFINITY. IT IS A SMALL REMINDER OF BUSTER KEATON'S VISIT TO THE ROW RIVER VALLEY.

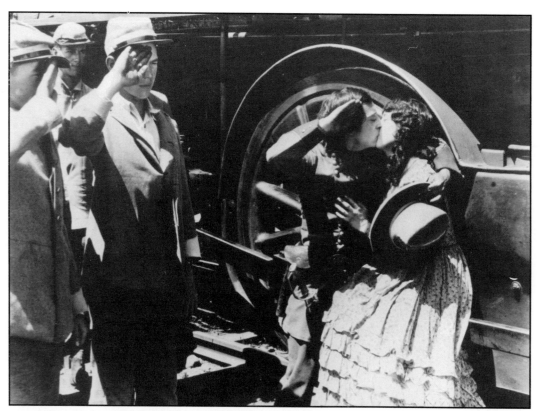

At the end of *The General*, Johnnie wins not only Annabelle, but an officer's commission. And like any army assignment, this one requires double duty.

After Buster and the film crew left Cottage Grove and went home to Hollywood, the real star of *The General*, Oregon Pacific and Eastern Railroad's #4, had to go back to work hauling lumber out of the Oregon forests. This photo was taken shortly after production was completed and shows the engine's modern headlight. Just below the bell on the boiler can be seen the straps that were added to carry the nameboard *General*. Old #4 went back into service without time for a coat of paint—it still wears its makeup on the tender; the letters W&A R R. The locomotive operated a few more years and was scrapped in 1941.

LANGUISHING A FEW YEARS AFTER THE END OF PRODUCTION, THE *TEXAS* AWAITS A SCRAPPER'S TORCH.

ANDREWS RAID TO BE PUT IN MOVIES

Nashville, Tenn.—Once again, the old "General" famous Civil War engine which figured in one of the most thrilling episodes of the War Between the States, is to feel the surge of steam through its ancient pipes.

The "General" is going into the movies.

The old engine of the Western & Atlantic Railroad is to be the principal character in reenacting the scene in which the "General" was captured sixty-four years ago at Marietta, Ga., by the Andrews Raiders, a band of disguised Federal soldiers. After a desperate chase in the "Texas," another historic engine, now at Grant Park, the trainmen and Confederate soldiers recaptured the stolen engine and brought eight of the raiders back to Atlanta, where they were shot as spies.

Buster Keaton will film the "Great Locomotive Chase" for United Artists and will spare no expense in making the picture. He himself will play the part of the young Confederate engineer in charge of the "General" when the engine was stolen.

Pittenger's "The Great Locomotive Chase" will be used as the basis for the picture, and all facts in it will be followed closely in order that the film may be historically accurate. Of course, says Buster, no young Confederate engineer, especially in Georgia, could be without a sweetheart, and, as a result, poetic license will be taken to the extent of presenting a love story to be interwoven with the picture.

WORK TO BEGIN NEXT MONTH

The film is to be named "The General," and work of producing it will begin next month, according to announcement.

Instead of being filmed in Georgia, the scene of the Andrews Raid, the picture is to be produced for the most part on a spur track near Cowan, Tenn., which already has been leased by Keaton. Other scenes will be made along various parts of the main line between Nashville and Atlanta. But the filming will be only a few miles from the place where the "General" was abandoned by the Federal raiders sixty four years ago, and the ancient engine may well feel again within its steel bones the thrill of that memorable day of '62.

And although the major part of the production will be done actually in Tennessee, Georgia citizens may well feel that the film is rightly theirs, portraying as it does an episode of Georgia history.

It was only through the chance of an excellent "location" being available in Tennessee that the picture is to be made in Georgia's neighbor state rather than in the old Empire State of the South itself.

A full force of technicians, numbering more than fifty, is to be brought to Nashville, where general headquarters will be established for the production. Actual "shooting" of scenes will be done mostly on the spur track at Cowan, half way between Nashville and Chattanooga.

W.S. Howland
Atlanta Journal   Sunday, May 9, 1926

Walt Disney's *The Great Locomotive Chase*

FESS PARKER, AS JAMES J. ANDREWS, AND HIS RAIDERS WATCH FOR PURSUERS IN *THE GREAT LOCOMOTIVE CHASE*. AMONG THOSE PLAYING VOLUNTEERS ARE EDDIE FIRESTONE, DON MEGOWAN, LENNIE GEER, CLAUDE JARMIN JR., JOHN LUPTON, MARC HAMILTON, JOHN WILEY, DICK SERGEANT AND JEFF YORK. WALT DISNEY PRODUCTIONS

BORED OF UNEXCITING PICKET
DUTY, WILLIAM PITTENGER
(JOHN LUPTON) ASKS THE
MYSTERIOUS UNION SPY
ANDREWS TO REMEMBER HIM
IF EVER HE NEEDS HELP ON A
SECRET MISSION. WALT DISNEY
PRODUCTIONS

One of the few films to tell the story of an actual incident of Civil War history, and to do it with few deviations, was Walt Disney's *The Great Locomotive Chase*, released in 1956. The movie, much like Buster Keaton's *The General*, was based on the daring exploits of James J. Andrews and his band of volunteers. Disney's film, however, was a straightforward drama, told from the viewpoint of one of the survivors, William Pittenger. Disney planned an elaborate production that would tell the whole story of the raid, even up to its tragic conclusion....

The award ceremony became the opening and closing sequence of *The Great Locomotive Chase*, which is told by Pittenger in flashback. The lead role of Andrews was played by Disney's newest star Fess Parker, fresh out of the coonskin cap role of Davy Crockett. The role of Fuller was capably handled by young Jeffrey Hunter. Disney assembled a first-rate cast of familiar character actors in other roles in the picture, including John Lupton as Pittenger, Jeff York, Harry Carey Jr., Claude Jarmin Jr., Dick Sergeant, Slim Pickens, Morgan Woodward and Kenneth Tobey.

Disney spared no expense for the filming of *The Great Locomotive Chase.* He approached the Baltimore and Ohio Railroad Museum in Baltimore for the use of two of its locomotives. The lead role of the *General* was played by the *William Mason*, a beautiful 4-4-0 American-style locomotive built in 1856 that had actually operated during the Civil War. For the lesser role of the yard engine *Yonah*, the B&O Museum lent its replica of the 1837 locomotive *Lafayette*. Since it did not have a cab, a false cab was added for the duration of filming.

The role of the *Texas* was given to a veteran of Hollywood films, #22, the *Inyo* of the cont. p 125.

DISGUISED AS LOYAL KENTUCKIANS
HEADING TO ATLANTA TO JOIN THE
CONFEDERATE ARMY, ANDREWS'
MEN COME UNDER SUSPICION WHEN
A CONFEDERATE CORPORAL
(MORGAN WOODWARD) DISCOVERS
A UNION ARMY ISSUE REVOLVER ON
BILL CAMPBELL (JEFF YORK). WALT
DISNEY PRODUCTIONS

ONCE ON BOARD THE TRAIN THEY INTEND TO STEAL, ANDREWS MEETS THE CONDUCTOR, WILLIAM A. FULLER (JEFFREY HUNTER) WHO HAS NOTICED THE FACT THAT SO MANY MEN HAVE BOARDED THE TRAIN AT THE LITTLE TOWN OF MARIETTA AND SEEMINGLY DON'T KNOW EACH OTHER. WALT DISNEY PRODUCTIONS

STAN JONES, GEORGE ROBOTHOM, FESS PARKER AND LENNIE GREER PREPARE TO STEAL THE *GENERAL* FROM THE STATION STOP AT BIG SHANTY, IN FULL VIEW OF A CONFEDERATE ENCAMPMENT. JONES' RESEMBLANCE TO ULYSSES S. GRANT, THE ROLE HE PLAYED IN *THE HORSE SOLDIERS* IS EVIDENT IN THIS VIEW. WALT DISNEY PRODUCTIONS

A SURPRISED WILLIAM FULLER DISCOVERS THAT HIS TRAIN HAS BEEN STOLEN WHILE STOPPED AT BIG SHANTY. ON THE LEFT IS VETERAN ACTOR KENNETH TOBEY, PLAYING ANTHONY MURPHY, FOREMAN OF MACHINERY AND MOTIVE POWER ON THE WESTERN AND ATLANTIC RAILROAD WHO JOINS IN THE PURSUIT. WALT DISNEY PRODUCTIONS

FULLER HAS COMMANDEERED A SMALL SWITCH LOCOMOTIVE, THE *YONAH* AND ARRIVES AT KINGSTON JUST SECONDS AFTER ANDREWS AND HIS MEN HAVE DEPARTED. WALT DISNEY PRODUCTIONS

DESTROYING THE RAILS OF THE WESTERN AND ATLANTIC RAILROAD WAS ONE OF THE MAIN OBJECTIVES OF ANDREWS' PLAN. HERE, FULLER AND MURPHY SURVEY THE DAMAGE BEFORE PROCEEDING ON FOOT TO STOP AN ONCOMING TRAIN. WALT DISNEY PRODUCTIONS

FULLER AND MURPHY FLAG DOWN PETE BRACKEN'S (SLIM PICKENS) EXPRESS TRAIN, PULLED BY THE *TEXAS* AND EXPLAIN THE SITUATION. BRACKEN WILL RUN THE *TEXAS* IN REVERSE AT FULL SPEED IN ORDER TO CAPTURE ANDREWS AND HIS MEN. WALT DISNEY PRODUCTIONS

FULLER'S DOGGED PURSUIT GAVE ANDREWS AND HIS
MEN NO TIME TO STOP AND FUEL THE *GENERAL*, AND
IT FINALLY ROLLED TO A STOP WITH THE RAIDERS
RUNNING FOR THE WOODS, WHERE THEY WERE SOON
CAPTURED. HERE, FULLER, MURPHY AND HANEY
SURVEY THE LOCOMOTIVE AND SATISFY THEMSELVES
THAT IT HASN'T BEEN DAMAGED. WALT DISNEY
PRODUCTIONS

A RELAXED MOMENT ON THE SET BETWEEN SLIM
PICKENS AND YOUNG DOUGLAS BLECKLY, WHO
PORTRAYED PICKENS' LOYAL FIREMAN, HENRY
HANEY. BLECKLY WAS A NATIVE OF CLAYTON,
GEORGIA, WHERE *THE GREAT LOCOMOTIVE
CHASE* WAS FILMED, AND GOT THE PART WHEN
DIRECTOR FRANCIS D. LYONS SPOTTED HIM
WORKING IN A SMALL LUNCHROOM IN THE TOWN.
WALT DISNEY PRODUCTIONS

SECRETARY OF WAR STANTON (ROY GORDON) PINS THE MEDAL OF HONOR ON CLAUDE JARMIN JR., DURING THE FINAL MOMENTS OF *THE GREAT LOCOMOTIVE CHASE*. GEORGE ROBOTHAM, EDDIE FIRESTONE AND JOHN LUPTON STAND AT ATTENTION, AWAITING THEIR TURN. WALT DISNEY PRODUCTIONS

Virginia & Truckee Railroad, a Nevada short line. The *Inyo* had been built in 1875 and had been starring in films since the late thirties. In addition, Disney built five period boxcars for the film, and the B&O museum also supplied two Civil War ammunition cars, two coaches, and a baggage car.

The locomotives were painted in colorful Western and Atlantic Railroad livery and all the equipment was shipped to Clayton, Ga. The railroad scenes were filmed on a fifty-seven-mile short line near Clayton, the Tallulah Falls Railway. It closely resembled a Civil War railroad with its rough and unkempt roadbeds. The railroad ran through some spectacular scenery, which was beautifully captured by the technicolor cameras. The Disney film crew made great use of the locomotives, filling the screen with exciting railroad shots. By the end of the production, both the *William Mason* and the *Inyo* had each logged more than a thousand miles.

The film portrays civilian raider William Campbell as a large hotheaded Yankee who, at various times, is in danger of blowing the whole scheme because of his propensity for fighting. The film follows Pittenger's book closely, and offers an excit-ing adventure full of intrigue and suspense. The chase itself occupies more than half the screen time giving railroad lovers a feast of steam, smoke, whistles and bells.

Critics enjoyed *The Great Locomotive Chase*, giving it acceptable reviews, yet it was not the success in the theaters that Disney himself had hoped. It may be that the story did not hold much for female audiences because there was no love interest, or female lead, in the picture. Also, the raiders fail in their task of destroying the railroad, and Andrews is hanged as a spy. Audiences may have found this too downbeat a storyline to appease their tastes.

As a historical recreation *The Great Locomotive Chase* comes closest to achieving what many Hollywood producers try to avoid. It didn't tell the story of the Civil War on a large scale, but it did relate history in an honest and entertaining manner. Like most films about history it has some minor flaws, but, along with *The Horse Soldiers,* it does give a feeling for the period. And at times, that feeling can make history more understandable and interesting than any textbook.

The West Salem News

Volume 38 West Salem, Ohio Thursday, July 5, 1956 5c a Copy, $2.00 Year
Entered as 2nd Class matter, Postoffice, West Salem, O. under Act of March 6, 1879 Published Thursdays, W. Buckeye St., West Salem, O., by Joseph W. and Edna E. Parrott, Publishers-Editors.

WALT DISNEY FILM LIES

MacLennan Roberts' Book Also Lies

by JOSEPH W. PARROTT

In the May 17, 1956 issue of the West Salem News I questioned whether or not Walt Disney's picture, "The Great Locomotive Chase" would tell the truth as to whom the First Congressional Medal of Honor was awarded. I now know that the picture does not truthfully portray this event in American history.

As a guest of Ed McGlone, manager of the RKO Palace theatre, in Columbus, June 25 I witnessed a special Ohio preview of "The Great Locomotive Chase." Except for the scene portraying the awarding of the First Congressional Medal of Honor the picture is a first-rate historical film and brings recognition to the deeds of these Civil War heroes in picture form.

The opening scene of Disney's picture is wrong, according to official records of the Department of the Army of the United States of America. The scene is wrong according to the writings of the very man to whom Disney's picture awards the first Congressional Medal of Honor, namely William Pittenger, who was the first to give my grandfather, Jacob Parrott, credit for being the one to receive the first medal.

Titles preceding the opening scene state that the picture is a true story and that names have not been changed. Advertisements in city dailies state thus: "Remarkable . . . because it is true! Capturing the authentic Drama, the suspense and adventure of our Nation's Strangest Spy Story." Theatre reporters have stated, "Walt Disney, as is well known, has a great passion for authenticity."

From Walt Disney Productions, Inc., Publicity Department I received a picture and copy to the effect that Claude Jarman Jr. would portray Jacob Parrott. The copy Disney sent to be used under the picture states, "Claude Jarman Jr., featured in Walt Disney's Civil War spy story, "The Great Locomotive Chase," receives the Nation's first Congressional Medal of Honor," etc. I published that picture June 21 complete with the copy, word for word as sent by Disney.

This picture, complete with the copy under it, as it appeared in the June 21 issue, is again printed in this issue. Because of the picture and copy, I stated in the June 21 issue that I believed Disney's picture would be authentic and that only MacLennan Robert's book would lie about this event in American history. I was misled.

In the first scene of "The Great Locomotive Chase" the actor playing the part of Secretary of War Stanton speaks to a group of soldiers, who had been part of the group who stole the General. He stated that Congress had just authorized the issuance of a new military medal and that they had been chosen to receive the first of the medals. It is at this point that William Pittenger, played by John Lupton in the film, is singled out by Stanton. The first medal is pinned on Pittenger's uniform. In the film's last scene Stanton congratulates Pittenger only.

This is where I, the official publication of the Department of the Army, and William Pittenger (deceased), the author and Methodist minister, disagree with Walt Disney. Pittenger himself never made any such claims. In fact his gravestone in Fallbrook cemetery, Fallbrook, California, bears the simple inscription, "One of the Andrews Raiders."

After seeing "The Great Locomotive Chase" film presented and reading, MacLennan Roberts book, which is based on the Disney production, I have no other choice than to state that both lie, one in the scene of the picture and the other in the chapter of the book, dealing with the awarding of the First Congressional Medal of Honor.

I will, however, in the interest of fairness to Walt Disney and MacLennan Roberts, apply the formula of Joseph Pulitzer in dealing with opposition editors. When Pulitzer caught the editor of another paper in a lie, he assumed editorially that the editor had not intentionally misled his readers but was probably misled himself.

A representative of Disney's studio, according to the Columbus Dispatch said he was certain the juggling of facts was not done deliberately and that "Mr. Disney will hate this more than anyone else." He said (according to the Dispatch story) he would make arrangements for Parrott to explain the discrepancy to Disney.

There is no explaining to be done by myself. I have been more than liberal with my efforts to correct the situation since first reading Roberts book. The explaining must come from Mr. Disney and Mr. Roberts—personally—and in as large a magnitude as their movie and book has spread the untruth. From here on it is entirely up to Mr. Disney and Mr. Roberts to classify their production and book, respectably. This is a job for each personally—not for their employees.

There is one point which I want the public to thoroughly understand. It is that when I refer to Walt Disney, in relation to this incident, it is as the one who heads Walt Disney Productions Inc. and not in a personal way; that when I refer to MacLennan Roberts, it is as the author of "The Great Locomotive Chase" book, based on Walt Disney's production. As head of his corporation Walt Disney has justly earned and received many Oscars for films. So, in his position, he must also receive the Oscars of criticism. Mr. Roberts, as an author, is open to fame as a writer, so he must also assume blame if something he writes is not true, even though he faithfully accepted writings of others for compiling his book.

I have purposely waited a week after seeing "The Great Locomotive Chase," before writing this article, criticising the scene awarding the medal. To make sure I was not predjudiced it was necessary that the public see the picture and that other members of the press also see the discrepancy. I herewith publish opinions of several newspapers in regards to the issue I have raised.

• • •

THE COLUMBUS DISPATCH

Norman H. Dohn, of the Columbus Dispatch, in that paper's June 28, 1956 issue writes the following about "The Great Locomotive Chase" medal awarding scene:

"The film's opening scene depicts Secretary of War Edwin M. Stanton addressing six of the soldiers who had participated in the engine theft. He tells them that for their act of daring, Congress has authorized a new military award and designated them to be the first to receive it.

"Then Stanton singles out a bespectacled young man, William Pittenger by name, and pins the first medal on his uniform. And that is where Joseph Parrott takes issue with Mr. Disney, and justly so.

"History specifically records the fact that the first Congressional Medal of Honor was awarded to Jacob Parrott of Kenton. In fact, markers erected by the Ohio Historical Society at the corporation limits of the Hardin county community read

"Home of Lt. Jacob Parrott, first Congressional Medal of Honor Winner."

"Historians maintain that Parrott was singled out for the honor because of his youth—he was barely 18—and the fact that he refused to divulge to his Confederate captors details of the raid even though he was stretched across a log and given 100 lashes in an effort to make him talk

"Pittenger, a native of Steubenville and a minister in New Jersey, following the war, wrote and published the most detailed and comprehensive account of the adventure, entitled "Daring and Suffering."

"It was from this book that Disney gleaned much of the information for "The Great Locomotive Chase." Consequently, Pittenger is assigned a major role in the film whereas Parrott is not mentioned once."

Copyright Walt Disney Productions

Claude Jarman Jr., featured in Walt Disney's Civil War spy story, "The Great Locomotive Chase," receives the Nation's First Congressional Medal of Honor. Jarman portrays Jacob Parrott, first man in history to get the medal. Roy Gordon portrays Secretary of War Stanton, who pinned it on. To the right of Jarman, left to right are George Robotham, Eddie Firestone and John Lupton in portraying other Andrew's Raiders who were similarly awarded.

• • •

Why didn't Disney show Jarman in the above true first award scene?

The reading matter under the above picture is exactly as it came from Disney Productions Inc. If this had been shown in the movie it would have been completely true as the title of the picture laid claim to being. John Lupton, extreme right and wearing glasses, portrayed William Pittenger. In the film the first medal is pinned on him not Jarman as shown above.

• • •

THE KENTON TIMES

An article in The Kenton Times, May 24, 1956, by Tom Cooper, remarks on Disney's show and the awarding of the first Congressional Medal as follows:

"The Kenton Times believes Jacob Parrott, late Kenton man and Civil War hero, was the first soldier ever to receive the Congressional Medal of Honor. The Times takes for its authority the Medal of Honor Book, official U. S. government publication which credits Jacob Parrott of Kenton with receiving the first Congressional Medal of Honor

"This writer has consulted the officia[illegible] [illegible]ent book as Oren [illegible] Hardin-co veterans [illegible] [illegible]btained a copy from Government Bureau of [illegible]uments.

"No better authority is available and the motion picture "The Great Locomotive Chase," which will premiere June 8 at Atlanta, Ga., is wrong if it says any other person than Lieut. Parrott was the first to receive the greatest honor.

"Joseph W. Parrott, a native of Kenton, now publisher of the West Salem News, weekly newspaper, is a grandson of Lieut Parrott His mother was the daughter of Wilson W. Brown, head railroad engineer in the famous Civil War raid.

"Mr. Parrott has taken up the matter on behalf of his grandfather and has written to the Walt Disney Productions.

"So The Kenton Times' faith in the official government publication is unshaken by the probable movie error and still believes that Lieut Parrott was the first to be honored. His gravestone in Grove cemetery says so, too."

• • •

AKRON BEACON JOURNAL

Art Cullison in his column "On with the Show" in the Akron Beacon Journal, Monday, June 2, 1956 writes the following criticism of the medal scene in "The Great Locomotive Chase."

"The motion picture shows Pvt. William Pittenger (as played by John Lupton) receiving the first Medal of Honor ever awarded to a private. This isn't exactly true.

"Pittenger, himself, reports in his book, "Daring and Suffering, or the Great Railroad Adventure," that Pvt. Parrott received the first award from the hands of Secretary of War Stanton. Pittenger received his a few moments later."

• • •

WILLIAM PITTENGER WROTE THIS

William Pittenger, member of the Andrews Raiders, reporter for a Steubenville paper before the Civil War, and while in service, a Methodist minister in Ohio and New Jersey, and author, wrote the following account of the awarding of the First Congressional Medal of Honor:

"Stanton seemed especially pleased with Parrott. He was the youngest of our number and of very quiet and simple manners. Stanton gave him the offer of a complete education if he would accept it—I understood him to mean at West Point. Parrott answered that while the war lasted he did not wish to go to school; but would rather go back and fight the Rebels who had used him so badly.

"At this Stanton smiled as if he greatly approved his spirit, and then said to him, "If you want a friend at any time be sure to apply to me." Then going into another room, he brought out a medal, and handed it to Parrott, saying, "Congress has by a recent law ordered medals to be prepared on this model, and your party shall have the first; they will be the first that have been given to private soldiers in this war!" Later all the survivors of the party received similar medals. Then he gave us a present of $100 each from the Secret Service fund."

FROM THE MEDAL OF HONOR BOOK

The Medal of Honor Book, Official Publication of the Department of the Army, gives this account of the awarding of the first Congressional Medal of Honor.

In the second and third paragraphs on page eight of "The Medal of Honor," official publication of the Department of the Army, it is stated as follows:

"Then Stanton turned to Pvt. Jacob Parrott, who had been beaten during his captivity, and spoke quietly about his appreciation of Parrott's devotion. Opening a morocco case, he explained the Congressional authorization for awards of medals of bravery.

"None of these medals," he said to Parrott, "have yet been awarded to any soldiers, and I now present you with the first one that has been issued by the authority of the late Act."

ART TEACHER IS STRICKEN

Mrs. Frank Ellis, art teacher of Northwestern schools, was taken seriously ill at her home in Wooster Thursday. She suffered a hemorrhage of the brain. She was first taken to Ashland hospital, then to the Elyria hospital. At present she is in St. Luke's hospital at Cleveland under the care of Dr. Spencer Braden. The Ellis family resided in West Salem until moving to Wooster last winter.

SHEARER WEST SALEM SOFTBALL SCHEDULE

Remainder of Season

Tuesday, July 3: West Salem at Holdmesville.

Friday, July 6: West Salem at New Pittsburg.

Tuesday, July 10: Perrysville at West Salem.

Friday, July 13: Jeromesville at West Salem.

Tuesday, July 17: West Salem at Wooster.

Friday, July 20: West Salem at Fredricksburg.

Tuesday, July 24: Berlin at West Salem.

Friday, July 27: West Salem at Dalton.

Tuesday, July 31: Kidron at West Salem.

Friday, Aug. 3: West Salem at Burbank.

Tuesday, Aug. 7: West Salem at Legion 68, Wooster,

JACOB PARROTT'S GRANDSON JOSEPH W. PARROT TAKES ISSUE WITH DISNEY'S PORTRAYAL IN THEIR MOVIE *THE GREAT LOCOMOTIVE CHASE* OF THE AWARDING OF THE FIRST MEDAL OF HONOR TO WILLIAM PITTENGER INSTEAD OF PARROTT.

Index (Captions are not indexed.)

Bibliography

Aiken Gene, *The Great Locomotive Chase As Told By Men Who Made It Happen*, Historic Press/South, Gatlinburg, Tenn., 1994.

Augle, Craig, *The Great Locomotive Chase*, Rouzerville, Pa. 1992.

Cassidy, John, *Civil War Cinema, A Pictorial History of Hollywood and The War Between the States*, Pictorial Histories Publishing Co., Missoula, Mont., 1986.

Gregg, Frank M., *Andrews Raiders*, Republican Job Print, Chattanooga, Tenn., 1891.

Head, Joe H., *The General, The Great Locomotive Dispute*, Bartow History Center, Cartersville, Ga., 1990.

Jones, Robert C., *Retracing the Route of the General*, Kennesaw Historical Society, Inc., 1996.

Louisville & Nashville Railroad Company, *The Great Locomotive Chase On The Western & Atlantic Railroad*, April 12, 1862, 1959.

McBryde, Randell: *The Historic "General,"*, McGowan & Cook, Chattanooga, 1904.

O'Neill, Charles, *Wild Train, The Story of the Andrews Raiders*, Random House, New York, 1956.

Pittenger, William, *Daring and Suffering,* J.W. Daughaday, Philadephia, Pa., 1863.

Pittenger, William, *Capturing A Locomotive*, J.P. Lippincott, Philadelphia, Pa., 1881.

_____, *Daring and Suffering, A History of the Andrews Railroad Raid into Georgia in 1862*, War Publ. Co., New York, 1887

_____, *The Great Locomotive Chase*, Penn. Publishing Co., 1893.

Wilson, John A., *Adventures of Alf Wilson*, Toledo, Ohio, Blade Printing and Paper Co., 1880.

Plus many newspapers, magazines and bulletins including *Blue and Gray Magazine* and *The Landmarker* Vols. 4 & 5 of the Cobb County Landmarks Society, Inc.

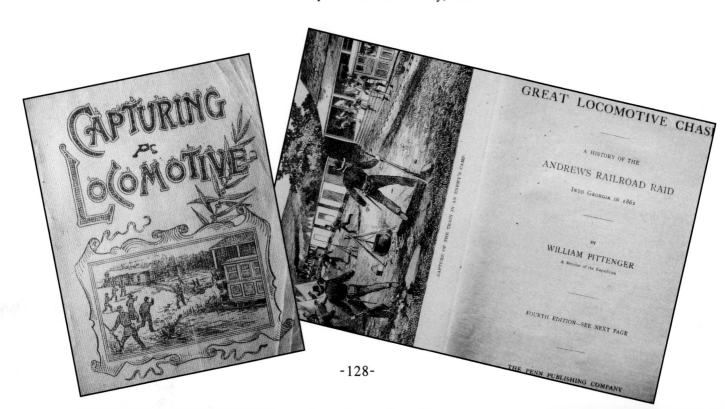

 # About the Authors

Stan Cohen is a native of Charleston, West Virginia, and a graduate of West Virginia University with a BS degree in geology. He established Pictorial Histories Publishing Company in 1976 with his first book, *The Civil War in West Virginia, A Pictorial History*. Since then he has authored or co-authored 66 books and published over 200. He moved to Missoula, Montana, in 1961 to work for the U.S. Forest Service and has been a full-time author/publisher since 1980. He lives in Missoula with his wife, Anne, but maintains an office in Charleston and travels extensively throughout the country, selling and researching new books.

WILBUR G. KURTZ AT LEFT, AND JAMES G. BOGLE AT THE OHIO MEMORIAL TO THE ANDREWS RAIDERS, NATIONAL CEMETERY, CHATTANOOGA, TENN., SEPT. 15, 1965.

Colonel James G. Bogle, U.S. Army, retired, is a native of Tennessee and has been a resident of Atlanta since 1956. He retired from the U.S. Army in 1967 with over 31 years of service. His decorations include the Legion of Merit, the Bronze Star Medal, and the Asiatic-Pacific Campaign Medal with one Battle Star. He served in the South Pacific during World War II and later in Korea during the Korean War. He graduated from the Army Transportation School, the Command and General Staff College, and the Armed Forces Staff College, while in the service, and also holds a degree from Georgia State University of Atlanta. His active service includes six years on the Army General Staff. Following his retirement from the U.S. Army, Colonel Bogle served as administrative aide to the Director of the Georgia Historical Commission for five years.

Colonel Bogle became interested in the "Great Locomotive Chase" or the "Story of the General" in his early years. His father was a long time employee of the Nashville, Chattanooga & St. Louis Railway, which for many years had custody of the locomotive *General* and went to great effort to publicize the story of the old locomotive and the men involved with it. Thus he started early collecting material relating to the Raid, learning all that he could about it, and seeking to solve some of the mysteries pertaining to the story. He has written several articles dealing with the men and the locomotives. They have been published in *Railroad History, The Atlanta Historical Journal*, and *The Landmarker*. In 1971, he was instrumental in securing a marker for the grave of Peter James Bracken, the engineer of the locomotive *Texas* during the Chase. In 1980, he assisted in the location and erection of a marker in Oakland Cemetery, Atlanta, indicating the site where seven of the Andrews Raiders were executed in 1862. In 1982, he supervised the restoration of the locomotive *Texas* on display in Atlanta's famous Cyclorama of the Battle of Atlanta. He also prevailed upon the State authorities to erect an historical marker at the site in Atlanta of the execution of James J. Andrews. In 1983, he assisted in locating the final resting place of James Ovid Smith, one of the raiders, and helped solve one of the remaining major mysteries dealing with the Raid.

Colonel Bogle is very interested in Civil War history, railroad history, and local history. He is a life member of the Railway & Locomotive Historical Society, a long time member and past president of the Atlanta Civil War Round Table, a charter member and past president of the Atlanta Chapter of the National Railway Historical Society. He is also an active member of several other historical societies including the Atlanta Historical Society, the DeKalb Historical Society, the Georgia Historical Society, and the Tennessee Historical Society.

Colonel Bogle is married to the former Mary Alice Clark of Atlanta, and they have two children, James G. Bogle Jr., of Columbia, S.C., and Mrs. Steven H. Lyons of Atlanta, and two grandsons, Michael James Bogle of Columbia, S.C., and John Robert Lyons of Atlanta, Ga.

The Art of Wilbur G. Kurtz Sr.

WILBUR KURTZ was born in Oakland, Illinois, in 1882. He was raised in Greencastle, Indiana, and studied at DePauw University and the Art Institute of Chicago. In his early years he worked as a draftsman and engraver. In 1910 he became a professional illustrator specializing in architectural renderings.

Kurtz first went to Atlanta in 1903 to investigate the story of the Andrews Raid. Here he interviewed Capt. William A. Fuller. In 1911 he married Fuller's daughter Annie Laurie. The couple made Atlanta their permanent home, where Kurtz created historical murals, which were in demand throughout the South. He also painted murals for the Georgia exhibits at the 1933 Chicago Century of Progress Exposition and the 1939 New York World's Fair.

His knowledge of early Atlanta took him to Hollywood for 13 months as a technical advisor for the epic movie *Gone With the Wind*. He was also an advisor for Walt Disney's 1945 saga *Song of the South* and the 1955 making of *The Great Locomotive Chase*.

Kurtz took part in the creation of the diorama in the foreground of the painting of the Battle of Atlanta at the Grant Park Cyclorama and also repaired the damaged parts of the immense scene. As a consultant for the Little White House—Franklin D. Roosevelt's house in Warm Springs, Georgia—he aided in its conversion into a landmark commemorating the World War II president.

During the 1950s he wrote the text for most of the Atlanta campaign markers, which the Georgia Historical Commission erected in the area. In 1962 he was asked by the Georgia Civil War Centennial Commission to be chairman of the observances that featured the *General*.

For ten years he was a member of the Atlanta City Planning Commission, an honorary member of the Atlanta Historical Society, and a member of the Atlanta Symposium and Atlanta Civil War Round Table.

Annie Laurie Kurtz, with whom Kurtz had five children, died in 1946. In 1949 he married Annie Rachell Pye. Kurtz died in Atlanta on Feb. 18, 1967, and is buried in Westview Cemetery.

Top: THE ATLANTA CAR SHED (RAILROAD STATION) IN THE EARLY 1860S, FACING WEST. *Above:* WILBUR KURTZ IN HIS STUDIO IN ATLANTA, GEORGIA, MAY 1961, HOLDING HIS PAINTING OF THE *GENERAL* AS SHE APPEARED IN 1862.

THE *GENERAL* AT THE ATLANTA CAR SHED THE MORNING OF APRIL 12, 1862.

THE *GENERAL* AT BIG SHANTY, GEORGIA, THE MORNING OF APRIL 12, 1862, JUST BEFORE BEING SEIZED BY THE ANDREWS RAIDERS.

Above: THE RAIDERS' FIRST STOP AT MOON'S STATION AS JOHN M. SCOTT CLIMBS A POLE TO CUT THE TELE-GRAPH WIRE.

Right: THE *YONAH* AT THE ETOWAH BRIDGE, THE COOPER IRON WORKS AND FURNACE, AND THE MONUMENT TO OWNER MARK COOPER.

Below: THE *YONAH* AT ETOWAH STATION AS THE *GENERAL* STEAMS NORTHWARD.

ALLATOONA PASS ON THE WESTERN
& ATLANTIC RAILROAD IN 1864.

Right: THE *WILLIAM R. SMITH*
AT KINGSTON.

Below: THE *TEXAS* RUNNING IN
REVERSE ON THE OOSTANAULA
RIVER BRIDGE AT RESACA.

THE END OF THE CHASE, TWO MILES NORTH OF RINGGOLD, GEORGIA.

Top: THE SWIMS JAIL AND WILLIAMS ISLAND IN CHATTANOOGA.
Bottom: JAMES J. ANDREWS GOING TO HIS EXECUTION IN
ATLANTA ON JUNE 7, 1862.

THE *TEXAS* AT THE TUNNEL.

WALT DISNEY presents
"THE GREAT LOCOMOTIVE CHASE"
An all - live action feature in CinemaScope

Color by Technicolor
Litho U.S.A.   56-211

WALT DISNEY presents
"THE GREAT LOCOMOTIVE CHASE"
An all - live action feature in CinemaScope

Color by Technicolor
Litho U.S.A.   56-211

WALT DISNEY presents

THE GREAT Locomotive CHASE

FESS PARKER
as ANDREWS
the mysterious spy.

JEFF HUNTER
as FULLER
the relentless pursuer.

JEFF YORK
as CAMPBELL
the rebellious giant.

JOHN LUPTON
as PITTENGER
heroic volunteer.

A REMARKABLE *TRUE* SPY STORY...
NOW A *GREAT* MOTION PICTURE!

Roaring across the CinemaScope screen comes Walt Disney's newest action filled motion picture — the story of a handful of desperate raiders who steal a train behind enemy lines and race for the biggest prize of all — a nation's fate. Filmed where it actually happened, capturing the authentic drama, suspense and adventure

... it is the memorable story of a mission so daring that the courageous men who volunteered were awarded America's highest tribute, the Congressional Medal of Honor. Here is exciting motion picture entertainment, remarkable because it is true. See Walt Disney's THE GREAT LOCOMOTIVE CHASE at your favorite theater.

THE FIRST CONGRESSIONAL MEDAL OF HONOR EVER AWARDED

starring **FESS PARKER**   **JEFF HUNTER**

with Jeff York · John Lupton · Eddie Firestone · Kenneth Tobey · Claude Jarman, Jr.

COLOR BY
TECHNICOLOR   CINEMASCOPE

WRITTEN AND PRODUCED BY LAWRENCE EDWARD WATKIN   DIRECTED BY FRANCIS D. LYON

COPYRIGHT WALT DISNEY PRODUCTIONS

DISTRIBUTED BY BUENA VISTA FILM DISTRIBUTION CO., INC.

The *General*

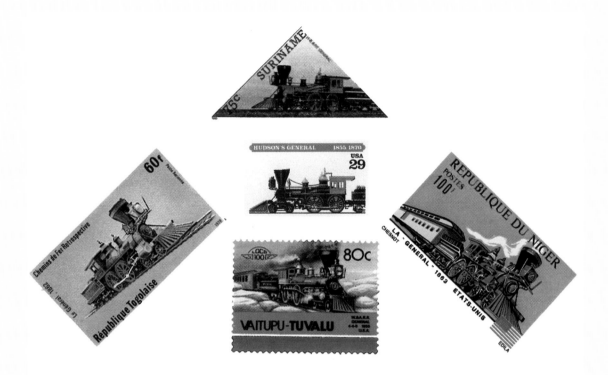

The *General* arrives at Big Shanty on April 14, 1962.

The *General* on its special flat car during the 1962 Civil War Centennial. LOUISVILLE & NASHVILLE RR

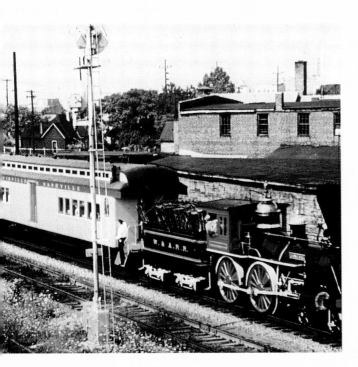

Left: THE *GENERAL* AT INDIANAPOLIS, INDIANA, AUGUST 1964. CHARLES CASTNER PHOTO *Right:* THE *GENERAL* BACK HOME IN KENNESAW, GEORGIA, FEB. 19, 1972.

THE *GENERAL* ON THE BEAR CREEK TRESTLE AT LOUISVILLE, KENTUCKY. LOUISVILLE & NASHVILLE RR

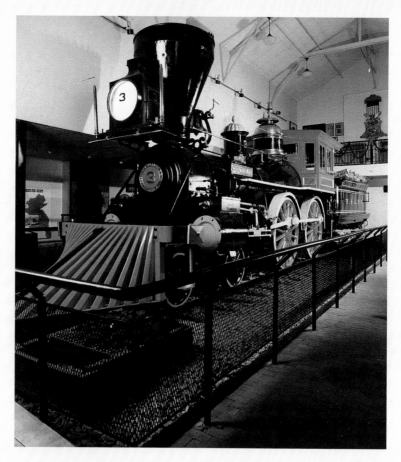

THE *GENERAL* HAS BEEN DISPLAYED IN THE KENNESAW CIVIL WAR MUSEUM IN KENNESAW, GEORGIA, SINCE 1972. THE MUSEUM, OPERATED BY THE CITY, IS LOCATED AT 2829 CHEROKEE STREET. PHOTO COURTESY KENNESAW CIVIL WAR MUSEUM

The *Texas*

Left: THE STEAM LOCOMOTIVE *TEXAS* DOMINATES THE MAIN FLOOR OF THE ATLANTA CYCLORAMA BUILDING AT 800 CHEROKEE AVE. SE IN ATLANTA'S GRANT PARK. THE CYCLORAMA OF THE BATTLE OF ATLANTA PAINTING WAS COMPLETED IN 1886 AND AFTER SEVERAL YEARS AS A TOURING EXHIBIT, WAS BROUGHT TO ATLANTA IN 1892. THE PRESENT CYCLORAMA BUILDING WAS CONSTRUCTED IN 1921 AND REMODELED IN1981. ALONG WITH THE PAINTING, DIORAMA (ADDED IN 1936) AND THE *TEXAS,* IS A 200-SEAT THEATER AND CIVIL WAR MUSEUM. PHOTO BY KEITH G. LAUER, COURTESY ATLANTA CYCLORAMA. *Above*: CIVIL WAR REENACTORS POSE IN FRONT OF THE CYCLORAMA BUILDING.

Present-Day Views along the Chase Route

PHOTOS BY
JAMES BOGLE AND STAN COHEN

MONUMENTS ACROSS THE RAILROAD TRACKS FROM THE MUSEUM. JIM BOGLE STANDS BY THE *GENERAL* STONE.

THE ANDREWS RAID

About 6 A.M., April 12, 1862, a Federal spy & contraband merchant, James J. Andrews, of Ky., together with 18 soldiers & one civilian of Ohio, seized the locomotive "General", & three box cars while the train-crew & passengers were breakfasting at the Lacy Hotel.

Intending to sabotage the State R.R. between Atlanta & Chattanooga, the raiders steamed N. to destroy track & burn bridges.

They were foiled in this attempt by the persistent pursuit of Capt. W.A. Fuller, Conductor of the train; Jeff Cain, Fireman; & Anthony Murphy, of the Atlanta R.R. shops, after a chase of eighty-seven miles.

SITE - LACY HOTEL

Eastward across R.R. stood the 2-story frame hotel, leased by George M. Lacy in 1859 - an eating house for passengers on the State-owned railway until June 9, 1864, at which time the Federal forces occupied Big Shanty.

April 12, 1862, the Andrews Raiders seized the locomotive "General" while train crew & passengers were breakfasting at the hotel.

Fortified by a stockade, it housed a Federal garrison from June 9 to Oct. 3, 1864, when it was captured by Confederate forces. Re-occupied by Federal troops it was maintained as a R.R. blockhouse until abandoned & burned by them, Nov. 14.

BIG SHANTY

In 1838-41, a construction camp of laborers, grading & building the State R.R., was located at the spring approximately 250 yds. W. of here, where temporary structures (shanties) housed the workmen.

Track level here, being some 345 ft. above the level at Cartersville, 19 mi. N., the grade was 18 ft. per mi. at time of construction.

In railroad parlance, this was known as "the big grade to the shanties" - later shortened to "big shanty grade", finally to "Big Shanty", which was changed to Kennesaw about 1870.

In June, 1864, Federal forces on the Kennesaw Mtn. front, drew supplies at this point.

TO THE MEMORY OF
WILLIAM A. FULLER,
1836-1905

HISTORICAL MARKERS AT KENNESAW, GEORGIA.

-142-

SITE-MOON'S STATION

A wood-shed, water-tank, siding & log house. Here, April 12, 1862, the pursuers of the Andrews Raiders — Fuller, Cain & Murphy — acquired a push-car from section foreman Jackson Bond, which carried them 14 mi. down grade to the Etowah River.

Oct. 3, 1864 A Federal stockade, garrisoned by 84 officers & men from the 14th & 15th Ill., was located on the high ground 50 yds. E. of the track.

The stockade was attacked & captured by Reynolds' brigade, Walthall's div., Stewart's A.C. Loring's div. captured the Acworth garrison, 4 mi. N., Oct. 4th.

MOON'S STATION, ABOUT TWO MILES NORTH OF THE MUSEUM ALONG THE OLD RAILROAD RIGHT-OF-WAY. THE RAIDERS STOPPED HERE TO BORROW TOOLS FROM A RAILROAD CREW AT THE SITE. FULLER AND MURPHY COMMANDEERED THEIR POLE CAR HERE AND USED IT ALL THE WAY TO THE ETOWAH RIVER.

REMAINS OF THE ETOWAH RIVER BRIDGE. THE BRIDGE WAS DESTROYED DURING GENERAL SHERMAN'S 1864 ATLANTA CAMPAIGN. THE BRIDGE WAS BUILT IN 1847.

THE COOPER IRON WORKS WAS BUILT ABOUT 1845 ON THE BANKS OF THE ETOWAH RIVER. TODAY THE BASE OF THE ALLATOONA DAM IS NEARBY. IT WAS OPERATED BY MAJ. MARK COOPER FROM 1847 TO 1862 AND THE ENGINE *YONAH* WAS USED HERE.

THE CASS STATION WAS BUILT IN 1857 AND DESTROYED IN 1969. THE RAIDERS STOPPED HERE FOR FUEL AND WATER.

SITE OF THE WESTERN & ATLANTIC RAILROAD DEPOT AT CASS, GEORGIA, AS IT APPEARS TODAY.

FOUNDATION REMAINS OF THE OLD KINGSTON DEPOT, FACING GENERALLY NORTH. THE ABANDONED SIDING IS IN THE FOREGROUND AND THE WYE IS TO THE LEFT BEHIND THE BUILDING. THE RAIDERS WERE DELAYED HERE FOR 65 MINUTES TO LET A SOUTHBOUND FREIGHTS PASS. THE *WILLIAM R. SMITH* WAS COMMANDEERED HERE BY FULLER AND MURPHY.

ABANDONED RIGHT-OF-WAY OF THE ROME RAILROAD WYE AT KINGSTON, FACING GENERALLY SOUTH. THE RIGHT LEG OF THE WYE CONTINUES ON TOWARD THE DEPOT REMAINS. THE LEFT LEG LEADS NORTHWARD. ROME IS DIRECTLY BEHIND THE CAMERA POSITION.

THE ADAIRSVILLE STATION, CIRCA 1891, FACING NORTH. FULLER AND MURPHY ABANDONED THE *WILLIAM R. SMITH* NEAR HERE AND PICKED UP THE *TEXAS.*

THE NORTH ABUTMENT OF THE ORIGINAL OOSTANAULA RIVER COVERED BRIDGE, DATING FROM 1847, IS STILL IN USE. THE BRIDGE WAS ANOTHER MAJOR TARGET OF THE RAIDERS BUT IT WAS TOO WET TO SET ON FIRE.

ORIGINAL STONEWORK, AT RIGHT AND LOWER SECTION, OF SOUTH ABUTMENT.

THE PRE-CIVIL WAR DEPOT AT TUNNEL HILL, BUILT OF LOCAL LIMESTONE IS NOW INCORPORATED INTO A LOCAL FEED MILL.

THE OLD TUNNEL THROUGH CHETOOGETA MOUNTAIN WAS COMPLETED IN 1850. A NEW TUNNEL WAS BORED TO THE LEFT BEHIND THE FENCE IN 1928. THE RAIDERS FAILED TO DESTROY THIS IMPORTANT SITE BECAUSE THE *TEXAS* WAS RIGHT BEHIND THEM.

THE 1849 WESTERN & ATLANTIC DEPOT AT RINGGOLD.

MARKER, TWO MILES NORTH
OF THE RINGGOLD DEPOT
THAT MARKS THE END OF THE
"GREAT LOCOMOTIVE
CHASE." THE MONUMENT WAS
PLACED AT THE SITE BY THE
NASHVILLE, CHATTANOOGA &
ST. LOUIS RAILWAY IN 1901.

Miscellaneous Sites

TENNESSEE STATE HISTORICAL MARKER NEAR SHELBYVILLE.

GRAVESTONE OF RAIDER
WILLIAM J. KNIGHT IN STRYKER, OHIO.

GRAVESTONE OF RAIDER
MARK WOOD IN FOREST CEMETERY, TOLEDO, OHIO.

ON APRIL 12, 1862 CAPTAIN
FULLER PURSUED AND AFTER
A RACE OF 90 MILES FROM
BIG SHANTY NORTHWARD
ON THE WESTERN & ATLANTIC
RAILROAD RECAPTURED
THE HISTORIC ENGINE
GENERAL WHICH HAD BEEN
SEIZED BY 22 FEDERAL
SOLDIERS IN DISGUISE,
THEREBY PREVENTING
THE DESTRUCTION OF
THE BRIDGES OF THE
RAILROAD AND THE
CONSEQUENT DISMEMBERMENT
OF THE CONFEDERACY.

GRAVESITE OF WILLIAM A. FULLER IN OAKLAND CEMETERY, ATLANTA, GEORGIA.

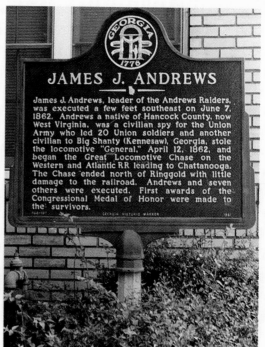

Left: ON THE EDGE OF ATLANTA'S OAKLAND CEMETERY IS A MONUMENT TO THE EIGHT EXECUTED RAIDERS. SEVEN OF THEM WERE HANGED ABOUT 100 YARDS IN THE DISTANCE. *Right:* MARKER AT THE SITE OF ANDREWS' HANGING AT THIRD AND JUNIPER IN ATLANTA.

THE HOTEL IN FLEMINGSBURG WHERE ANDREWS LIVED.

GRAVESTONES OF JEFF CAIN AND HIS WIFE, ELIZABETH, IN OAKLAND CEMETERY, ATLANTA, GEORGIA.
CAIN WAS THE ENGINEER ON THE *GENERAL*.

HISTORICAL MARKER AT
MORROW, GEORGIA,
SOUTH OF ATLANTA.

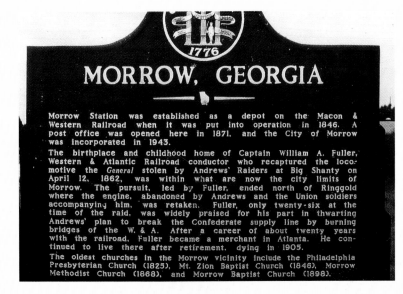

PRESENT VIEW OF GEORGIA
RR (CSX) EAST OF ATLANTA
ABOUT WHERE THE *GENERAL*
STOOD WHEN PHOTOGRAPHED
BY GEORGE BARNARD IN 1864
(SEE PAGE 42), AFTER THE BIG
FIRE OF SEPT. 1, 1864.

OHIO MEMORIAL TO THE ANDREWS RAIDERS IN THE NATIONAL CEMETERY,
CHATTANOOGA, TENNESSEE, DEDICATED ON MAY 31, 1891.

GRAVES OF THE EIGHT RAIDERS WHO WERE EXECUTED IN 1862. THEY FORM A SEMI-CIRCLE AROUND THE MEMORIAL.